Gasoline Dreams

GASOLINE DREAMS

WAKING UP FROM PETROCULTURE

SIMON ORPANA

FORDHAM UNIVERSITY PRESS · NEW YORK · 2021

This research was supported by funding from the Canada First
Research Excellence Fund as part of the University of Alberta's
Future Energy Systems research initiative.

Fordham University Press has no responsibility for the persistence
or accuracy of URLs for external or third-party Internet websites
referred to in this publication and does not guarantee that any
content on such websites is, or will remain, accurate or appropriate.

Fordham University Press also publishes its books in a variety of
electronic formats. Some content that appears in print may not be
available in electronic books.

Visit us online at www.fordhampress.com.

Library of Congress Control Number: 2021911747

Printed in the United States of America

23 22 21   5 4 3 2 1

First edition

CONTENTS

FOREWORD

Just what does it mean to say we live in a "petroculture"?

It probably doesn't come as a surprise to say that historical periods differ from one another. It might come as a surprise to hear that one of the big ways our own historical period differs from others is the sheer amount of energy in use. In 1850, we depended almost entirely on the energy of people and animals to get things done. By 1950, the vast majority of our activities—production, consumption, travel, and all the ins and outs of everyday life—were powered by fossil fuels. Over this century, an incredible shift occurred in how societies work. And despite the shiny promise of a future powered by solar panels and electric cars, with each passing year we continue to depend on energy from the ground—and a lot of it: in 2020, we used roughly *ten* times the amount of oil we did in 1950.

"Petroculture" means, simply, the society we inhabit today—a global society made possible by the energies afforded by burning fossil fuels. The amount of energy used around the globe differs greatly. Some people—Americans, Australians, and Canadians—use enormous amounts; others, even today, still depend on the energy of living bodies and on animal power to help with their daily work. Even so, it's clear the heavy users have set the terms for how all of us are supposed to live in relation to energy. The ideologies that rationalize ever-growing production and consumption mean that the power available to those in the global North has become a metric for modernization and economic development in the global South. Among the networks and shiny devices to which they give life, fossil fuels power cell phones and social media. These have acted as forms of soft power even more effective than their Cold War counterparts (film, television) in cementing the energy-intensive desires condensed into the phrase "the American way of life."

Two cars in every driveway, vacation flights for the whole family, a house full of every imaginable consumer object: the American dream is a social fantasy so well known that it doesn't really require explanation. The process of globalization has transformed it into a deeply-sedimented set of desires, with more people than ever conceding to the personal imperatives and hopes it drives, and to its multiple and seemingly never-ending consumerist temptations. If access to fossil fuels has produced more life opportunities for many, they are opportunities that appear to flourish and expand only if ever more fuel is added to the economic fire.

The limits and problems of the social fantasy we inhabit, and the forms of violence and exclusion it necessitates, have been criticized and challenged from a wide range of perspectives. Indeed, a sizable segment of post-war U.S. cultural production has done little but inventively and relentlessly interrogate this fantasy and explore its consequences for the individuals who live it, consciously or unconsciously, willingly or not. The inanity and insanity of consumer lifestyles are all too well known. Until recently, what has been far less evident is that making stuff and buying stuff, creating experiences and inhabiting them, filling driveways with cars and stuffing planes with vacationers, all require a lot of fuel.

Even if we take these practices to be normal parts of everyday life, high-energy petrocultures are actually strange ones to live in. Time is stretched in improbable ways. Our high-tech societies depend on the energies of *millions* of years of solar energy, absorbed by ancient fossilized plants, and just waiting for us to discover. Filling up a gas tank is a banal task—a chore to be crossed off a list. It should instead be an event filled with wonder and amazement. Every squeeze of the lever on a gas pump to fill 'er up should be accompanied by a destabilizing insight into how we mess with time. It has been estimated that one U.S. gallon of gas (a little under four liters) is produced out of *ninety-eight tons* of prehistoric plant matter—the equivalent in today's terms of forty acres of wheat, stalks and all.* In a very real sense, we are burning time, using condensed ancient time to open up space in our jam-packed calendars. It saves a lot of time to drive somewhere instead of trudging the vast distances of cities that have been shaped by fossil fuels.

Time is not the only thing stretched by fuel from the earth. So, too, is space. Fossil fuels bring the world closer. A new continent is only hours away via airplanes, as are neighboring cities via automobiles. The rich and privileged expect to be able to easily access goods and services that originate on the other side of the planet. The collapse of distance is as wondrous as our reuse of ancient time to speed up experience. But the way we mess with space has become commonplace, too—a part of daily life about which one might think deeply only when chatting with friends while stoned or on those few occasions when one runs headfirst into an existential wall because one can't traverse the distances needed to visit friends and family.

One of the many wonderful things about Simon Orpana's *Gasoline Dreams*—and its wonders abound—is how its words and images explode our comfortable, *laissez-faire*, unreflective use of energy. We wear fossil fuels like a second skin, as part of the very make-up of who and what we are. The insights and ideas crowded onto every page of *Gasoline Dreams* can't help but make us squirm. Even those of us who might have imagined themselves alert to the multiple ways in which energy constitutes us can't help but develop new itches, rashes, and scratches. Some pages even bring about burns. Orpana wants his words and images to produce ontological discomfort, an anxiety about modern being and its ways of believing and behaving. He wants us to recognize that to be human is to be fossil fueled—indeed to *be* fossil fuel—in ways we are only now beginning to grasp.

But this book is more than ontological exposé. *Gasoline Dreams* offers a detailed account of a historical crime in which all of us are implicated, even if only some of us have benefited, whether by using fossil fuels to excess or by lining our pockets as vendors of energy snake oil. Ever-increasing access to and use of energy fueled the growth of Western capitalist modernity and its incalculable violence toward others and to the natural world. This is a crime for which there is no easy restitution, no way to simply return the stolen goods.

---

* Jeff Dukes, "Burning Buried Sunshine: Human Consumption of Ancient Solar Energy," *Climatic Change* 61 (November 2003): 31-44.

Despite all the evidence that has turned up, the scene of this particular crime is in the process of being burned to the ground.

What did those who had energy ever do with it? Did they ever use it to ameliorate poverty? To help others, if cautiously, being attentive to the implications of the use of fossil fuels on the environment? Of course not. In the *Accursed Share*, one of the great interrogations of the causes and consequences of the fossil fuel era, French philosopher Georges Bataille proposed an obvious solution to the existing state of global affairs: there should be an immediate transfer of American wealth to India "without reciprocation"—a synecdoche intended to name the disproportion of wealth between the global North and global South as a whole and to name, too, the possibility of things being otherwise. What did those with energy do instead? They used it to bend others to their will through military might, trade deals, and labor regimes, and they used it to get ever more of the stuff at whatever cost. From Abdul Rahman Munif's *Cities of Salt* trilogy to Annie Proulx's *Barkskins*, fiction writers have shown us the brutal results of drilling into sand or slashing timber on the communities living in and with sand and forest. This basic fact of history can't be reiterated enough. Fossil fuels fucked things over.

When one thinks about the traumas of mass energy use, what immediately comes to mind is the state and fate of the environment. Burning fossil fuels constitutes the single biggest source of human-produced carbon dioxide in the atmosphere. The planet is warming, with disastrous implications for all its inhabitants. Adding new forms of renewable energy into the mix of energy we use might do the trick, by limiting the addition of carbon dioxide to the atmosphere. Orpana draws our attention to why this isn't nearly enough. He insists we confront all the ways in which we are petrocultural people, the ways in which our bodies and minds are saturated in the social expectations, opportunities, capacities, and beliefs that we developed over the century in which we moved from doing things with our bodies and animals, to a time when much of the work in the world is done by machines (physical and digital) powered by fossil fuels. To really take on climate change, we collectively need to do something very difficult. Solar panels on rooftops and wind farms in fields and oceans are only the first meek steps toward what undoing petroculture demands of us. It demands a revolution.

A revolution? Yes—an event in which one system dramatically gives way to another. In common parlance, the word "revolution" has become attached to political change; just as commonly, it is used to demarcate a change from right to left, from conservative to socialist (the events that bring about populisms like those of Viktor Orbán in Hungary or Recep Erdoğan in Turkey are rarely described as revolutions). Revolution is also about speed—a rapid change, a flip of the switch from minus to plus. Climate change certainly demands a reset of political priorities and even of our understanding of the conditions under which political decisions are made (and by whom, and for whom). The revolution *Gasoline Dreams* points to is deeper and more challenging. Orpana tells us we need to reset our bodies, selves, desires, hopes, and dreams. If it seems like an impossible task, it is. The circumstances we find ourselves in demand nothing less than taking up the challenge of flipping the impossible to the possible and do so with the speed of a revolution.

Gasoline Dreams is a manifesto for this revolution. Orpana offers us a detailed map of the fossil-fueled reality we inhabit. He presents us with ideas for action. He doesn't hesitate to explain why our deep commitment to fossil fuels makes action difficult. This is not a book that thrives on doom and naysaying. Nor does it employ critical blinders so that it might rally people to do, well, something. *Gasoline Dreams* is an honest account of being-in-relation to fossil fuels. Orpana traces the impact of the use of dirty fuel on almost every element of our lives, patiently connecting the dots while unnerving the solidity of the day-to-day. He interrogates the strange mirage of historical certainty, the perverse sense that things couldn't have been any different and that we were always heading down the path we took, no matter how utterly destructive this drama has been. Orpana stands face to face with the abiding fiction of wonders bequeathed to us by the steam engine and prompts us to think about what might have been otherwise had we been able to do without it. Despite everything, despite all its unblinking criticism of who and what we are, *Gasoline Dreams* gives us hope that we are not all already sliding to a tragic denouement, but that there are still more, better stories to be told.

Imre Szeman
Salt Spring Island, B.C.
December 2020

Gasoline Dreams

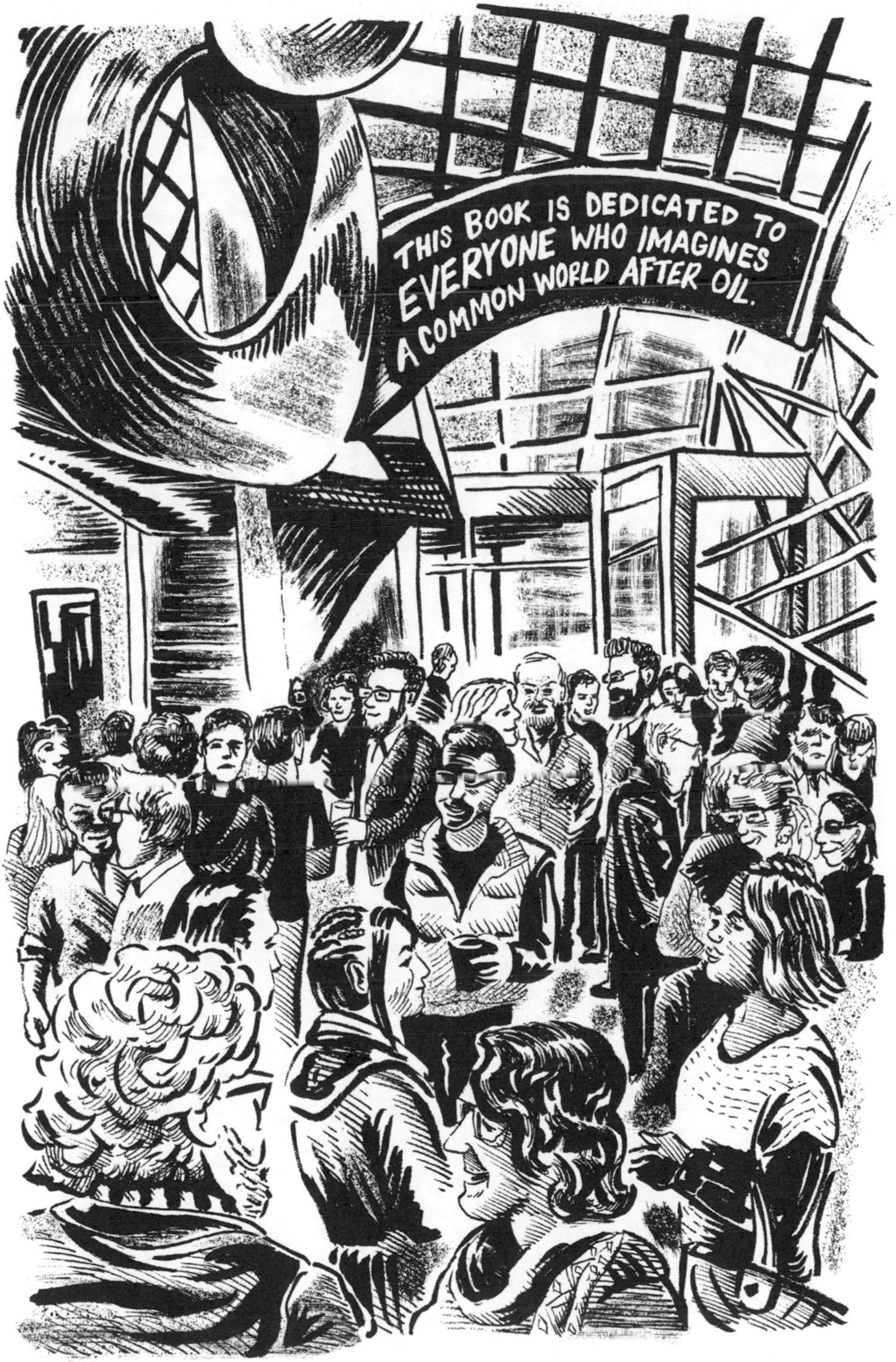
THIS BOOK IS DEDICATED TO
EVERYONE WHO IMAGINES
A COMMON WORLD AFTER OIL.

THE FALSE LIBERATION OF THE ON-RAMP

IN AUGUST OF 2018, MY FRIEND EVAN MAURO AND I WENT FOR A DRIVE...

THIS IS THE **GRANDVIEW** HIGHWAY ON-RAMP. IT'S A PORTION OF **HIGHWAY ONE**, WHICH GOES ACROSS THE COUNTRY.

'COUGH'

IT'S THE MAIN COMMUTING **CORRIDOR** FOR MOST PEOPLE WHO WORK IN DOWNTOWN **VANCOUVER.**

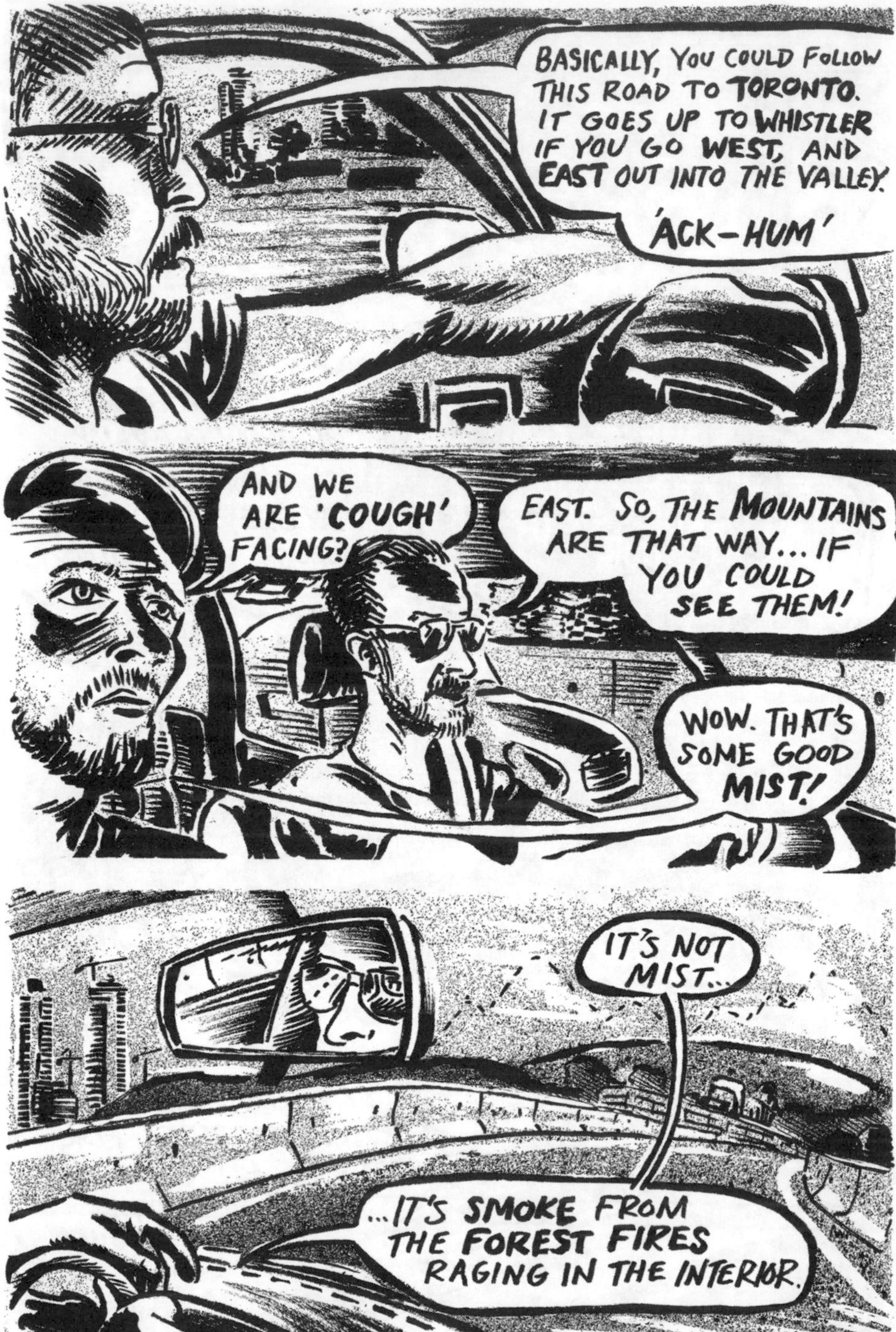
BASICALLY, YOU COULD FOLLOW THIS ROAD TO TORONTO. IT GOES UP TO WHISTLER IF YOU GO WEST, AND EAST OUT INTO THE VALLEY.
'ACK-HUM'
AND WE ARE 'COUGH' FACING?
EAST. SO, THE MOUNTAINS ARE THAT WAY... IF YOU COULD SEE THEM!
WOW. THAT'S SOME GOOD MIST!
IT'S NOT MIST...
...IT'S SMOKE FROM THE FOREST FIRES RAGING IN THE INTERIOR.

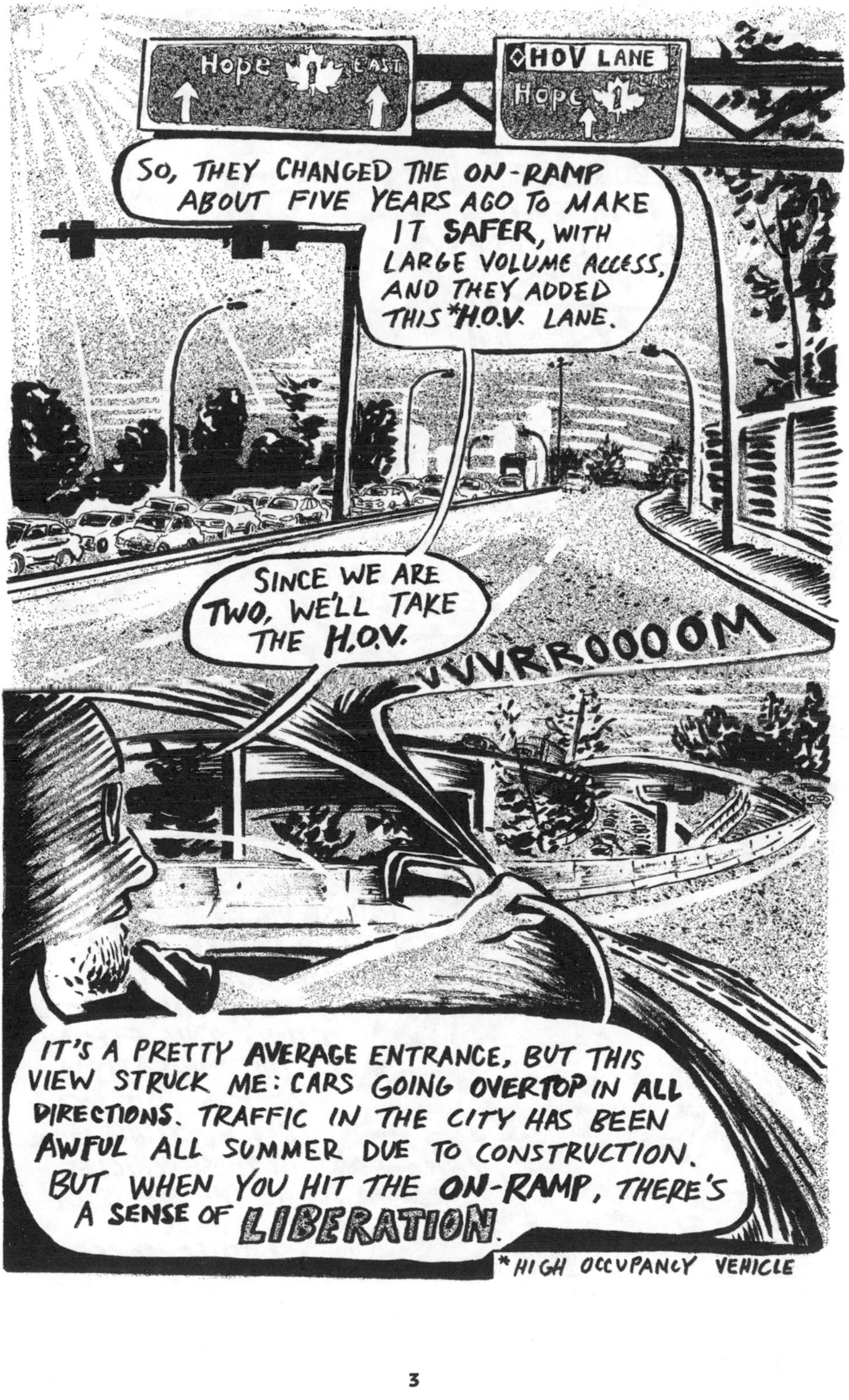
Hope EAST
HOV LANE
Hope
SO, THEY CHANGED THE ON-RAMP ABOUT FIVE YEARS AGO TO MAKE IT SAFER, WITH LARGE VOLUME ACCESS, AND THEY ADDED THIS *H.O.V. LANE.
SINCE WE ARE TWO, WE'LL TAKE THE H.O.V.
VVVRROOOOOM
IT'S A PRETTY AVERAGE ENTRANCE, BUT THIS VIEW STRUCK ME: CARS GOING OVERTOP IN ALL DIRECTIONS. TRAFFIC IN THE CITY HAS BEEN AWFUL ALL SUMMER DUE TO CONSTRUCTION. BUT WHEN YOU HIT THE ON-RAMP, THERE'S A SENSE OF LIBERATION.
*HIGH OCCUPANCY VEHICLE

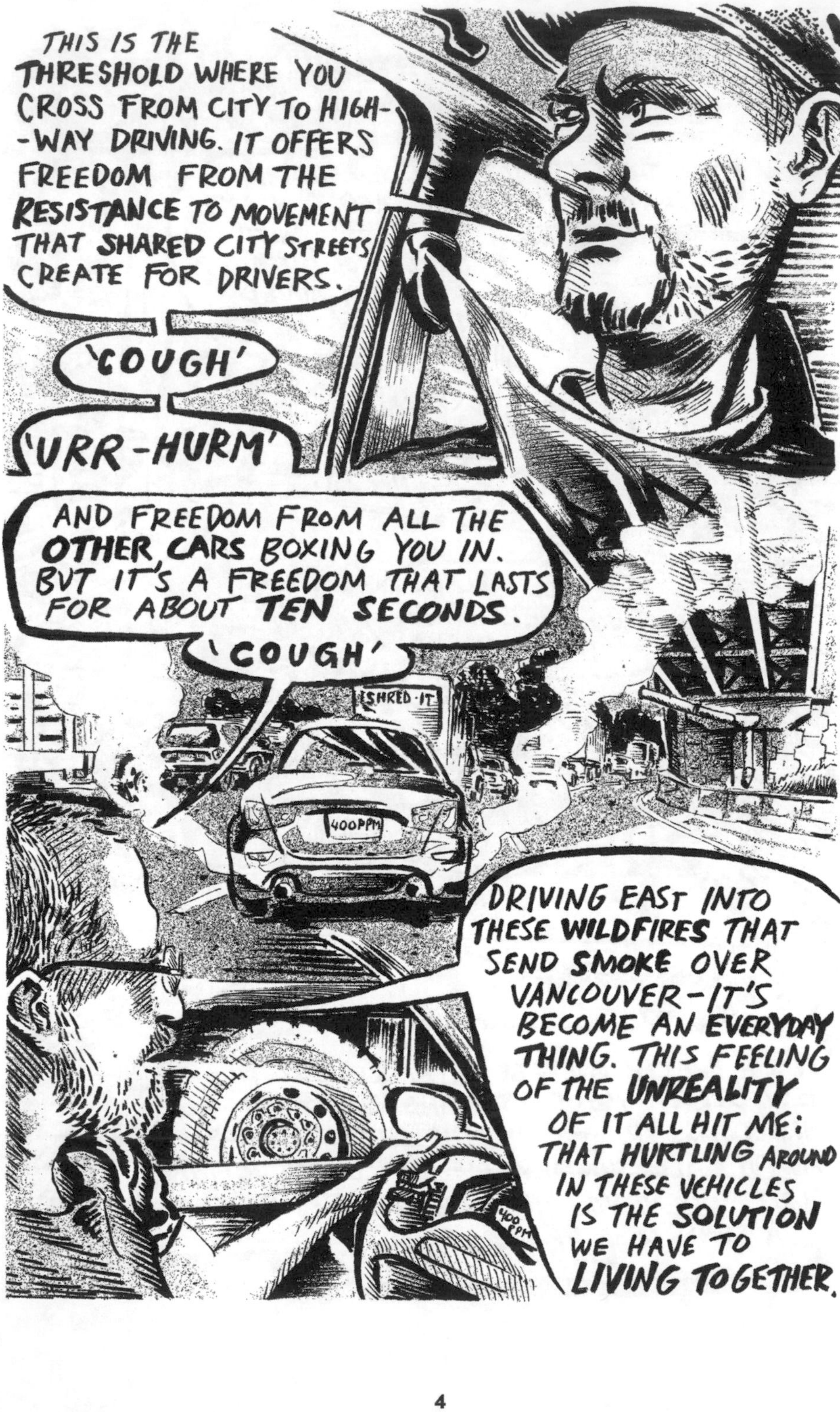
THIS IS THE THRESHOLD WHERE YOU CROSS FROM CITY TO HIGH--WAY DRIVING. IT OFFERS FREEDOM FROM THE RESISTANCE TO MOVEMENT THAT SHARED CITY STREETS CREATE FOR DRIVERS.
'COUGH'
'URR-HURM'
AND FREEDOM FROM ALL THE OTHER CARS BOXING YOU IN. BUT IT'S A FREEDOM THAT LASTS FOR ABOUT TEN SECONDS.
'COUGH'
SHRED-IT
400PPM
DRIVING EAST INTO THESE WILDFIRES THAT SEND SMOKE OVER VANCOUVER-IT'S BECOME AN EVERYDAY THING. THIS FEELING OF THE UNREALITY OF IT ALL HIT ME: THAT HURTLING AROUND IN THESE VEHICLES IS THE SOLUTION WE HAVE TO LIVING TOGETHER.
400 PPM

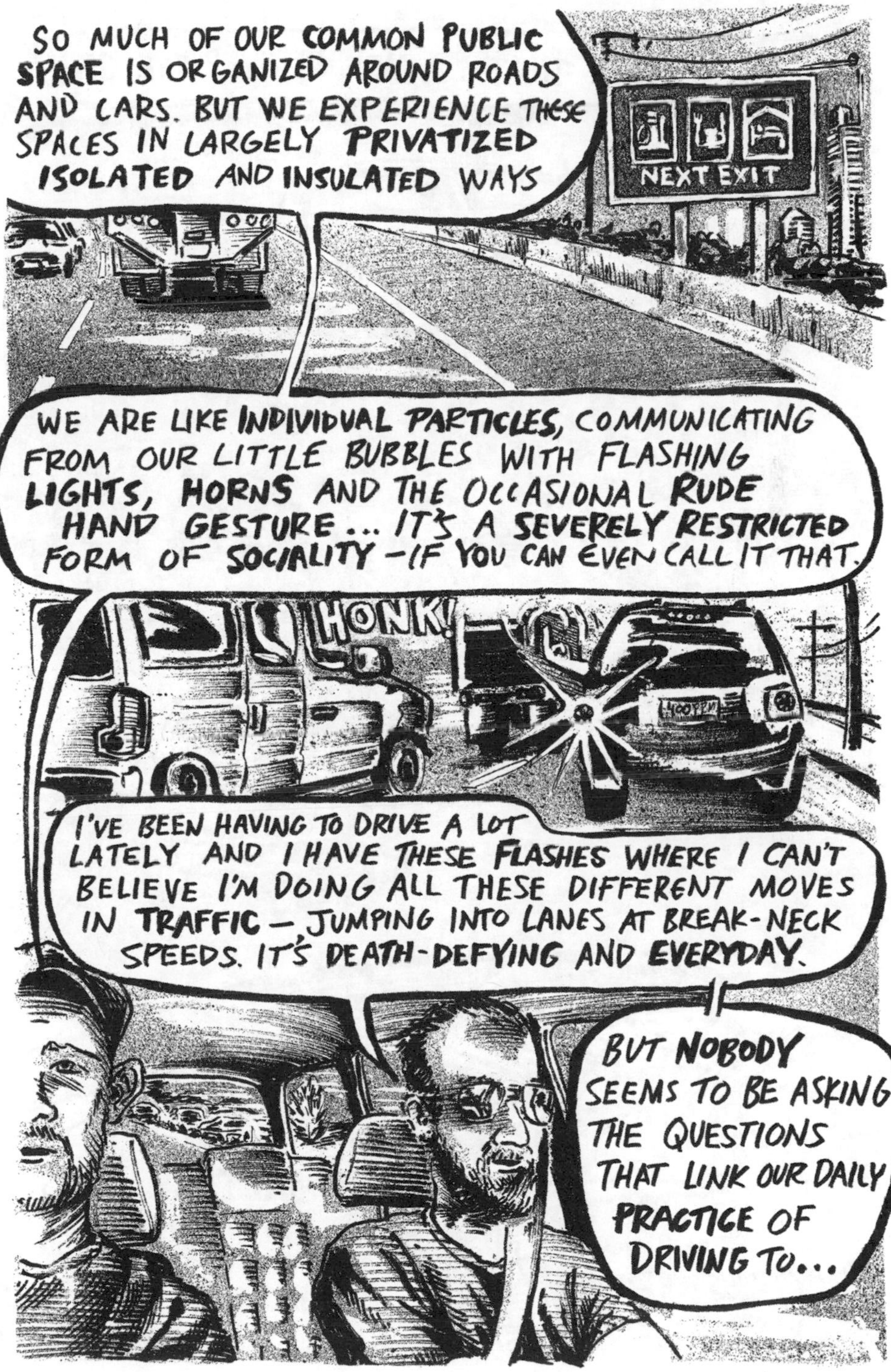
SO MUCH OF OUR COMMON PUBLIC SPACE IS ORGANIZED AROUND ROADS AND CARS. BUT WE EXPERIENCE THESE SPACES IN LARGELY PRIVATIZED ISOLATED AND INSULATED WAYS
NEXT EXIT
WE ARE LIKE INDIVIDUAL PARTICLES, COMMUNICATING FROM OUR LITTLE BUBBLES WITH FLASHING LIGHTS, HORNS AND THE OCCASIONAL RUDE HAND GESTURE ... IT'S A SEVERELY RESTRICTED FORM OF SOCIALITY — IF YOU CAN EVEN CALL IT THAT.
HONK!
I'VE BEEN HAVING TO DRIVE A LOT LATELY AND I HAVE THESE FLASHES WHERE I CAN'T BELIEVE I'M DOING ALL THESE DIFFERENT MOVES IN TRAFFIC — JUMPING INTO LANES AT BREAK-NECK SPEEDS. IT'S DEATH-DEFYING AND EVERYDAY.
BUT NOBODY SEEMS TO BE ASKING THE QUESTIONS THAT LINK OUR DAILY PRACTICE OF DRIVING TO...

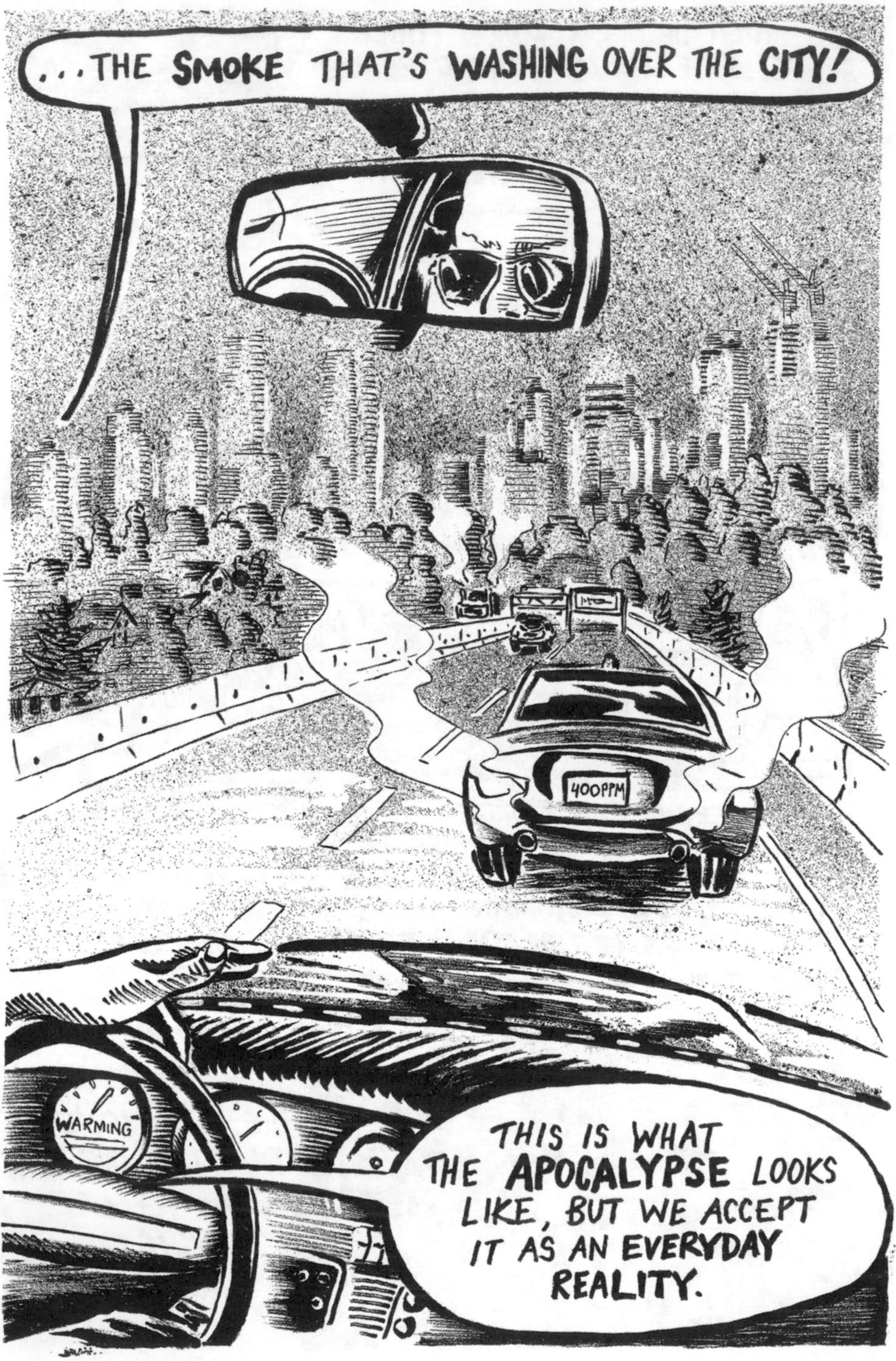
...THE SMOKE THAT'S WASHING OVER THE CITY!
400PPM
WARMING
THIS IS WHAT THE APOCALYPSE LOOKS LIKE, BUT WE ACCEPT IT AS AN EVERYDAY REALITY.

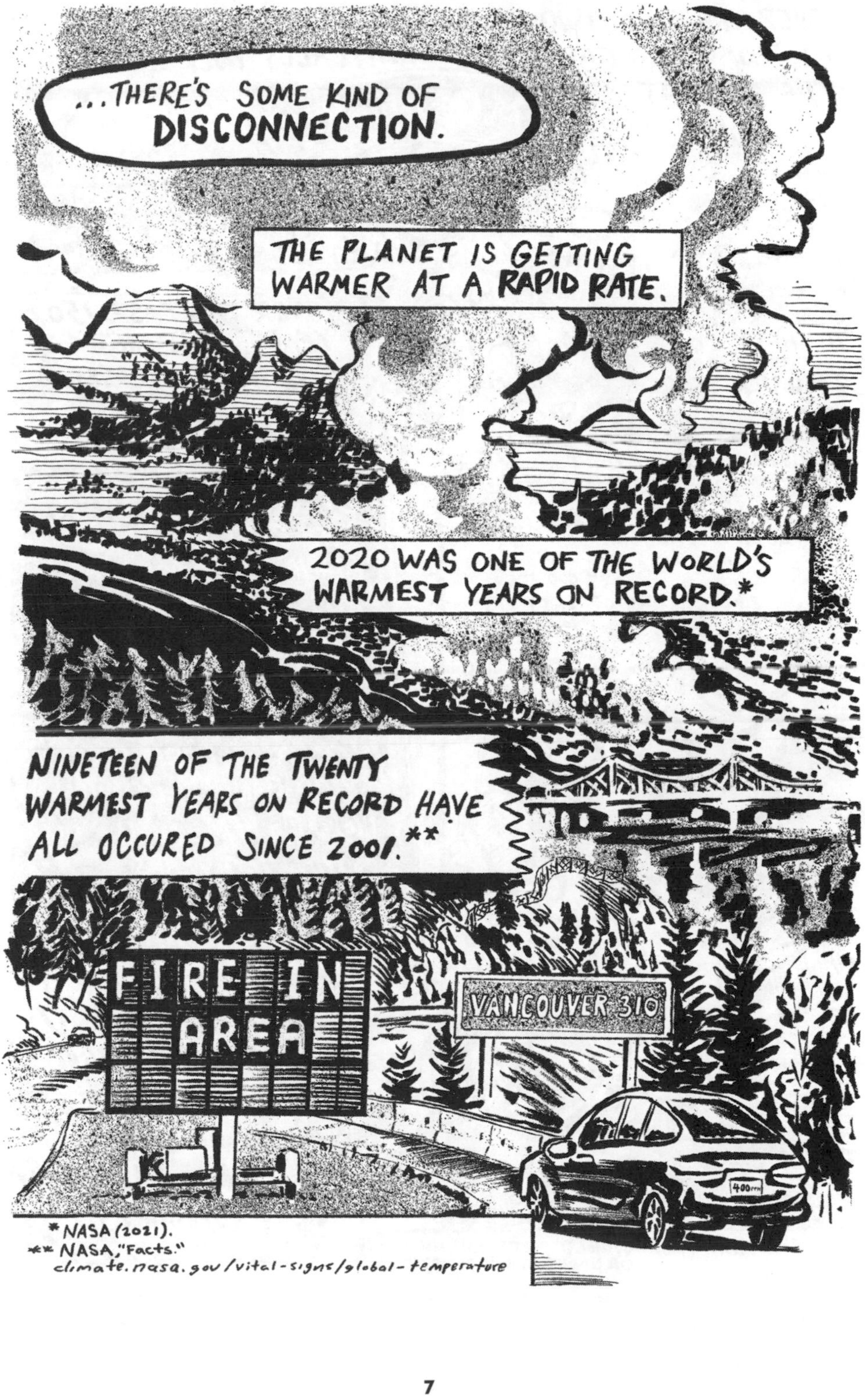
...THERE'S SOME KIND OF DISCONNECTION.
THE PLANET IS GETTING WARMER AT A RAPID RATE.
2020 WAS ONE OF THE WORLD'S WARMEST YEARS ON RECORD.*
NINETEEN OF THE TWENTY WARMEST YEARS ON RECORD HAVE ALL OCCURED SINCE 2001.**
FIRE IN AREA
VANCOUVER 310

*NASA (2021).

** NASA, "Facts." climate.nasa.gov/vital-signs/global-temperature

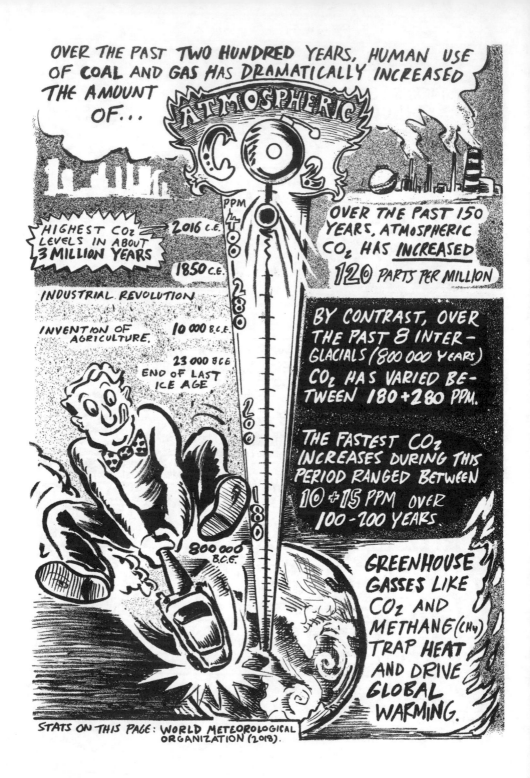

OVER THE PAST **TWO HUNDRED** YEARS, HUMAN USE OF **COAL** AND GAS HAS DRAMATICALLY INCREASED THE AMOUNT OF...

ATMOSPHERIC CO_2

HIGHEST CO_2 LEVELS IN ABOUT 3 MILLION YEARS

2016 C.E.

1850 C.E.

INDUSTRIAL REVOLUTION

INVENTION OF AGRICULTURE. 10 000 B.C.E.

23 000 BCE END OF LAST ICE AGE

800 000 B.C.E.

PPM

400

280

200

180

OVER THE PAST 150 YEARS, ATMOSPHERIC CO_2 HAS __INCREASED__ 120 PARTS PER MILLION

BY CONTRAST, OVER THE PAST 8 INTER-GLACIALS (800 000 YEARS) CO_2 HAS VARIED BETWEEN 180+280 PPM.

THE FASTEST CO_2 INCREASES DURING THIS PERIOD RANGED BETWEEN 10+15 PPM OVER 100-200 YEARS

GREENHOUSE GASSES LIKE CO_2 AND METHANE (CH4) TRAP **HEAT** AND DRIVE GLOBAL WARMING.

STATS ON THIS PAGE: WORLD METEOROLOGICAL ORGANIZATION (2018).

THE LAST TIME EARTH'S CO₂ LEVELS REACHED 400 WAS THE MID-PLIOCENE ROUGHLY THREE MILLION YEARS AGO. AT THIS TIME, THE AVERAGE GLOBAL TEMPERATURE WAS 2-3°C HIGHER THAN TODAY.

IN 2018, THE WORLD'S LEADING CLIMATE SCIENTISTS WARNED THAT MORE THAN A 1.5°C CHANGE WILL...

"SIGNIFICANTLY WORSEN THE RISKS OF DROUGHT, FLOODS, EXTREME HEAT AND POVERTY FOR HUNDREDS OF MILLIONS OF PEOPLE."*

ANOTHER STUDY WARNS OF POSSIBLE FEEDBACK-LOOPS

THE COMBINED EFFECTS OF CLIMATE CHANGE EVENTS COULD TIP THE EARTH INTO A HOTHOUSE STATE, BEYOND OUR ABILITY TO INTERVENE IF WE DON'T INTERRUPT CURRENT TRENDS.**

* "WE HAVE 12 Years to limit climate change catastrophe, warns UN" WATTS, The GUARDIAN Oct. 8, 2018.

+2°C

MELTING ICE   SHIFTING TIDES   ACIDIC OCEANS   DYING FORESTS   CORAL REEFS   METHANE GAS   HEAT WAVES   EXTINCTIONS

** STEFFEN et al. (2018).

9

FOR THE PAST TEN THOUSAND YEARS, HUMAN CIVILIZATION HAS UNFOLDED IN A PERIOD OF RELATIVE **CLIMATE STABILITY** CALLED THE **HOLOCENE** THAT FOLLOWED THE LAST ICE AGE.

HUMAN ALTERATIONS TO THE CO_2 CYCLE HAVE LIKELY ALREADY PUSHED EARTH OUT OF THE **GLACIAL CYCLES** THAT HAVE DICTATED PLANETARY TEMPERATURE LIMITS FOR THE PAST TEN ICE AGES, OR ABOUT **1.2 MILLION YEARS**

RECENT PROJECTIONS WARN THAT HUMAN CO_2 EMISSIONS COUPLED WITH CASCADING **BIOSPHERE DAMAGE** COULD SEND THE PLANET PAST A CRUCIAL **TIPPING POINT**...

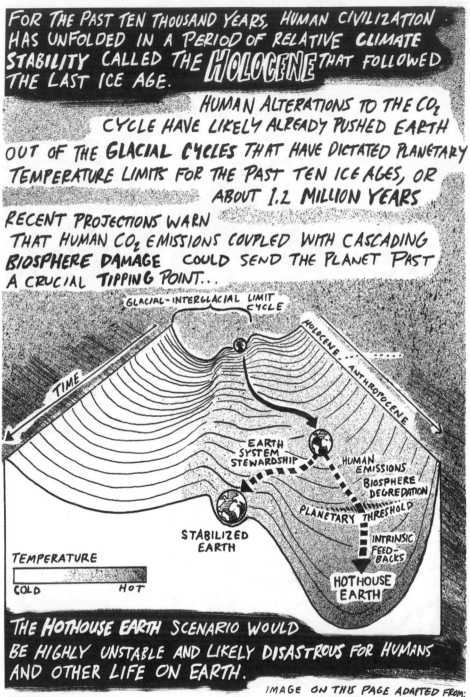

GLACIAL-INTERGLACIAL LIMIT CYCLE

TIME

HOLOCENE · ANTHROTOCENE

EARTH SYSTEM STEWARDSHIP

HUMAN EMISSIONS

BIOSPHERE DEGREDATION

PLANETARY THRESHOLD

STABILIZED EARTH

INTRINSIC FEED-BACKS

HOTHOUSE EARTH

TEMPERATURE

COLD   HOT

THE **HOTHOUSE EARTH** SCENARIO WOULD BE HIGHLY UNSTABLE AND LIKELY **DISASTROUS** FOR HUMANS AND OTHER LIFE ON EARTH.

IMAGE ON THIS PAGE ADAPTED FROM: STEFFEN et al. (2018).

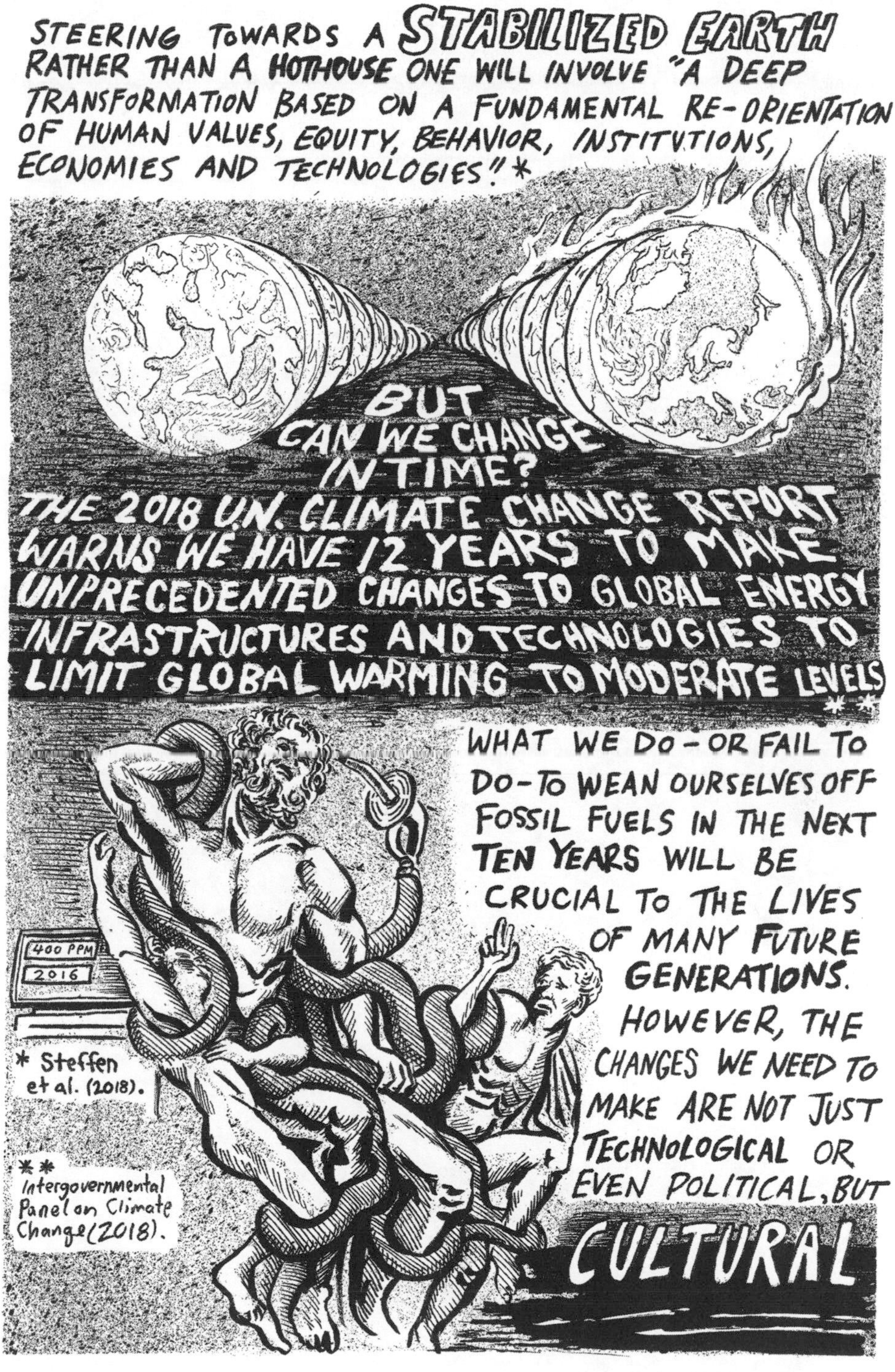
STEERING TOWARDS A STABILIZED EARTH RATHER THAN A HOTHOUSE ONE WILL INVOLVE "A DEEP TRANSFORMATION BASED ON A FUNDAMENTAL RE-ORIENTATION OF HUMAN VALUES, EQUITY, BEHAVIOR, INSTITUTIONS, ECONOMIES AND TECHNOLOGIES." *
BUT CAN WE CHANGE IN TIME?
THE 2018 U.N. CLIMATE CHANGE REPORT WARNS WE HAVE 12 YEARS TO MAKE UNPRECEDENTED CHANGES TO GLOBAL ENERGY INFRASTRUCTURES AND TECHNOLOGIES TO LIMIT GLOBAL WARMING TO MODERATE LEVELS **
WHAT WE DO - OR FAIL TO DO - TO WEAN OURSELVES OFF FOSSIL FUELS IN THE NEXT TEN YEARS WILL BE CRUCIAL TO THE LIVES OF MANY FUTURE GENERATIONS. HOWEVER, THE CHANGES WE NEED TO MAKE ARE NOT JUST TECHNOLOGICAL OR EVEN POLITICAL, BUT
CULTURAL
400 PPM
2016
* Steffen et al. (2018).
** Intergovernmental Panel on Climate Change (2018).

Chapter 1
Petroculture

HIGHLY PETROL-DEPENDENT CULTURES LIKE NORTH AMERICA MIGHT IMAGINE ENERGY **TRANSITION** AS MERELY A SHIFT IN **TECHNOLOGY**

THE BELIEF THAT SCIENCE AND TECHNOLOGY WILL SAVE US OVERLOOKS THE WAYS OUR RELATIONSHIPS, LIFESTYLES AND LIFEWORLDS ARE **SOAKED** IN OIL...

FOOD FABRICS COSMETICS TRANSPORT PRINT MEDIA PLASTICS TECHNOLOGY CONSTRUCTION EYE GLASSES MEDICINE ENTERTAINMENT

MODERN **LIFE** FOR MOST PEOPLE IS THOROUGHLY A...

PETROCULTURE

OIL IS NOT JUST AN ENERGY SOURCE OR RAW MATERIAL, BUT A SET OF **PRACTICES, HABITS, INSTITUTIONS, BELIEFS** AND **HISTORIES**

WE ARE **PETRO-SUBJECTS** THROUGH AND THROUGH.

PETROCULTURE **STRUCTURES** HOW WE **RELATE** TO OURSELVES, EACH OTHER, THE LARGER ENVIRONMENT AND THE FUTURE.
THE TASK OF **TRANSITIONING** FROM FOSSIL FUELS, WHILE DAUNTING, IS AN **OPPORTUNITY** TO **RE-IMAGINE** OUR SOCIETY AND SELVES.

HOW MIGHT WORK, FAMILY, RECREATION, POLITICS, ECONOMICS, SOCIAL LIFE AND CULTURE LOOK IN A **POST-OIL FUTURE?**

FOR MORE ON PETROCULTURE SEE:
AFTER OIL, BY THE PETROCULTURE RESEARCH GROUP, 2016. AVAILABLE FREE AT: AFTEROIL.CA.

PERHAPS WE WOULD SPEND LESS TIME COMMUTING...

... OR HAVE WE BECOME ATTACHED TO THE EXPERIENCE OF BEING **STUCK?**

THE HOURS I SPEND LOCKED IN TRAFFIC ARE THE ONLY MOMENTS OF UNDISTRACTED **PRIVATE** TIME I HAVE LEFT.

SIGH SIGH SIGH SIGH SIGH SIGH SIGH

PERHAPS WE COULD **LOCALLY** AND **COOPERATIVELY** HARVEST AND MANAGE **RENEWABLE ENERGY...**

... OR WILL WE JUST LET LARGE CORPORATIONS CONTINUE TO **MONOPOLIZE** OUR SHARED RESOURCES?

410 PPM

PERHAPS WE COULD HAVE LESS **EXPLOITATIVE**, MORE **JUST** AND **SUSTAINABLE** RELATIONSHIPS WITH EACH OTHER AND THE WORLD THAT SUPPORTS US...

... OR HAVE WE LOST THE ABILITY TO **LIVE** AND **DREAM** DIFFERENTLY?

17

DESPITE A GREAT POTENTIAL FOR TRANSITIONING TO MORE
EQUITABLE, SUSTAINABLE AND DEMOCRATIC SOCIETIES,
IT IS DIFFICULT TO IMAGINE WHAT OUR LIVES AND
RELATIONSHIPS MIGHT LOOK LIKE

*PETROCULTURES RESEARCH GROUP
(2016), PG. 41.

CULTURAL THEORIST IMRE SZEMAN DESCRIBES HOW THE MODERN SUBJECT

...HAS HAD HER CAPACITIES RADICALLY REDEFINED BY CHEAP ENERGY.

THE PETROCULTURAL SUBJECT'S LIFE IS CONFIGURED AROUND THE ENERGIES OF MILLIONS OF YEARS OF DEAD MATTER.

WHAT SHE UNDERSTANDS AS BANAL, QUOTIDIAN REALITY IS IN FACT A BENDING AND STRETCHING OF TIME TO GIVE THE SUBJECT POWERS OF MOVEMENT, VISION AND KNOWLEDGE AKIN TO THE DEMIGODS FOUND IN ANCIENT MYTH.*

ENERGY CULTURE SHIFT AHEAD

ENERGY JUSTICE

BUSINESS AS USUAL

ENERGY 101

* SZEMAN (2019) Pg. 10.

DESPITE BEING ONE OF THE SINGLE MOST **DETERMINATIVE** SUBSTANCES, THE POLITICS AND ECONOMICS OF WHICH SHAPE THE LIVES OF **BILLIONS OF PEOPLE** IN EMPHATICALLY DIVERSE AND UNEVEN WAYS, FOSSIL FUELS HAVE LARGELY REMAINED AN **UN-THEORIZED** AND TAKEN-FOR-GRANTED REALITY...

...UNTIL **NOW.**

WITH THE NEED TO **TRANSITION** AWAY FROM FOSSIL FUELS BECOMING DAILY MORE EVIDENT...

...THERE IS AN IMPERATIVE TO EXAMINE AND REIMAGINE OUR RELATION- SHIP TO ENERGY.

THIS TASK IS QUITE POSSIBLY...

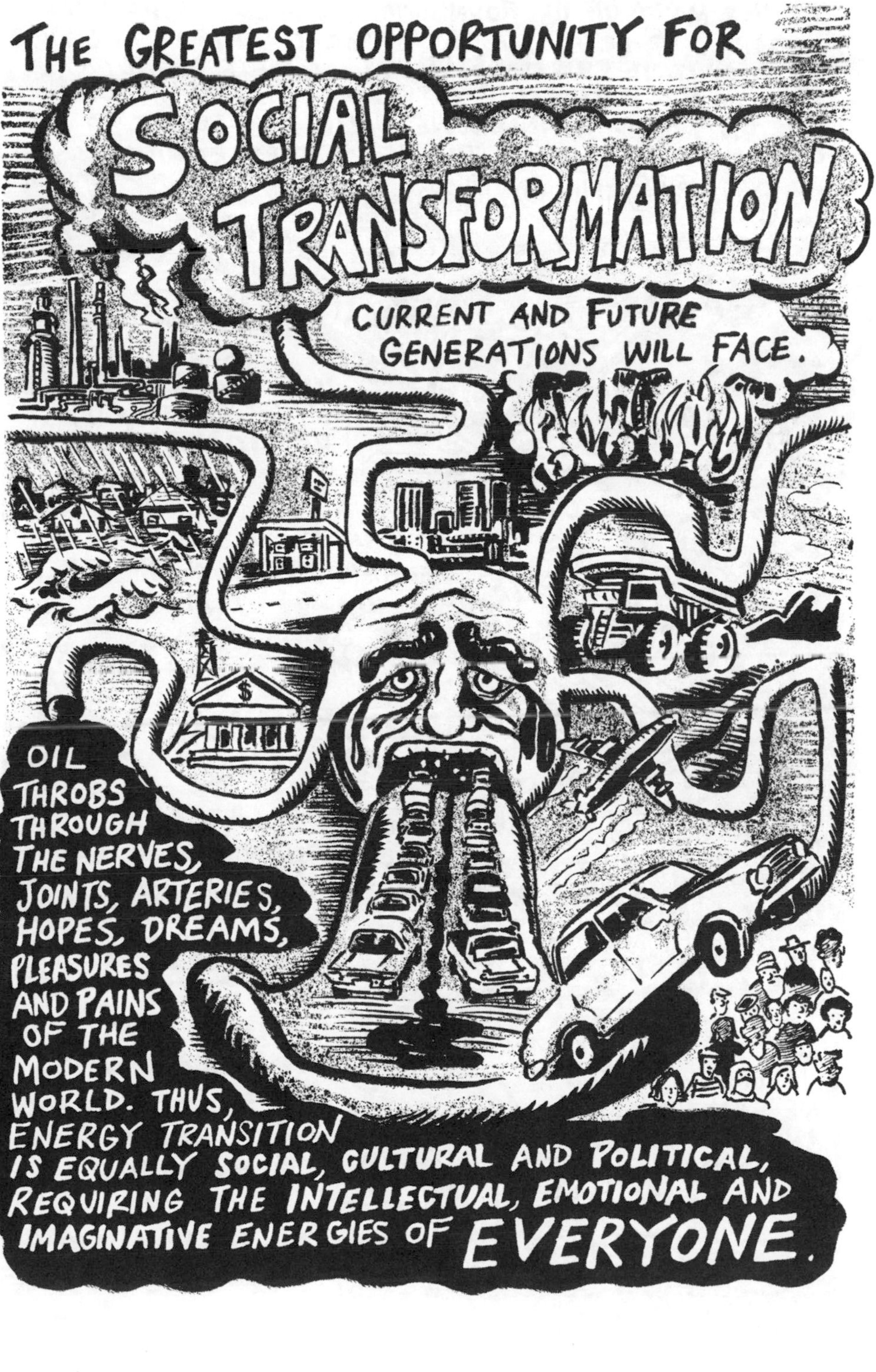

THE GREATEST OPPORTUNITY FOR
SOCIAL TRANSFORMATION
CURRENT AND FUTURE GENERATIONS WILL FACE.
$
OIL THROBS THROUGH THE NERVES, JOINTS, ARTERIES, HOPES, DREAMS, PLEASURES AND PAINS OF THE MODERN WORLD. THUS, ENERGY TRANSITION IS EQUALLY SOCIAL, CULTURAL AND POLITICAL, REQUIRING THE INTELLECTUAL, EMOTIONAL AND IMAGINATIVE ENERGIES OF EVERYONE.

YET, FOR MANY OF US BORN INTO A WORLD WHERE CHEAP, ACCESSIBLE ENERGY IS A TAKEN-FOR-GRANTED REALITY, THE MOUNTING CRISES OF GLOBAL CLIMATE CHANGE CAN SEEM LIKE A **PARALYZING** SITUATION — TOO BIG, CLOSE AND ENTWINED WITH WHO WE BELIEVE OURSELVES TO BE TO DO ANYTHING ABOUT. THUS, SOME TAKE REFUGE IN OUTRIGHT DENIAL

...USUALLY GROUNDED IN PATRIARCHAL AND OFTEN RACIST FORMS OF NOSTALGIA.

OTHERS FOSTER A TECHNO-UTOPIAN BELIEF THAT SCIENCE WILL SAVE US, PERHAPS BY COLONIZING OTHER PLANETS.

WHILE THESE TWO POSITIONS DIFFER IN THEIR RELATIONSHIP TO THE FACTS ABOUT ANTHROPOGENIC CLIMATE CHANGE, THEY BOTH TAKE REFUGE IN APPEALS TO AUTHORITARIAN AND MASCULINIST POWER FIGURES TO SAVE US.

BOLDLY TRANSFORMING NATURE INTO STUFF WE CAN **CONSUME** AND **DISCARD** IS WHAT DEFINES HUMAN LIFE.

ALL THESE SISSY ENVIRONMENTALISTS SHOULD BE ROUNDED UP AS THE FIRST TEST SUBJECTS FOR THE MARS MISSION.

22

WHILE WE MIGHT TEND TO THINK OF ENERGY TRANSITION
AS A TECHNOLOGICAL PROBLEM, MORE LIKELY IT IS
THE CULTURAL NEXUS WHERE ENERGY REGIMES
AND MEANING-MAKING PROCESSES CONVERGE THAT
PROVIDES THE GREATEST BARRIER TO IMAGINING
AND WORKING TOWARDS A WORLD BEYOND
FOSSIL FUELS.

DESPITE THE WORLD
BEING IN FLAMES AROUND US, OUR OIL-SOAKED
CULTURE, WITH ALL ITS SPEED, DISTRACTIONS AND
EXCITEMENT, LARGELY WORKS TO
KEEP US ASLEEP.

WHAT KINDS OF ANALYSIS, CRITIQUE AND CREATIVITY MIGHT HELP OPEN A SPACE WHERE WE CAN BEGIN BUILDING AND DREAMING A NEW AND BETTER WORLD?

TO BORROW AND ADAPT SOME TERMS FROM PSYCHOANALYSIS, WHAT IF OUR DEPENDENCIES AND ANXIETIES OVER ENERGY ARE THE **LATENT CONTENT**, THE OBSCURED MATRIX THAT SHAPES MUCH OF **CONTEMPORARY CULTURE**?

PERHAPS THE FANTASIES AND NARRATIVES WITH WHICH WE **IDENTIFY** ARE, THEMSELVES, SHAPED BY WHAT PATRICIA YEAGER CALLS AN

ENERGY UNCONSCIOUS

... SINCE FUEL SOURCES HOVER IN THE BACKGROUND OF TEXTS, IF THEY SPEAK AT ALL, TO PURSUE AN **ENERGY UNCONSCIOUS** MEANS A COMMITMENT TO THE REPRESSED, THE **NON-DIT**, AND TO THE TEXT AS A **TISSUE OF CONTRADICTIONS.***

* YEAGER (2011) Pg. 310, FN 1.

IN DREAMING, OUR IMAGINATIONS DRESS UP OUR FEARS, ANXIETIES AND DESIRES IN DISGUISED FORM, PROVIDING STRIKING AND BIZARRE, BUT ALSO STRANGELY FAMILIAR NARRATIVES THAT HELP PREVENT US FROM BEING WOKEN UP DUE TO THE NIGHTTIME ECHOES OF OUR DAYTIME LIVES.

JUST AS THE WEIRD, SHIFTING IMAGES OF OUR DREAMS ATTEMPT TO CAPTURE AND MANAGE THE DISCORDANT ENERGIES THAT WOULD OTHERWISE DISTURB OUR SLEEP...

FAMILIES HAVE NO BORDERS

LET US BE PART OF THE AMERICAN DREAM

...SO TOO DO THE COLLECTIVE DREAMS, NOT JUST OF POPULAR CULTURE, BUT OF POLITICS, HISTORY AND EVERYDAY LIFE, ATTEMPT TO SHAPE AND MANAGE HOPES, FEARS AND DESIRES IN SERVICE OF HABITUATED MODES OF EXISTENCE.

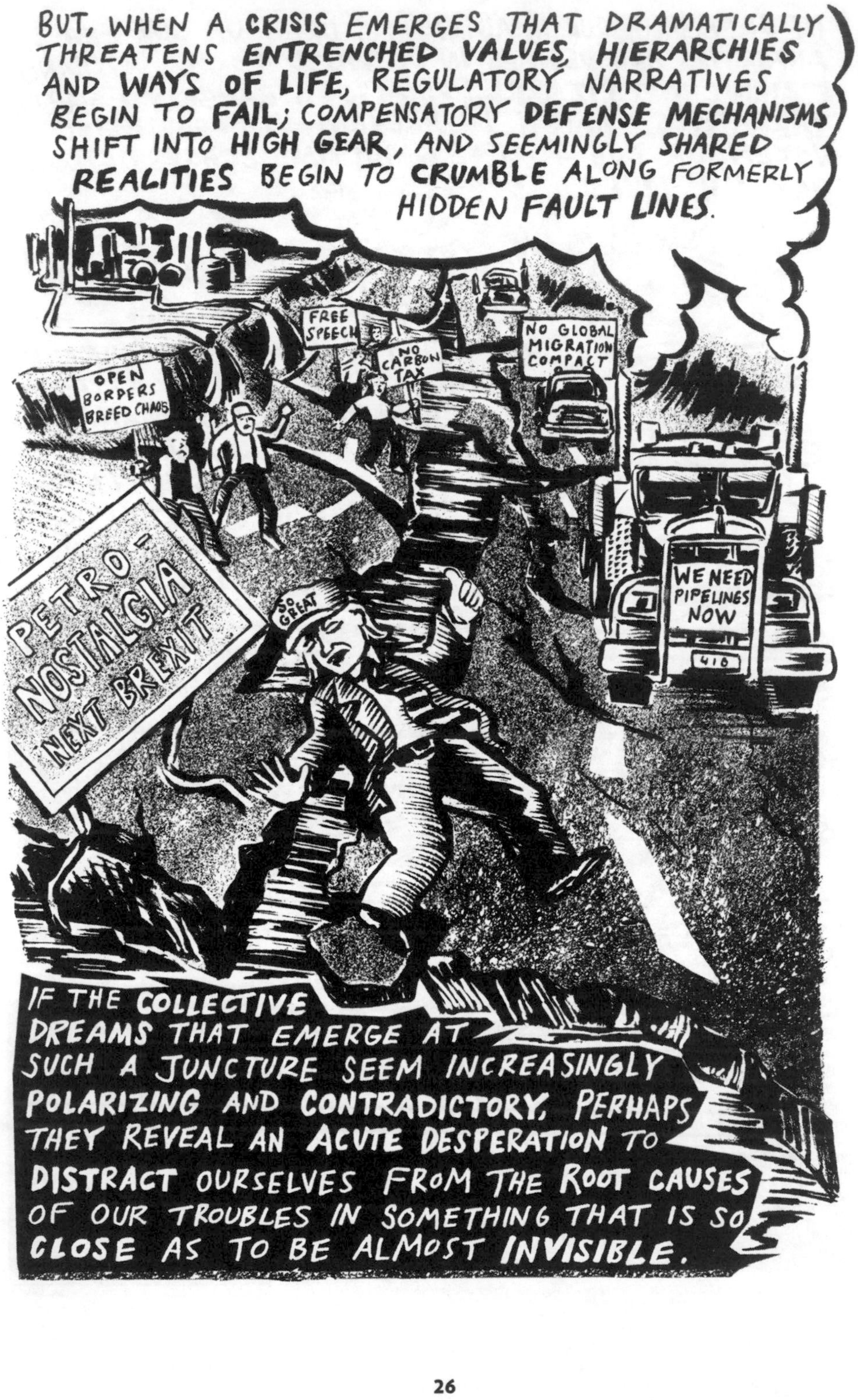
BUT, WHEN A CRISIS EMERGES THAT DRAMATICALLY THREATENS ENTRENCHED VALUES, HIERARCHIES AND WAYS OF LIFE, REGULATORY NARRATIVES BEGIN TO FAIL; COMPENSATORY DEFENSE MECHANISMS SHIFT INTO HIGH GEAR, AND SEEMINGLY SHARED REALITIES BEGIN TO CRUMBLE ALONG FORMERLY HIDDEN FAULT LINES.
FREE SPEECH
NO CARBON TAX
NO GLOBAL MIGRATION COMPACT
OPEN BORDERS BREED CHAOS
PETRO-NOSTALGIA NEXT BREXIT
SO GREAT
WE NEED PIPELINES NOW
410
IF THE COLLECTIVE DREAMS THAT EMERGE AT SUCH A JUNCTURE SEEM INCREASINGLY POLARIZING AND CONTRADICTORY, PERHAPS THEY REVEAL AN ACUTE DESPERATION TO DISTRACT OURSELVES FROM THE ROOT CAUSES OF OUR TROUBLES IN SOMETHING THAT IS SO CLOSE AS TO BE ALMOST INVISIBLE.

OUR SENSE OF SELFHOOD, IDENTITY, AGENCY, GENDER AND POLITICAL POSSIBILITIES AND OUR RELATIONSHIPS TO EACH OTHER AND THE LARGER ENVIRONMENT HAVE ALL BEEN CONDITIONED BY PETROCULTURE, OFTEN TO THE POINT OF BECOMING "SECOND NATURE."

THE WORLD MAY BE ENDING, BUT I'VE STILL GOT MY CAR!

PERHAPS THIS IS THE REASON THE COLLECTIVE CHALLENGES POSED BY THE PROSPECT OF ENERGY TRANSITION ARE MET BY SUCH A HOST OF REACTIONARY, EMOTIONAL, RESENTFUL AND ANXIOUS RESPONSES

... SOME OF WHICH ARE CAPTURED AND MANAGED BY POPULAR CULTURE. TAKE JOHN KRASINSKI'S 2018 THRILLER A QUIET PLACE.

HERE, BLIND EXTRA-TERRESTRIALS WITH SENSITIVE EARS MAKE THE USE OF PETROLEUM IMPOSSIBLE: ANY LOUD NOISE WILL ATTRACT THEM. THE EMBATTLED ABBOTT FAMILY MUST STRUGGLE TO REPRODUCE ITSELF IN OPRESSIVE -BUT SOMETIMES UTOPIAN- SILENCE.

TO WHAT HIDDEN WISHES AND ANXIETIES MIGHT THESE STRANGE MONSTERS GIVE DISGUISED EXPRESSION?

LET'S CONSIDER, FIRST OF ALL, THE YOUNG MARCUS ABBOTT (NOAH JUPE), WHO IS SHOWN, EARLY IN THE FILM, IN A FORD PICK-UP TRUCK, LONGINGLY MIMING THE ACTIONS OF DRIVING, A RITUAL OF **MOBILITY** AND **MANHOOD** DENIED HIM BY THE MONSTERS' REGIME OF **SILENCE**.

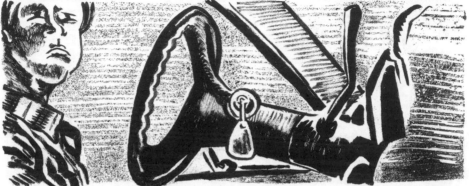

TOWARDS THE **CLIMAX** OF THE FILM, WHEN MARCUS AND HIS SISTER ARE **TRAPPED** IN THE SAME VEHICLE BY ONE OF THE **ALIENS**, HIS FATHER **SACRIFICES HIMSELF**, DRAWING THE CREATURE AWAY FROM THE TRUCK AND ALLOWING MARCUS TO **ROLL THE CAR** TO THE SAFETY OF THE HOUSE.

YEEAGHH!

AT PRECISELY THE MOMENT THAT **MALE AUTHORITY** IS **TRANSFERRED** FROM FATHER TO SON IN AN ACT OF **SELF-SACRIFICE**, MARCUS' DREAM OF **PILOTING** THE FAMILY TRUCK IS REALIZED (EVEN THOUGH IT IS ACTUALLY THE DAUGHTER, REGAN, WHO WILL ULTIMATELY **DISCOVER** THE MONSTERS' **FATAL WEAKNESS**).

SUCH ASSOCIATIONS OF MASCULINITY, COMING-OF-AGE AND THE SURVIVAL OF THE WHITE, NUCLEAR FAMILY WITH DRIVING ARE NOT NATURAL. RATHER, THEY ARE THE HISTORICAL PRODUCTS OF POST-WWII PETROCULTURE. IN ONLY A FEW SHORT GENERATIONS, THIS COMPLEX HAS BECOME SO ENTRENCHED THAT THREATS TO ITS REPRODUCTION CAN CAUSE GREAT COLLECTIVE ANXIETY.

IF THEY HEAR YOU THEY HUNT YOU

HORROR
COMEDY
ROMANCE

JUST AS THE ACT OF FUELLING A VEHICLE PUTS US IN CONTACT WITH DARK, CHTHONIC ENERGIES THAT ARE USUALLY HIDDEN, SO TOO DOES POPULAR CULTURE FUEL OUR IMAGINATIONS, GIVING SHAPE TO UNCONSCIOUS FORCES.

OFTEN, SUCH FANTASIES ENGAGE OUR DESIRES FOR CHANGE WHILE NEGOTIATING WITH OUR FEARS OF THE UNKNOWN, THUS RETRENCHING THE SAME OLD PARADIGMS.

TAKE THE OPENING SCENES OF A QUIET PLACE. HERE, FOUR-YEAR-OLD BEAU ABBOTT IS KILLED WHEN A TOY HIS SISTER HAS GIVEN HIM MAKES NOISES THAT ATTRACT ONE OF THE MONSTERS.

THE TOY RESPONSIBLE FOR BEAU'S DEMISE IS A SPACE SHUTTLE.

JUST AS THE MONSTERS BAR MARCUS FROM DRIVING, SO TOO DO THEY PUNISH YOUNG BEAU'S DREAMS OF SPACE TRAVEL.

ALREADY, THE FILM TAPS INTO AND HELPS REINFORCE A TANGLE OF CULTURALLY CONSTRUCTED ASSOCIATIONS...

29

THE FILM'S OPENING IMAGERY COUPLES YOUTH, INNOCENCE AND IMAGINATION WITH ADVENTURE, NATIONHOOD AND THE FRONTIER OF SPACE, ALL OF WHICH IS CODED AS MASCULINE AND THEN DRAMATICALLY SUPPRESSED BY BEAU'S DEATH AT THE HANDS OF ONE OF THE ALIENS.

FURTHERMORE, THE GUILT THAT REGAN FEELS OVER THE DEATH OF HER BROTHER PROVIDES ONE OF THE CENTRAL PSYCHOLOGICAL DRAMAS OF THE PLOT.

IF THE ALIENS GIVE EXPRESSION TO ANXIETIES REGARDING THREATS TO PETROCULTURAL NORMS — SPECIFICALLY, A MASCULINE SENSE OF AGENCY IN PHYSICAL SPACE AND THE WAY THESE RELATE TO THE REPRODUCTION OF THE WHITE, NUCLEAR FAMILY AND THE STATE — THEN REGAN'S GUILT OVER HER UNINTENTIONAL PARTICIPATION IN THIS THREAT IS MEANINGFUL.

COULD THE FILM HERE BE TAPPING INTO CULTURAL STEREOTYPES BY WHICH ENVIRONMENTAL CONCERNS ARE CODED AS 'FEMININE,' WHILE BURNING GAS AND DRAMATICALLY TRANSFORMING ENVIRONMENTS ARE CODED AS 'MANLY'?

CAN THE ALIEN MONSTERS THUS BE READ AS VEHICLES FOR THE ANXIETIES A LARGELY MASCULINIST PETROCULTURE FEELS OVER ITS REPRODUCTION?

CONSIDER HOW PUBLIC CRITIQUES OF CLIMATE ACTIVISM ARE OFTEN COUPLED WITH MISOGYNISTIC INVECTIVE, SUGGESTING THAT CHALLENGES TO PETROCULTURE ARE PERCIEVED BY SOME AS ATTACKS UPON SPECIFIC VARIETIES OF MASCULINE IDENTITY, FREEDOM AND PRIVILEGE.

GERRY RITZ, M.P.
CONSERVATIVE
PARTY OF CANADA

CATHERINE McKENNA,
CANADIAN ENVIRONMENT
& CLIMATE CHANGE MINISTER

IN SEPT. 2017, RITZ CALLED McKENNA A "CLIMATE CHANGE BARBIE" ON TWITTER, PROVOKING THE USE OF THE SLUR ON SOCIAL MEDIA BY McKENNA'S DETRACTORS EVER SINCE.

MAXIME BERNIER, LEADER
PEOPLE'S PARTY OF CANADA

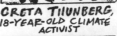

GRETA THUNBERG,
18-YEAR-OLD CLIMATE
ACTIVIST

IN 2019, BERNIER DISPARAGED THUNBERG IN A TWEET, CALLING THE ACTIVIST, WHO IS AUTISTIC, "MENTALLY UNSTABLE" AMONGST OTHER SLIGHTS AIMED AT HER CHARACTER.

CHARLES COOKE, EDITOR,
NATIONAL REVIEW

ALEXANDRIA OCASIO-
CORTEZ, U.S. CONGRESSWOMAN

AFTER OCASIO-CORTEZ REVEALED HER GREEN NEW DEAL PROPOSAL, COOKE CALLED HER AN "UNMARRIED, CHILDLESS BARTENDER" UNFIT FOR PUBLIC OFFICE.

WHILE THESE GENDERED, PERSONAL ATTACKS AGAINST WOMEN WHO TAKE PUBLIC POSITIONS ON ENVIRONMENTAL ISSUES REVEAL PERVASIVE BIASES INHERENT IN PETROCULTURE, WHAT IS MOST TELLING IN TERMS OF INTERPRETING A QUIET PLACE IS THE WAY THIS SAME PATRIARCHAL COMPLEX RESPONDS TO BEING CHALLENGED FOR ITS DEPLOYMENT OF SEXIST STEREOTYPES...

QUOTES ON THIS PAGE FROM:
RANEY, T. & M. GREGORY, "WOMEN CLIMATE LEADERS FACE 'GREEN RAGE' ATTACKS,"
THE TYEE. CA, SEPT 16, 2019.

WHEN RIGHT-WING SPOKESPEOPLE ARE CRITICIZED FOR THEIR USE OF DISCRIMINATORY, AD HOMINEM ATTACKS AGAINST CLIMATE ACTIVISTS, THEY OFTEN FURTHER ATTEMPT TO DERAIL REASONABLE DISCUSSION OF FACTS BY CLAIMING THEY ARE BEING **SILENCED**

"I'M PERSONALLY DISGUSTED AT EFFORTS BY CLIMATE ACTIVISTS TO SHUT DOWN CRITICISM BY ACCUSING THEIR CRITICS OF BEING RACISTS OR MISOGYNISTS." *

* ERIC WORRALL, "CLAIM..." WHATSUPWITHTHAT.COM, SEPT 13, 2019

ONE OF THE MOST GRIPPING SCENES OF **A QUIET PLACE** HAS EVELYN ABBOTT (EMILY BLUNT) TRYING TO REMAIN **SILENT** AS SHE IS ABOUT TO **GIVE BIRTH**, WITH ONE OF THE **MONSTERS** CREEPING TOWARDS HER.

THIS SCENE PROVIDES A **METAPHOR** THAT SUPERIMPOSES TWO PREDOMINANT ANXIETIES ASSOCIATED WITH CLIMATE CHANGE AND ACTIVISM: THE FEAR OF BEING **PREVENTED** FROM HAVING **CHILDREN**, AND THE FEAR THAT FORMERLY **PRIVILEGED** SUBJECTS, SUCH AS THE **WHITE MIDDLE CLASS**, HAVE OF BEING **SILENCED** WHEN THEY ATTEMPT TO **DEFEND** A NOW **EMBATTLED** WAY OF **LIFE** DEPENDENT ON **FOSSIL FUELS.**

THE FILM'S **POPULARITY** LIKELY HAS MUCH TO DO WITH THE WAY IT **WEAVES** THESE OTHERWISE **DIFFUSE** AND **NEBULOUS** ANXIETIES INTO THE **CONCRETE** IMAGE OF FEARSOME **MONSTERS** THAT CAN THEN BE **SLAIN.**

REGAN (MILLICENT SIMMONDS) ATONES FOR HER ROLE IN BEAU'S DEATH BY DISCOVERING THAT THE FREQUENCY OF HER HEARING AID, WHEN AMPLIFIED, RENDERS THE ALIENS INCAPACITATED AND **VULNERABLE**.

WHAT COULD THIS MEAN ACCORDING TO THE **DREAM LOGIC** OF THE **FILM?**

IF THE MONSTERS POSE A BARRIER TO THE MASCULINE ENJOYMENT OF PETROCULTURE, THEN THE AMPLIFIED SIGNAL MAKES THEM LOSE THEIR **HEADS** – OR AT LEAST THEIR HEAD'S ARMOUR PLATING.

THE DEMONIZATION OF CARBON DIOXIDE IS JUST LIKE THE DEMONIZATION OF THE POOR JEWS UNDER **HITLER.** *

AND IF THE ALIENS ARE FOCAL POINTS FOR REAL-WORLD ANXIETIES ABOUT ANTI-PETROLEUM ACTIVISM, THEN WHAT KINDS OF SIGNALS DRIVE CLIMATE CHANGE ACTIVISTS CRAZY?

YREEEAAGH!!

97% OF CLIMATE SCIENTISTS KNOW YOU ARE WRONG!

CO₂ FOR LIFE

*PHYSICIST **WILLIAM HAPPER** SAID THIS ON **CNBC** IN 2014. HE SERVED AS DONALD TRUMP'S ASSISTANT OF EMERGING TECHNOLOGIES IN 2018. THOUGH NOT TRAINED IN **CLIMATE SCIENCE**, THE PRINCETON PROF. ADAMANTLY **DENIES** ANTHROPOGENIC CLIMATE CHANGE. FOR THE ORIGINAL QUOTE, SEE: STRAUS (2014).

BENEATH THEIR ARMOUR PLATING, THE ALIENS' EXTREMELY SENSITIVE EARS ARE UNABLE TO BEAR A CERTAIN KIND OF STATIC.

ZZZSSST

AND CREATING STATIC IN THE FORM OF DOUBT, MISINFORMATION AND DISCRIMINATORY RHETORIC IS ONE OF THE COMMON DISCURSIVE STRATEGIES OF PRO-OIL PUNDITS.

FURTHERMORE, IN THE CULTURALLY CONSTRUCTED ECONOMY OF THE FIVE SENSES, HEARING IS STEREOTYPICALLY CODED AS FEMININE, WHILE SIGHT IS THE DOMINANT MALE SENSE ORGAN...

MY BIONIC VISION MAKES ME MASTER OF ALL I SURVEY.

MY BIONIC EAR MAKES ME GOOD AT EAVESDROPPING.

BIONIC WOMAN

$6 MIL MAN

POPULAR CULTURE REFLECTS AND REINFORCES THESE ASSOCIATIVE STRUCTURES.

THUS, WHILE THE MONSTERS FROM A QUIET PLACE ARE GIVEN NO DETERMINATIVE GENDER, THEIR DEFINING TRAIT OF SUPERIOR HEARING IS PART OF A LARGER PATTERN THAT CULTURALLY CODES THEM AS FEMININE.

THESE ASSOCIATIVE MEANINGS, SUCH AS IDENTIFYING THE ALIENS AS TAPPING INTO PETROCULTURAL ANXIETIES ABOUT THREATS TO THE PATRIARCHAL WHITE MIDDLE-CLASS FAMILY, ARE NOT EXPLICIT OR EVEN NECESSARILY INTENTIONAL NARRATIVES ON THE PART OF THE FILM'S PRODUCERS.

DREAM DISPLACEMENT AND DREAM CONDENSATION ARE THE TWO CRAFTSMEN IN CHARGE OF MOULDING THE DREAM.*

IN FACT, SUCH RESOURCES WORK MOST EFFECTIVELY AS THE BACKGROUND OR LATENT CONTENT THAT CONTRIBUTES TO THE FILM'S EMOTIONAL CHARGE, EXPRESSING FEARS AND DESIRES THAT WE MIGHT NOT BE ABLE TO FULLY RECOGNIZE IN OURSELVES OR OTHERS.

MY FREEDOM TO SPEAK IS BEING ERODED BY LEFTIES.

CONDENSER UNIT

THE REAL THREAT TO THE FLOURISHING OF MY FAMILY IS NOT GLOBAL WARMING BUT ALL OF THESE SOCIAL JUSTICE WARRIORS WHO WANT TO DESTROY OUR WAY OF LIFE.

DISPLACER RAY

* FREUD (1995), Pg. 286.

35

A QUIET PLACE BEGINS WITH THE ABBOTT FAMILY BEING PUNISHED FOR THE TRANSGRESSION OF THE YOUNGEST SON, WHO SUCCUMBS TO THE TEMPTATIONS OF A FORBIDDEN PETROCULTURE

AS BEAU REACHES FOR THE BATTERIES THAT WILL CAUSE HIS DEMISE, NOTICE THE CAR IN THE BACKGROUND.

BY THE FILM'S FINALE, AS THE ABBOTT WOMEN SQUARE OFF AGAINST THE ENERGY-DAMPENING ALIENS, THE FREEDOM TO BURN GASOLINE IS SET TO BE REINSTATED AS THE REPRESSIVE REGIME OF SILENCE IS ENDED BY GUNSHOTS.

WHEN EVELYN ABBOTT CONFRONTS THE MONSTER WHO HAS THREATENED HER PROGENY, SHE FACES AND VANQUISHES THE SPECTRE OF A FEMINIZED ENVIRONMENTALISM —BLIND BUT HEARING EVERYTHING.

THE FILM'S ENDING THUS OFFERS A PRO-PETROCULTURE STANCE THAT APPEARS PROGRESSIVE FOR ITS STRONG WOMAN CHARACTERS, WHILE ALSO CLEANSING THIS IDENTITY OF ITS ASSOCIATIONS WITH GREEN ACTIVISM.

SUCH MESSAGES ARE NOT NECESSARILY INTENTIONALLY ENCODED INTO POPULAR CULTURE.

FOR INSTANCE, JOHN KRASINSKI, WHO DIRECTED A QUIET PLACE, ALSO CO-WROTE AND CO-PRODUCED PROMISED LAND, A 2014 FILM THAT CRITQUES THE FRACKING INDUSTRY.

BUT THE REACTIONARY TENDENCIES OF A QUIET PLACE AND SO MANY OTHER FILMS ILLUSTRATE HOW FOSSIL FUELS AND THE VALUES ASSOCIATED WITH THEM HAVE BECOME A

BACKGROUND MATRIX FOR CULTURE AND SUBJECTIVITY.

PETROCULTURE IS THE JUNCTURE WHERE EXTRACTIVE INDUSTRIES, ECONOMIES AND INFRASTRUCTURES WARP NARRATIVE, MEANING, IDENTITY AND PERCEPTION ITSELF.

SUCH DISTRACTIONS MIGHT TAKE THE FORM OF XENOPHOBIC NATIONALISM, OR THEY MIGHT BE CLOAKED IN MORE SUBTLE AND SEEMINGLY PROGRESSIVE FORMS OF NOSTALGIA...

DO YOU EVER FEEL LIKE YOU ARE TRAPPED IN FANTASIES OF A BYGONE ERA BEING MARKETED TO AN EXPANDED DEMOGRAPHIC, TO SELL MORE PRODUCTS?

THE CRAPPY PART IS, KYLO REN STILL SELLS MORE ACTION FIGURES.

ROYALTIES

SO MUCH CONTEMPORARY POP-CULTURE, FOR INSTANCE, EVOKES LATE 20TH-CENTURY STRUCTURES OF FEELING, RECASTING THE EMANCIPATORY PROMISES OF PAST MOMENTS TO APPEAL TO A LIBERAL ETHICS OF INCLUSION.

I'M CONFUSED. WHAT DECADE ARE WE SUPPOSED TO BE IN?

IT'S LIKE THE 1980s BUT WITH CELL PHONES AND A MORE THAN TOKENISTIC TREATMENT OF DIVERSITY.

THESE POPULAR, POLITICALLY ASTUTE ENTERTAINMENTS REIMAGINE THE MISSED UTOPIAN POTENTIAL OF PAST ERAS, BUT THEY SHARE A HIDDEN CONNECTION WITH LESS PROGRESSIVE, REACTIONARY TENDENCIES AS A REFUGE FROM A SET OF PROBLEMS AND POTENTIALS THAT LACKS ADEQUATE MODES OF REPRESENTATION AND NARRATIVE.

PERHAPS THESE REIMAGININGS OF THE RECENT PAST REVEAL HOW WE WOULD LIKE THE FUTURE TO REMEMBER US. BUT, LIKE THE CHARACTERS FROM THE HIT NETFLIX SERIES **STRANGER THINGS**, OUR ESCAPIST NOSTALGIA IS HAUNTED BY AN UNCANNY REALM OF **MILDEW, FEAR, DEATH** AND **DECAY.**

LAST GAS FOR EVER

THE DECOMPOSING MIRROR WORLD OF "THE UPSIDE DOWN" IS WHERE THE SERIES ATTEMPTS TO CONTAIN THE SUPPRESSED ENTROPY OF THE SAME MELANCHOLIC ATTACHMENTS THAT MAKE THE SHOW SO SEDUCTIVELY APPEALING.

AND, LIKE SO MANY CONTEMPORARY POPULAR MONSTERS, THE DENIZENS OF THE UPSIDE DOWN FORM A **HIVE MIND.** PERHAPS WE ARE FRIGHTENED BY, BUT UNABLE TO CONFRONT, THE **COLLECTIVE EFFECTS AND REALITIES** OF OUR **INDIVIDUALIZED EXISTENCES.**

INTERESTINGLY, MANY *ZOMBIE FILMS* CONTAIN A GRIPPING SCENE WHERE THE PROTAGONISTS, IN AN EFFORT TO ACCESS A SMELLY FLUID MADE FROM THE DECOMPOSED BODIES OF *PAST LIFE FORMS*, ARE EXPOSED TO *ATTACK* FROM SMELLY, DECOMPOSED BODIES...

EXCEPTIONAL THOUGHT, IMAGINATION AND *RESOURCES* GO INTO MAKING THESE IMAGES

BUT WHY ARE DIRECT, EXPLICIT ENGAGEMENTS WITH ISSUES OF ENERGY AND ENVIRONMENT *ABSCENT* FROM THEM?

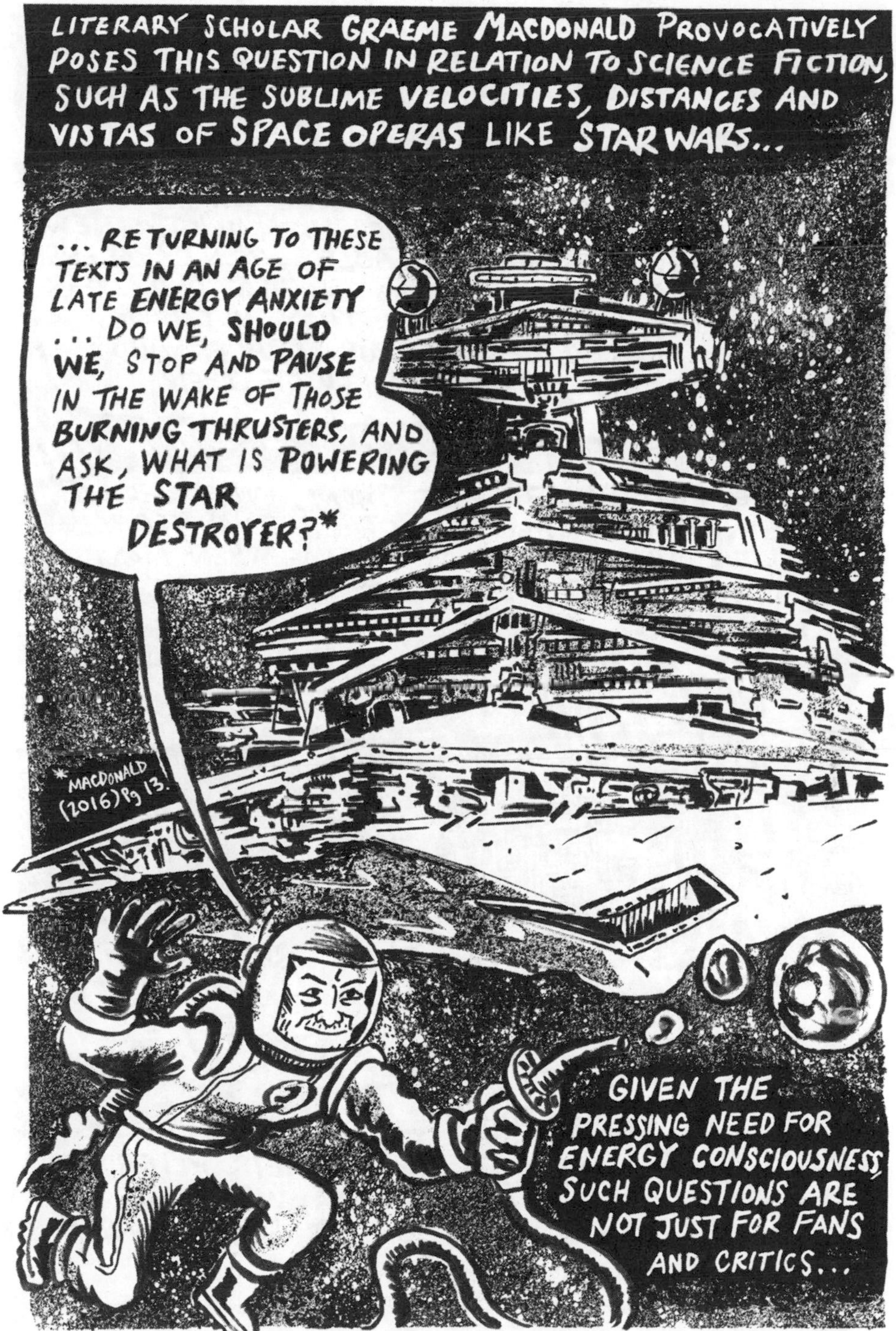
LITERARY SCHOLAR GRAEME MACDONALD PROVOCATIVELY POSES THIS QUESTION IN RELATION TO SCIENCE FICTION, SUCH AS THE SUBLIME VELOCITIES, DISTANCES AND VISTAS OF SPACE OPERAS LIKE STAR WARS...
... RETURNING TO THESE TEXTS IN AN AGE OF LATE ENERGY ANXIETY ... DO WE, SHOULD WE, STOP AND PAUSE IN THE WAKE OF THOSE BURNING THRUSTERS, AND ASK, WHAT IS POWERING THE STAR DESTROYER?*
* MACDONALD (2016) Pg 13.
GIVEN THE PRESSING NEED FOR ENERGY CONSCIOUSNESS, SUCH QUESTIONS ARE NOT JUST FOR FANS AND CRITICS...

FOR NOVELIST AND ESSAYIST AMITAV GHOSH, OUR (IN)ABILITY TO FIND NARRATIVE FORM TO ADDRESS CLIMATE CHANGE AND ENERGY WILL DETERMINE HOW FUTURE GENERATIONS WILL VIEW AND JUDGE US...

IN A SUBSTANTIALLY ALTERED WORLD WHEN SEA-LEVEL RISE HAS ... MADE CITIES LIKE KOLKOTA, NEW YORK, AND BANKOK UNINHABITABLE, WHEN READERS AND MUSEUM-GOERS TURN TO THE ART AND LITERATURE OF OUR TIME, WILL THEY NOT LOOK, FIRST AND MOST URGENTLY, FOR TRACES AND PORTENTS OF THE ALTERED WORLD OF THEIR INHERITANCE?

AND WHEN THEY FAIL TO FIND THEM, WHAT SHOULD THEY — WHAT CAN THEY — DO OTHER THAN TO CONCLUDE THAT OURS WAS A TIME WHEN MOST FORMS OF ART AND LITERATURE...

...WERE DRAWN INTO MODES OF CONCEALMENT THAT PREVENTED PEOPLE FROM RECOGNIZING THE REALITY OF THEIR PLIGHT? QUITE POSSIBLY, THEN. THIS ERA, WHICH SO CONGRATULATES ITSELF ON ITS SELF-AWARENESS, WILL COME TO BE KNOWN AS...

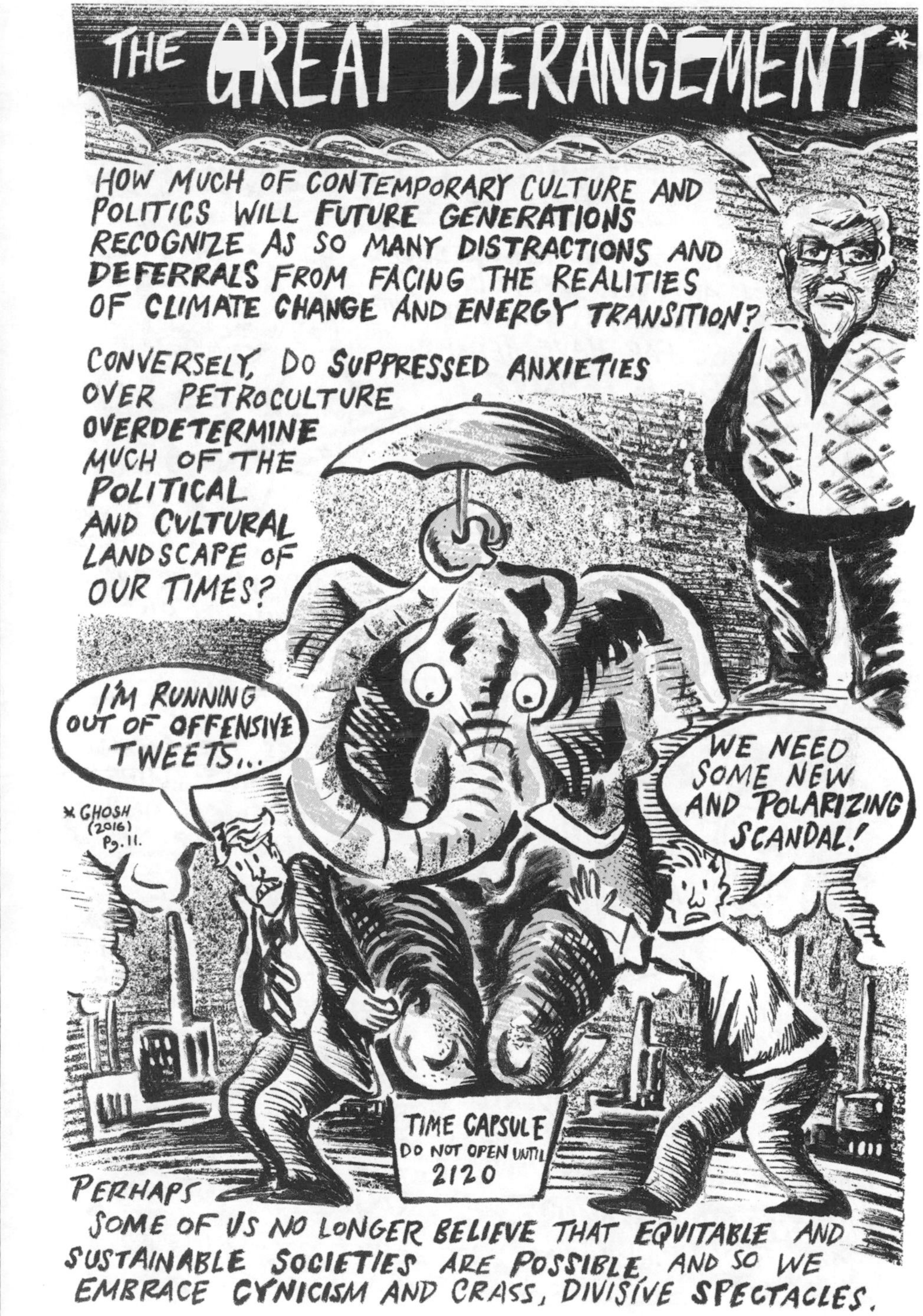
THE GREAT DERANGEMENT*
HOW MUCH OF CONTEMPORARY CULTURE AND POLITICS WILL FUTURE GENERATIONS RECOGNIZE AS SO MANY DISTRACTIONS AND DEFERRALS FROM FACING THE REALITIES OF CLIMATE CHANGE AND ENERGY TRANSITION?
CONVERSELY, DO SUPPRESSED ANXIETIES OVER PETROCULTURE OVERDETERMINE MUCH OF THE POLITICAL AND CULTURAL LANDSCAPE OF OUR TIMES?
I'M RUNNING OUT OF OFFENSIVE TWEETS...
WE NEED SOME NEW AND POLARIZING SCANDAL!
* GHOSH (2016) Pg. 11.
TIME CAPSULE DO NOT OPEN UNTIL 2120
PERHAPS SOME OF US NO LONGER BELIEVE THAT EQUITABLE AND SUSTAINABLE SOCIETIES ARE POSSIBLE AND SO WE EMBRACE CYNICISM AND CRASS, DIVISIVE SPECTACLES.

IF SUPPRESSED ANXIETIES ABOUT ENERGY AND CLIMATE ARE SHAKING SOCIETIES TO THEIR FOUNDATIONS, PERHAPS THIS IS BECAUSE WE HAVE NEVER FULLY AND COLLECTIVELY ACKNOWLEDGED THE DEGREE TO WHICH FOSSIL FUELS HAVE SHAPED MODERNITY. AS DIPESH CHAKRABARTY POINTS OUT...

THE MANSION OF MODERN FREEDOMS STANDS ON AN EVER-EXPANDING BASE OF FOSSIL FUEL USE. MOST OF OUR FREEDOMS SO FAR HAVE BEEN **ENERGY INTENSIVE.** *

FACED WITH THE URGENT NEED TO TRANSITION TO NEW, RENEWABLE ENERGY SYSTEMS...

*(2009) Pg. 208.

MIND YOUR OWN UTERUS

KEEP ABORTION LEGAL

NO PIPELINES ON UNCEDED TERRITORY.

BLACK LIVES MATTER

...IS IT ANY WONDER THAT RIGHTS FOUGHT FOR AND WON BY PAST GENERATIONS ARE NOW AGAIN UNDER DISPUTE, WHILE ONGOING STRUGGLES FOR SOCIAL JUSTICE HAVE GAINED NEW URGENCY AND MOMENTUM?

LET'S ENCOURAGE WHITE, MASCULINE AGGRESSION AGAINST WOMEN AND MINORITIES TO WEAKEN RESISTANCE AND KEEP PROFITS FLOWING.

FOR OIL AND COUNTRY!

IT OFTEN SEEMS AS IF, IN RESPONSE TO THE CHALLENGE OF RETHINKING OUR RELATIONSHIPS TO ENERGY, THE ACCUMULATED **INERTIA** OF **PETROCULTURE** WOULD RATHER **DOUBLE DOWN** ON ENGRAINED FORMS OF **EXPLOITATION AND ABUSE.**

44

However, as a **TOTTERING** edifice of compromises and managed **Injustice** is newly exposed to its **entangled roots**, mounting forms of **unrest** and **protest** can find new opportunities for solidarity, intersection and action.

THE HISTORICAL ANOMALY OF A HIGHLY POTENT, NON-RENEWABLE ENERGY SOURCE ALLOWED MULTITUDES TO IMAGINE, AND FIGHT FOR, MORE SECURE AND SATISFYING LIFESTYLES.

AT THE SAME TIME, FOSSIL FUELS ALSO ENABLED RAPACIOUS GREED, PATHOLOGICAL COMPETITION, VAST INEQUALITY, AND COLOSSAL WASTE AND DEVASTATION.

TO THIS EXTENT, WE STILL DO NOT KNOW 'HUMAN NATURE', ONLY HUMAN POTENTIALS UNDER PETRO-CULTURE.

DON'T LOOK BACK KIDS.

PETROCULTURE
NEXT 10,000 EXITS

WHO WE MIGHT BECOME UNDER A DIFFERENT ENERGY REGIME?

THE ANSWER REMAINS TO BE DETERMINED.

TO EMBARK UPON THIS ADVENTURE, WE FIRST NEED TO FULLY AND FEARLESSLY CONFRONT THE WAYS PETROCULTURE HAS SHAPED OUR HOPES, FEARS, RELATIONSHIPS, EXPECTATIONS AND SELVES. IT IS TIME FOR US TO...

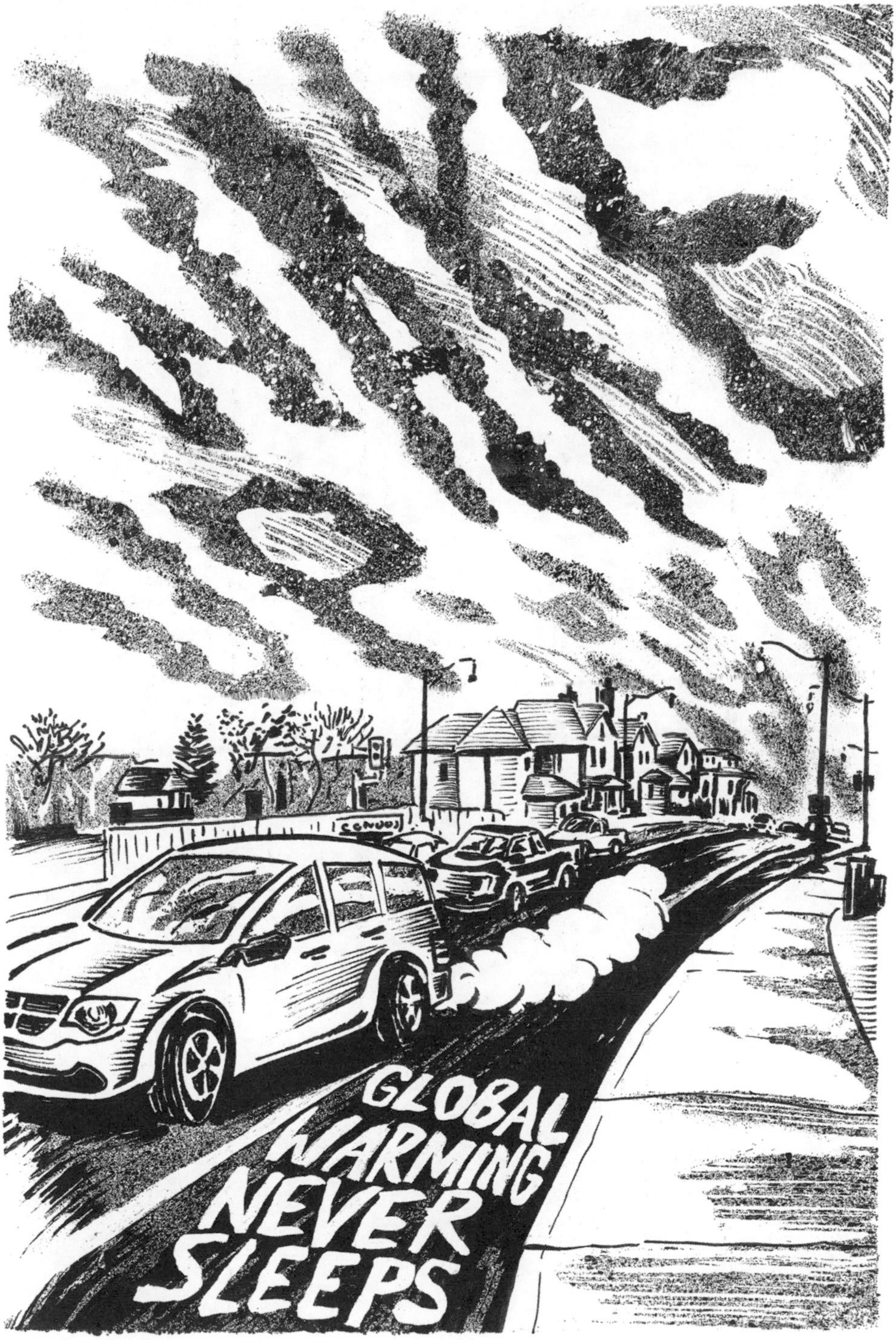
CONDOS
GLOBAL WARMING NEVER SLEEPS

Chapter 2
Big, Oily Dreams

SO, WHERE DO WE START? FOR WELL OVER A CENTURY POWERFUL INTERESTS HAVE BEEN SHAPING OUR DESIRES, HOPES, DREAMS AND EXPERIENCES ACCORDING TO THE LOGIC OF PETRO-CARBONS.

IN THE WESTERN WORLD, AND NORTH AMERICA IN PARTICULAR, WE HAVE BECOME ENERGY VAMPIRES

SUCKING UP MORE THAN OUR FAIR SHARE OF ENERGY RESOURCES IN PURSUIT OF LIFESTYLES THAT RARELY DELIVER ON THE PROMISES OF PROSPERITY AND HAPPINESS THAT ARE SOLD TO US.

MEANWHILE, MAJOR PRODUCERS LIKE **NIGERIA**, THE FIFTH-LARGEST EXPORTER OF OIL TO NORTH AMERICA, HAVE SUFFERED POVERTY, ENVIRONMENTAL DEVASTATION AND POLITICAL UNREST, DESPITE HAVING GENERATED ABOUT **$600 BILLION** USD IN OIL REVENUE SINCE THE FIRST WELL WAS DRILLED IN 1956 (WURTHMANN 2006).

RESOURCE CURSE

DESPITE OIL'S ASSOCIATION WITH IDEAS OF **PROGRESS** AND **PROSPERITY**, ITS PRODUCTION, DISTRIBUTION AND CONSUMPTION ARE **FRAUGHT** WITH **CONTRADICTION**.

PEOPLE LIVING IN **EXTRACTION** ZONES, FROM THE NIGER DELTA TO THE ATHABASKA TAR SANDS TO TEXAS SHALE FIELDS, SUFFER EXAMPLES OF WHAT **ROB NIXON** CALLS **SLOW VIOLENCE** DUE TO ENVIRONMENTAL DEGRADATION, POVERTY, ILL HEALTH AND INEQUALITY.

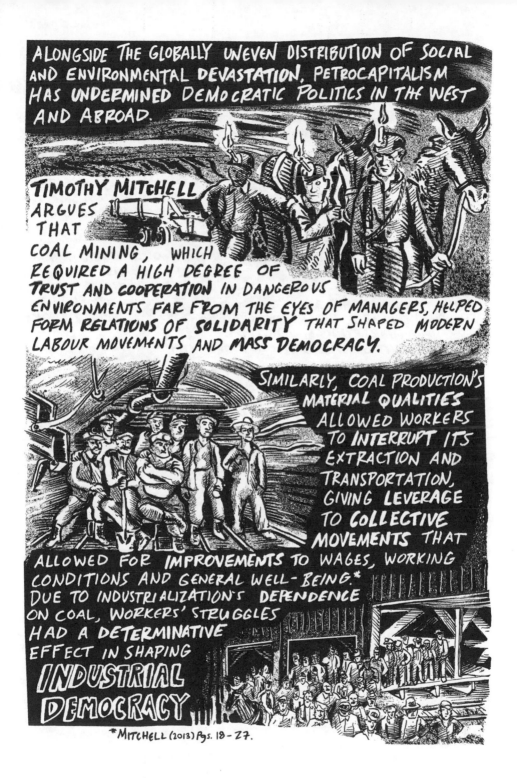

ALONGSIDE THE GLOBALLY UNEVEN DISTRIBUTION OF SOCIAL AND ENVIRONMENTAL **DEVASTATION**, PETROCAPITALISM HAS UNDERMINED DEMOCRATIC POLITICS IN THE WEST AND ABROAD.

TIMOTHY MITCHELL ARGUES THAT COAL MINING, WHICH REQUIRED A HIGH DEGREE OF **TRUST** AND **COOPERATION** IN DANGEROUS ENVIRONMENTS FAR FROM THE EYES OF MANAGERS, HELPED FORM **RELATIONS OF SOLIDARITY** THAT SHAPED MODERN LABOUR MOVEMENTS AND **MASS DEMOCRACY.**

SIMILARLY, COAL PRODUCTION'S **MATERIAL QUALITIES** ALLOWED WORKERS TO **INTERRUPT** ITS EXTRACTION AND TRANSPORTATION, GIVING **LEVERAGE** TO **COLLECTIVE MOVEMENTS** THAT ALLOWED FOR **IMPROVEMENTS** TO WAGES, WORKING CONDITIONS AND GENERAL WELL-BEING.* DUE TO INDUSTRIALIZATION'S DEPENDENCE ON COAL, WORKERS' STRUGGLES HAD A **DETERMINATIVE** EFFECT IN SHAPING **INDUSTRIAL DEMOCRACY**

*MITCHELL (2013) Pgs. 18-27.

53

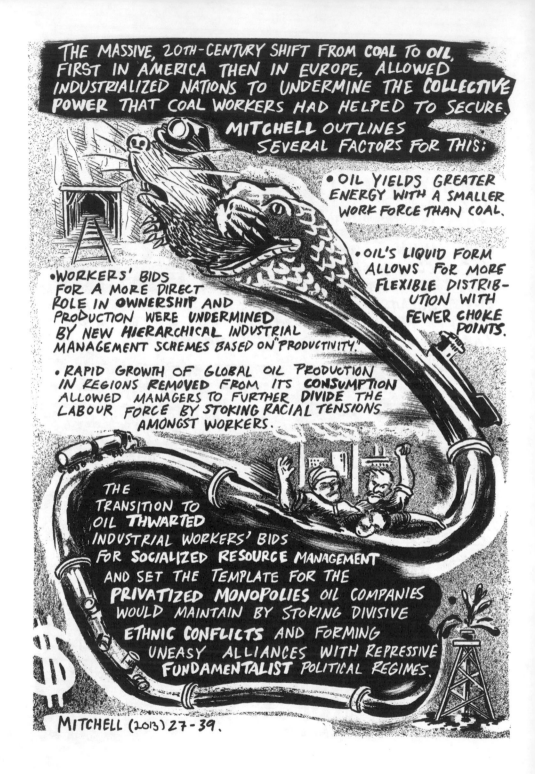

THE MASSIVE, 20th-CENTURY SHIFT FROM **COAL** TO **OIL**, FIRST IN AMERICA THEN IN EUROPE, ALLOWED INDUSTRIALIZED NATIONS TO UNDERMINE THE **COLLECTIVE** POWER THAT COAL WORKERS HAD HELPED TO SECURE.

MITCHELL OUTLINES SEVERAL FACTORS FOR THIS:

• OIL YIELDS GREATER ENERGY WITH A SMALLER WORK FORCE THAN COAL.

• OIL'S **LIQUID FORM** ALLOWS FOR MORE **FLEXIBLE DISTRIBUTION** WITH FEWER CHOKE POINTS.

• WORKERS' BIDS FOR A MORE DIRECT ROLE IN **OWNERSHIP** AND PRODUCTION WERE UNDERMINED BY NEW **HIERARCHICAL INDUSTRIAL** MANAGEMENT SCHEMES BASED ON "PRODUCTIVITY."

• RAPID GROWTH OF GLOBAL OIL PRODUCTION IN REGIONS REMOVED FROM ITS **CONSUMPTION** ALLOWED MANAGERS TO FURTHER **DIVIDE** THE LABOUR FORCE BY STOKING RACIAL TENSIONS AMONGST WORKERS.

THE TRANSITION TO OIL **THWARTED** INDUSTRIAL WORKERS' BIDS FOR **SOCIALIZED RESOURCE** MANAGEMENT AND SET THE TEMPLATE FOR THE **PRIVATIZED MONOPOLIES** OIL COMPANIES WOULD MAINTAIN BY STOKING DIVISIVE **ETHNIC CONFLICTS** AND FORMING UNEASY ALLIANCES WITH REPRESSIVE **FUNDAMENTALIST** POLITICAL REGIMES.

MITCHELL (2013) 27-39.

WHAT MITCHELL CALLS... **McJihad** BILLIONS PUMPED DESCRIBES HOW WESTERN PETROCAPITAL HAS MADE ALLIANCES WITH REPRESSIVE, FUNDAMENTALIST REGIMES, HELPING **OVERTHROW** DEMOCRATIC AND **PROGRESSIVE** GOVERNMENTS, IN SERVICE OF **CONTROLLING** GLOBAL OIL FLOWS.

OIL RENTS

BECAUSE THE ISSUE FOR PRODUCERS, FOR MOST OF THE 20TH CENTURY, WAS NOT OIL **SCARCITY** BUT **SURPLUS**, MITCHELL ARGUES THAT WESTERN GOVERNMENTS AND CORPORATIONS BUTTRESSED **REACTIONARY FUNDAMENTALISTS** WITH THE AIM OF **PREVENTING** MIDDLE EASTERN OIL FROM **REACHING** THE **MARKET** AND CHALLENGING WESTERN **MONOPOLIES**, A TACTIC HE CALLS...

SABOTAGE

MITCHELL (2013), Chs. 6 & 8.

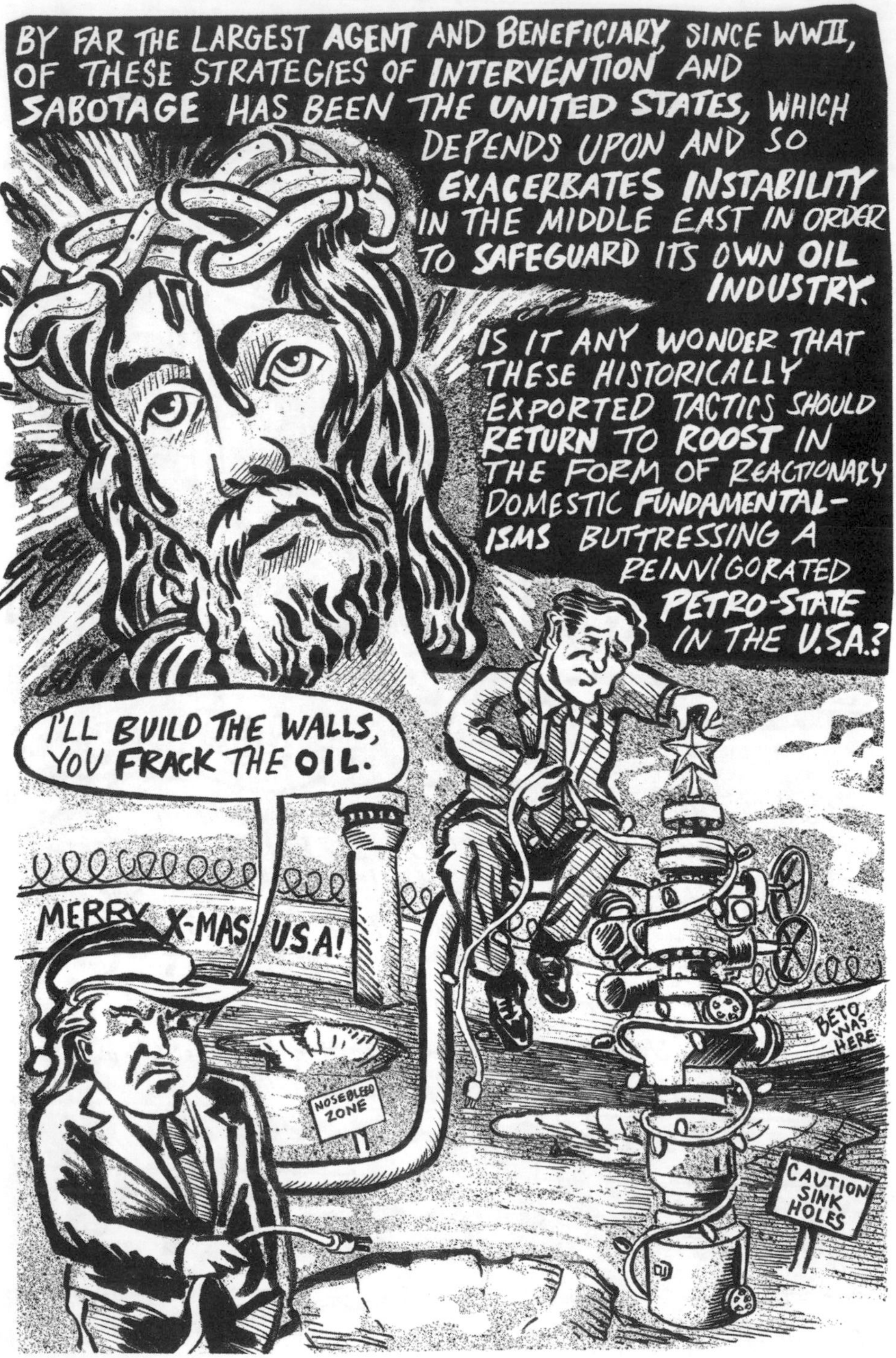
BY FAR THE LARGEST AGENT AND BENEFICIARY, SINCE WWII, OF THESE STRATEGIES OF INTERVENTION AND SABOTAGE HAS BEEN THE UNITED STATES, WHICH DEPENDS UPON AND SO EXACERBATES INSTABILITY IN THE MIDDLE EAST IN ORDER TO SAFEGUARD ITS OWN OIL INDUSTRY.
IS IT ANY WONDER THAT THESE HISTORICALLY EXPORTED TACTICS SHOULD RETURN TO ROOST IN THE FORM OF REACTIONARY DOMESTIC FUNDAMENTALISMS BUTTRESSING A REINVIGORATED PETRO-STATE IN THE U.S.A.?
I'LL BUILD THE WALLS, YOU FRACK THE OIL.
MERRY X-MAS U.S.A!
NOSEBLEED ZONE
BETO WAS HERE
CAUTION SINK HOLES

GILLES DELEUZE USED THE FIGURES OF THE **MOLE** AND SNAKE TO CHARACTERIZE THE TRANSITION, IN THE MID 20TH C., FROM **DISCIPLINARY SOCIETIES** WITH THEIR DISCRETE AND DISRUPTABLE SITES OF **ENCLOSURE** TO THE CURRENT **SOCIETIES OF CONTROL** WITH THEIR MORE FLUID, CONTINUOUS AND **PERMISSIVE** FORMS OF **DOMINATION** AND **EXPLOITATION.**

WE HAVE PASSED FROM ONE ANIMAL TO THE OTHER, FROM THE **MOLE** TO THE **SERPENT**, IN THE SYSTEM UNDER WHICH WE **LIVE**, BUT ALSO IN OUR MANNER OF LIVING AND IN OUR **RELATIONS** WITH OTHERS.

THE DISCIPLINARY MAN WAS A **DISCONTINUOUS** PRODUCER OF **ENERGY**, BUT THE **MAN OF CONTROL** IS **UNDULATORY**, IN ORBIT, IN A CONTINUOUS **NETWORK**.

THE **COILS** OF THE SERPENT ARE EVEN MORE **COMPLEX** THAN THE **BURROWS** OF THE **MOLE.***

*DELEUZE (1992) Pgs. 5-7.

57

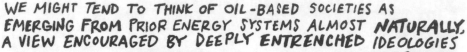

WE MIGHT TEND TO THINK OF OIL-BASED SOCIETIES AS EMERGING FROM PRIOR ENERGY SYSTEMS ALMOST **NATURALLY**, A VIEW ENCOURAGED BY DEEPLY **ENTRENCHED** IDEOLOGIES OF **PROGRESS**.

MITCHELL AND DELEUZE HELP US **CHALLENGE** THIS NOTION BY EMPHASIZING HOW **ENERGY SYSTEMS** ARE CONDITIONED AND TRANSFORMED BY **HISTORICAL STRUGGLES**.

PAST **MAJOR** SHIFTS IN ENERGY REGIMES WERE DECISIONS MADE BY **SPECIFIC AGENTS** WITH PARTICULAR INTERESTS, SUCH AS THE **PRIVATIZED CONTROL** OF LABOUR AND RESOURCES.

ANDREAS MALM PROVIDES A GOOD EXAMPLE OF THIS BY REVEALING HOW THE TRANSITION OF THE BRITISH TEXTILE INDUSTRY FROM WATER TO STEAM POWER WAS PRECIPITATED BY THE STRUGGLES BETWEEN EXPLOITED WORKERS AND INDUSTRIALISTS.

WATER POWER WAS CHEAP AND PLENTIFUL IN 19TH-CENTURY ENGLAND. BUT MILL WORKERS, MANY OF WHOM WERE CHILDREN, WORKED UP TO 16 HOURS A DAY.

THIS WAS PARTLY BECAUSE OF THE UNPREDICTABLE NATURE OF THE FLOW OF WATER; THE IMPERATIVE TO COMPETITION MEANT MILL OWNERS HAD TO MAKE UP FOR LOST PRODUCTIVITY BECAUSE OF UNEVEN WEATHER.

MALM POINTS OUT HOW SCHEMES TO COORDINATE MANAGEMENT OF THE FLOW THROUGH SHARED RESERVOIRS WERE REJECTED BECAUSE OF MILL OWNERS' FEARS OF BEING SUBJECTED TO CENTRALIZED, COLLECTIVE REGULATION. *

* MALM (2016) Ch. 6.

THIS AVERSION TO SHARED WATER USAGE MEANT MILL OWNERS FOUND THEMSELVES UP AGAINST A WALL WHEN WORKERS FINALLY SUCCEEDED IN INSTITUTING A TEN-HOUR DAY WITH PENALTIES FOR MILLS THAT DID NOT COMPLY, IN 1847. **

**MALM (2016) Ch. 8.

SHIFTING TO COAL-BURNING STEAM ENGINES ALLOWED CAPITALISTS TO AVOID COOPERATING WITH EACH OTHER OVER ENERGY. IT ALSO ALLOWED THE REMOVAL OF FACTORIES FROM THE COUNTRY-SIDE TO TOWNS, WHERE CHEAPER, MORE REPLACE-ABLE AND DOCILE LABOURERS COULD BE ACCESSED.

WHAT MALM CALLS THE STOCK OF CARBON-BASED FUEL PROMISED TO RELEASE FACTORY OWNERS FROM VULNERABILITY TO THE TWIN VICISSITUDES OF WEATHER AND LABOURERS.

WORKERS MIGHT GO ON STRIKE AND WATER FREEZE; WORKERS MIGHT DEPART IN A RESTLESS AND MIGRATORY SPIRIT AND WATER RUN FASTER IN FARAWAY HILLS; WORKERS MIGHT REFUSE ORDERS AND WATER DRY OUT; WORKERS COULD EMBEZZLE MATERIALS AND WATER FLOOD PREMISES; ALL VEXATIONS OF HUMAN LABOUR WERE MIRRORED IN THE FLOW.*

IN PERFECT CONTRAST TO THE MASSES OF UNDISCIPLINED, UNRULY, UNRELIABLE WORKERS, STEAM PROVIDES MASSIVE, DEPENDABLE FORCE WITH GENTLE, ELEGANT DOCILITY.

EXCEPT WHEN THE ENGINES EXPLODE, OF COURSE!

*MALM, P. 213.

60

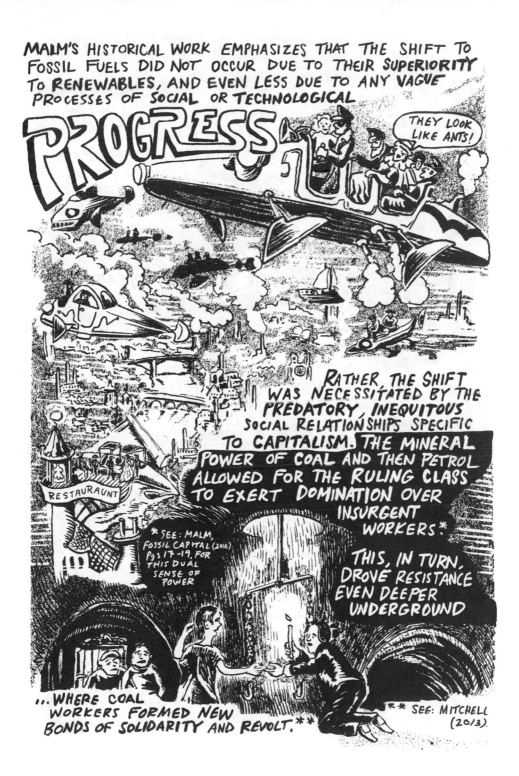

MALM'S HISTORICAL WORK EMPHASIZES THAT THE SHIFT TO FOSSIL FUELS DID NOT OCCUR DUE TO THEIR SUPERIORITY TO RENEWABLES, AND EVEN LESS DUE TO ANY VAGUE PROCESSES OF SOCIAL OR TECHNOLOGICAL

PROGRESS

THEY LOOK LIKE ANTS!

RATHER, THE SHIFT WAS NECESSITATED BY THE PREDATORY, INEQUITOUS SOCIAL RELATIONSHIPS SPECIFIC TO CAPITALISM. THE MINERAL POWER OF COAL AND THEN PETROL ALLOWED FOR THE RULING CLASS TO EXERT DOMINATION OVER INSURGENT WORKERS.*

RESTAURAUNT

* SEE: MALM, FOSSIL CAPITAL (2016) Pgs 17-19, FOR THIS DUAL SENSE OF POWER

THIS, IN TURN, DROVE RESISTANCE EVEN DEEPER UNDERGROUND

...WHERE COAL WORKERS FORMED NEW BONDS OF SOLIDARITY AND REVOLT.**

** SEE: MITCHELL (2013).

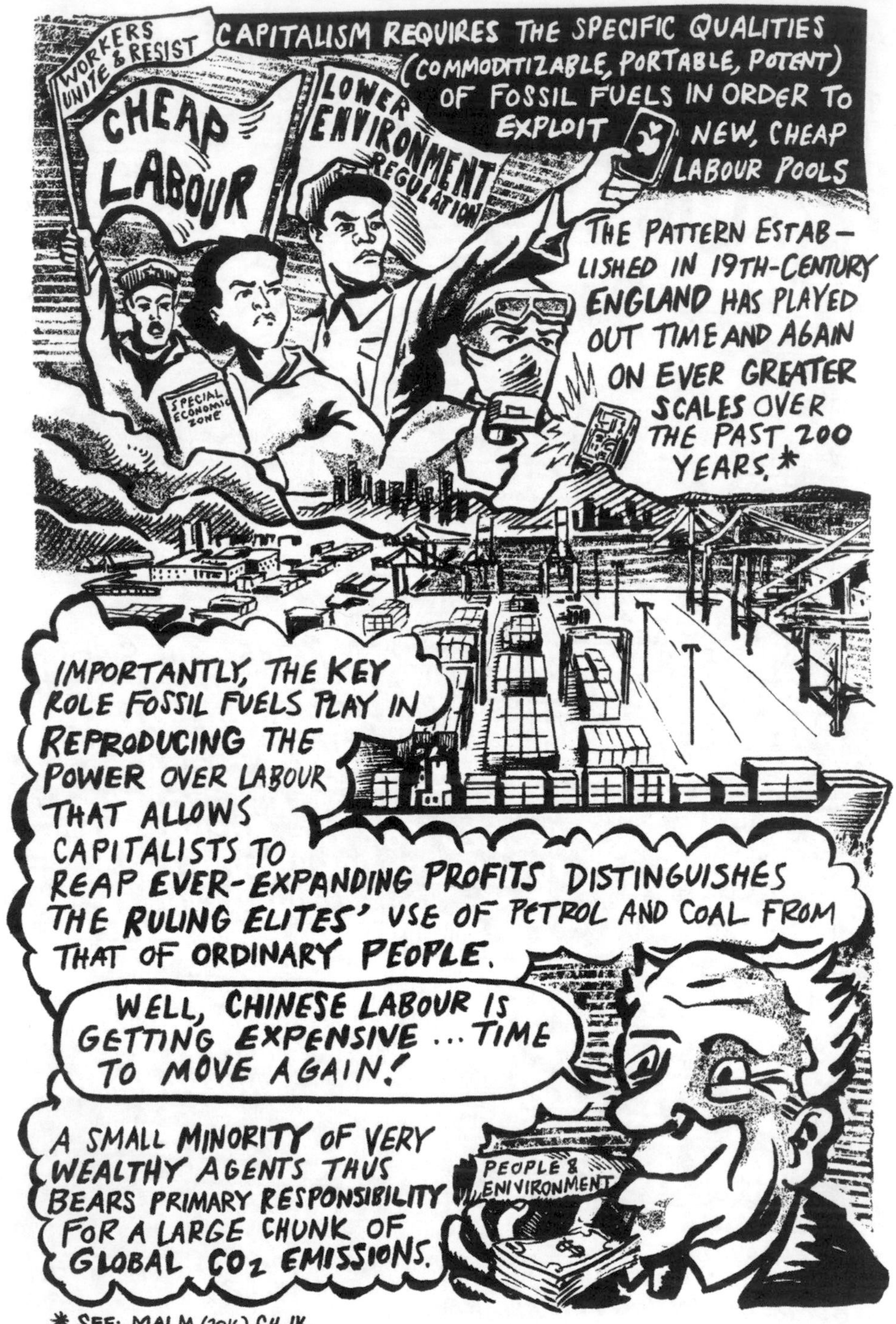
CAPITALISM REQUIRES THE SPECIFIC QUALITIES (COMMODITIZABLE, PORTABLE, POTENT) OF FOSSIL FUELS IN ORDER TO EXPLOIT NEW, CHEAP LABOUR POOLS
WORKERS UNITE & RESIST
CHEAP LABOUR
LOWER ENVIRONMENT REGULATION
SPECIAL ECONOMIC ZONE
THE PATTERN ESTABLISHED IN 19TH-CENTURY ENGLAND HAS PLAYED OUT TIME AND AGAIN ON EVER GREATER SCALES OVER THE PAST 200 YEARS.*
IMPORTANTLY, THE KEY ROLE FOSSIL FUELS PLAY IN REPRODUCING THE POWER OVER LABOUR THAT ALLOWS CAPITALISTS TO REAP EVER-EXPANDING PROFITS DISTINGUISHES THE RULING ELITES' USE OF PETROL AND COAL FROM THAT OF ORDINARY PEOPLE.
WELL, CHINESE LABOUR IS GETTING EXPENSIVE ... TIME TO MOVE AGAIN!
A SMALL MINORITY OF VERY WEALTHY AGENTS THUS BEARS PRIMARY RESPONSIBILITY FOR A LARGE CHUNK OF GLOBAL CO_2 EMISSIONS.
PEOPLE & ENIVIRONMENT

* SEE: MALM (2016) CH. 14.

WHILE A PERVASIVE **IDEOLOGY** FAVOURABLE TO THIS SAME MINORITY TRIES TO ARGUE THAT **EVERYONE** PARTICIPATES IN AND BENEFITS FROM THE PETRO-ECONOMY, THE INVESTOR CLASS BENEFITS IN A DISTINCT AND DISPROPORTIONATE WAY.

WHAT MALM CALLS **FOSSIL CAPITAL**

...[BECOMES] FUEL ON A FIRE THAT PROGRESSIVELY ELEVATES SOME HUMANS TO POWERFUL **KINGS** ON THE BACKS OF OTHERS, IN CONTRAST TO THE SPHERE OF FOSSIL CONSUMPTION.

IF YOU PAY 500 EUROS FOR A LONG-HAUL FLIGHT, YOUR ACTION CERTAINLY INDUCES EMISSIONS, BUT IT DOES NOT IN ITSELF AUGMENT YOUR FUTURE CLAIMS ON THE **TIME** AND RESOURCES OF OTHER PEOPLE (YOU HAVE SPENT YOUR MONEY, NOT INVESTED IT).

ONLY IF COMBUSTION IS A MOMENT IN THE **ACCUMULATION** OF CAPITAL — ONLY IF IT PLAYS ITS PART IN GENERATING **PROFIT** — WILL THE ACTOR POSSESS RENEWED, EXPANDED POWER TO PURCHASE AND COMMAND HUMAN LIFE AT THE END OF THE PROCESS*

THE BLACK STUFF SUCKED FROM THE EARTH HAS BEEN USED AGAINST US, PUTTING MASSIVE POWERS OF LIFE AND DEATH IN THE HANDS OF A FEW.

*MALM (2016) Pg. 315.

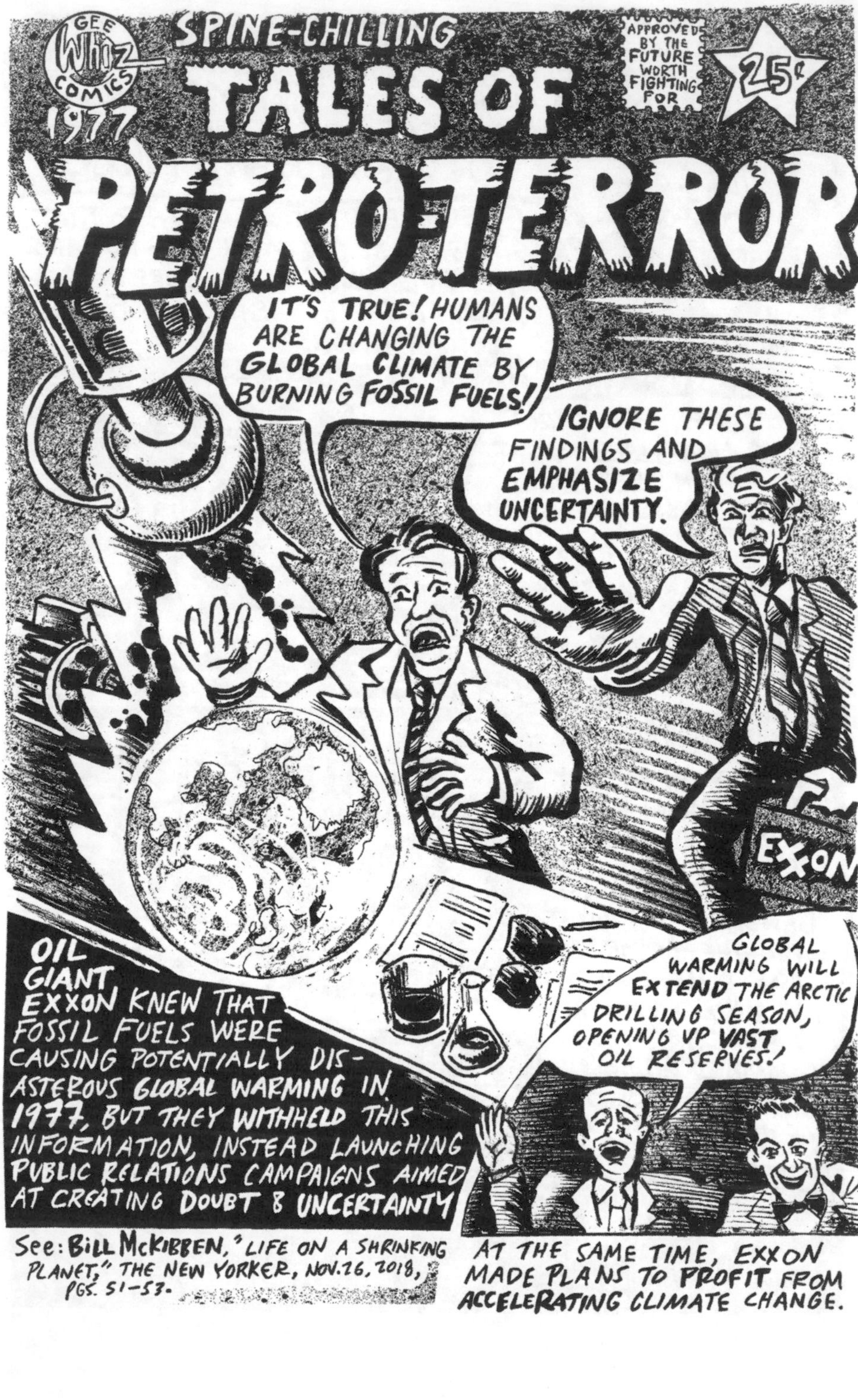
GEE WHIZ COMICS
1977
SPINE-CHILLING
TALES OF
PETRO-TERROR
APPROVED BY THE FUTURE WORTH FIGHTING FOR
25¢
IT'S TRUE! HUMANS ARE CHANGING THE GLOBAL CLIMATE BY BURNING FOSSIL FUELS!
IGNORE THESE FINDINGS AND EMPHASIZE UNCERTAINTY.
EXXON
OIL GIANT, EXXON KNEW THAT FOSSIL FUELS WERE CAUSING POTENTIALLY DIS-ASTEROUS GLOBAL WARMING IN 1977, BUT THEY WITHHELD THIS INFORMATION, INSTEAD LAUNCHING PUBLIC RELATIONS CAMPAIGNS AIMED AT CREATING DOUBT & UNCERTAINTY
GLOBAL WARMING WILL EXTEND THE ARCTIC DRILLING SEASON, OPENING UP VAST OIL RESERVES!
See: BILL McKIBBEN, "LIFE ON A SHRINKING PLANET," THE NEW YORKER, NOV. 26, 2018, PGS. 51-53.
AT THE SAME TIME, EXXON MADE PLANS TO PROFIT FROM ACCELERATING CLIMATE CHANGE.

EXXON'S **DUPLICITOUS** PUBLIC SUPPRESSION OF CLIMATE CHANGE SCIENCE (EVEN WHILE THEY BEGAN **ACTING** UPON THIS INFORMATION INTERNALLY) **DELAYED** EFFORTS TO ADDRESS THE CRISIS BY **DECADES**, COMPRISING WHAT **BILL** McKIBBEN CALLS "PERHAPS THE MOST CONSEQUENTIAL **DECEPTION** IN MANKIND'S HISTORY."*

* NEW YORKER, NOV. 26, 2018, P6.51

Victory Will Be Achieved When

- Average citizens "understand" (recognize) uncertainties in climate science; recognition of uncertainties becomes part of the "conventional wisdom"
- Media "understands" (recognizes) uncertainties in climate science
- Media coverage reflects balance on climate science and recognition of the validity of viewpoints that challenge the current "conventional wisdom"
- Industry senior leadership understands uncertainties in climate science, making them stronger ambassadors to those who shape climate policy
- Those promoting the Kyoto treaty on the basis of extant science appear to be out of touch with reality.

From: https://climateinvestigations.org/top-ten-documents-every-reporter-covering-exxon-should-know/

Davis (2016)

A 1998 PLAN BY EXXON REPS. RESPONDED TO THE KYOTO PROTOCOL BY TRYING TO INSTALL "UNCERTAINTY" IN THE PUBLIC SPHERE.

EXXON ACTED ON ITS KNOWLEDGE OF CLIMATE CHANGE BY **INVESTING** IN **ARCTIC DRILLING**, INCLUDING A 2011 DEAL WITH **RUSSIA** TO EXPLORE THE WORLD'S **LARGEST OIL SHALE DEPOSITS**, IN **WEST SIBERIA**.

WE MIGHT **EXPECT** CORPORATIONS TO PERSUE SHORT-TERM **PROFITS** OVER THE INTERESTS OF **PEOPLE** AND THE **PLANET**. BUT THE **BIGGER QUESTION**, AND THE PLACE WHERE ISSUES OF **CULTURE** BECOME **CRUCIAL**, IS...

WHY DO WE **COLLECTIVELY** CONTINUE TO ALLOW **FUEL** COMPANIES AND THE POLITICIANS WHO SUPPORT THEM TO **DESPOIL** THE PLANET AND **OBSCURE** OUR VISIONS OF A BETTER FUTURE?

PETROCULTURE AS WE KNOW IT TODAY, WITH ITS **CARS, HIGHWAYS, MEGA-CITIES,** GLOBALIZED **PRODUCTION** AND MECHANIZED MASS AGRICULTURE, IS SCARCELY MORE THAN **SEVENTY** YEARS OLD, AND YET IT HAS SO RESHAPED OUR **WORLD, RELATIONSHIPS** AND **EXPECTATIONS** THAT WE HAVE DIFFICULTY IMAGINING OTHERWISE.

AT A MOMENT WHEN OUR **FUTURE SURVIVAL** DEMANDS A POSSIBLY UNPRECEDENTED DEGREE OF IMAGINATION, COURAGE, COLLECTIVE **EFFORT** AND **COLLABORATIVE** POLITICAL STEWARDSHIP...

...CULTURE IS EVERYWHERE **RETREATING** INTO **NOSTALGIC** APPEALS TO UNTENABLE LIFESTYLES, OUTMODED INDUSTRIES, **EXCLUSIONARY** TRIBAL IMAGINARIES AND **INDIVIDUALISTIC** FANTASIES OF AGENCY AND **ESCAPE.** SOME TAKE REFUGE IN AUTHORITARIAN **LEADERS** WHO TELL US WHAT WE WANT TO HEAR, AGAINST OUR **BETTER KNOWLEDGE** AND SENSE OF **HUMANITY.** AND WE CLING TO THE BELIEF THAT THE WORLD WE KNOW IS **SUSTAINABLE** AND BETTER THAN **ALTERNATIVES,** EVEN WHILE...

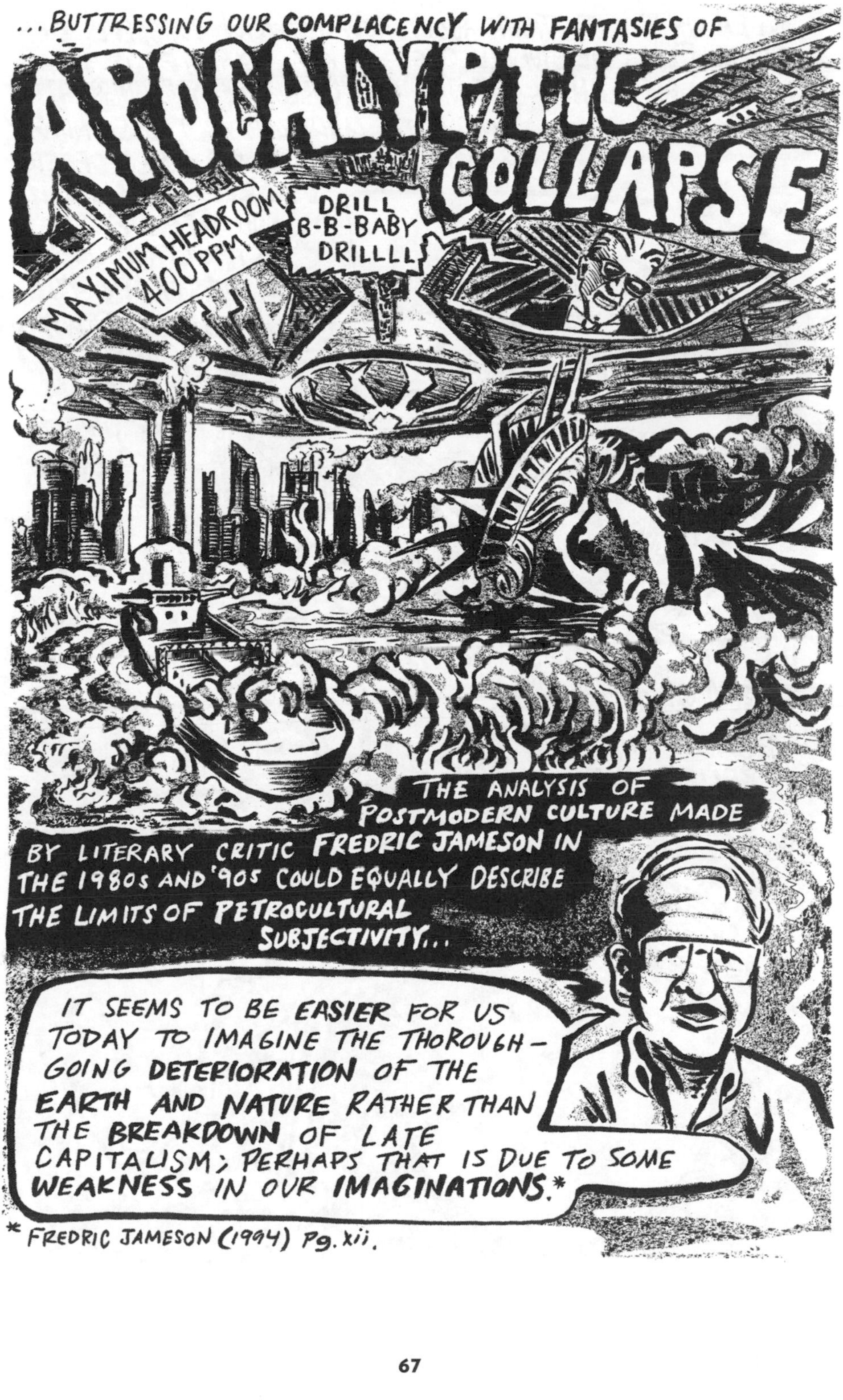

...BUTTRESSING OUR COMPLACENCY WITH FANTASIES OF
APOCALYPTIC COLLAPSE
MAXIMUM HEADROOM 400PPM
DRILL B-B-BABY DRILLLLL
THE ANALYSIS OF POSTMODERN CULTURE MADE BY LITERARY CRITIC FREDRIC JAMESON IN THE 1980s AND '90s COULD EQUALLY DESCRIBE THE LIMITS OF PETROCULTURAL SUBJECTIVITY...
IT SEEMS TO BE EASIER FOR US TODAY TO IMAGINE THE THOROUGH-GOING DETERIORATION OF THE EARTH AND NATURE RATHER THAN THE BREAKDOWN OF LATE CAPITALISM; PERHAPS THAT IS DUE TO SOME WEAKNESS IN OUR IMAGINATIONS.*
* FREDRIC JAMESON (1994) Pg. xii.

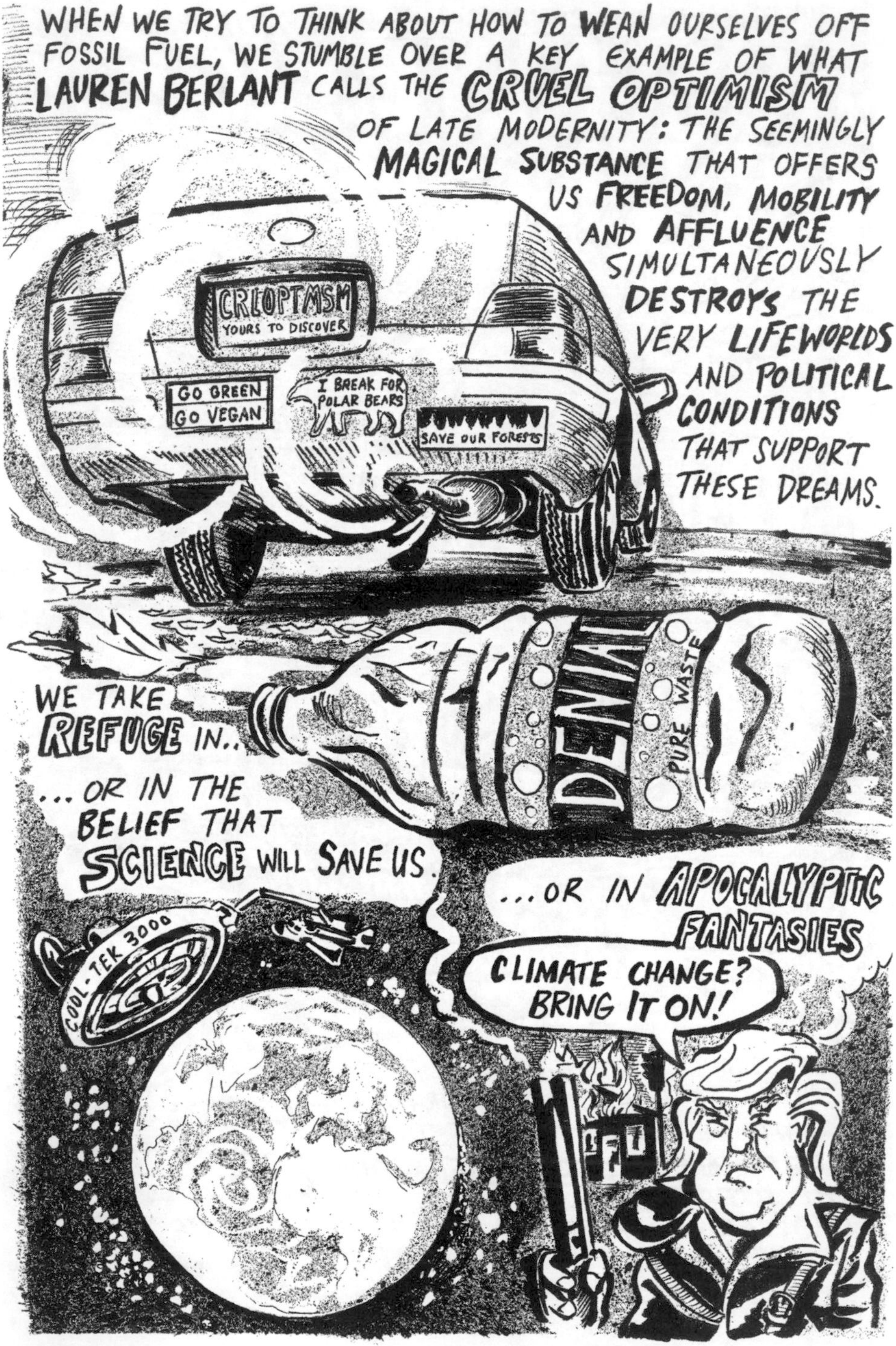
WHEN WE TRY TO THINK ABOUT HOW TO WEAN OURSELVES OFF FOSSIL FUEL, WE STUMBLE OVER A KEY EXAMPLE OF WHAT LAUREN BERLANT CALLS THE CRUEL OPTIMISM OF LATE MODERNITY: THE SEEMINGLY MAGICAL SUBSTANCE THAT OFFERS US FREEDOM, MOBILITY AND AFFLUENCE SIMULTANEOUSLY DESTROYS THE VERY LIFEWORLDS AND POLITICAL CONDITIONS THAT SUPPORT THESE DREAMS.
CRLOPTMSM
YOURS TO DISCOVER
GO GREEN
GO VEGAN
I BREAK FOR POLAR BEARS
SAVE OUR FORESTS
WE TAKE REFUGE IN..
DENIAL
PURE WASTE
...OR IN THE BELIEF THAT SCIENCE WILL SAVE US.
COOL-TEK 3000
...OR IN APOCALYPTIC FANTASIES
CLIMATE CHANGE? BRING IT ON!

PERHAPS LESS DRAMATIC BUT EQUALLY **SPURIOUS**, SETTLER NATIONS LIKE CANADA, WHOSE ECONOMIES HAVE GREATLY DEPENDED ON **RESOURCE EXTRACTION**, INDULGE WHAT

MARK SIMPSON CALLS **SMOOTH OIL'S LUBRICATING FANTASIES**

LUBRICITY, THE TEXTURE AND MOOD REQUISITE TO THE OPERATIONS OF NEOLIBERAL PETROCULTURE ... OFFERS **SMOOTHNESS** AS CULTURAL COMMON SENSE, PROMOTING THE FANTASY OF A **FRICTIONLESS** WORLD CONTINGENT ON THE CONTINUED, **INTENSIFYING** USE OF PETRO-CARBONS FROM UNDEREXPLOITED RESERVES IN NORTH AMERICA.

ONLY **SMOOTH SOCIETIES**, ONES **SUPPOSEDLY** WITHOUT **CONFLICT** OR **CRISIS**, CAN ENSURE OIL'S ETHICALLY CLEAN PRODUCTION AND CONSUMPTION.*

GOVERNMENTS, CORPORATIONS AND THEIR SUPPORTERS ADVANCE THE **FICTIONS** OF **SMOOTHNESS** AND `ETHICAL OIL´ WHILE HARVESTING SOME OF THE MOST **DIRTY ENERGY** ON THE PLANET, EFFECTIVELY DUMPING **BILLIONS** OF TONS OF CARBON INTO THE ATMOSPHERE. *SIMPSON (2017) Pg. 289.

69

THESE VARIOUS MODES OF **DENIAL** AND **IMPASSE** REVEAL THAT OUR INABILITY TO IMAGINE AND **WORK** TOWARDS A WORLD **AFTER OIL** IS NOT PRIMARILY A **TECHNOLOGICAL** OR EVEN **POLITICAL** PROBLEM...

... AND THEN **BRAVE** AND **INNOVATIVE MEN** TOOK THIS **MAGICAL SUBSTANCE** THAT WAS JUST **LYING IN** THE GROUND, **UNUSED**, AND BUILT A **WONDROUS** WORLD OUT OF IT, TO THE **BENEFIT OF ALL!**

PERHAPS IT IS **FIRST** AND **FOREMOST** AN ISSUE OF **NARRATIVE**.

THE OIL STORY

J·D·R

WE OFTEN LIKE TO **THINK** OF OURSELVES AS **BEYOND** THE **GRAND NARRATIVES** AND **IDEOLOGIES** THAT INFORMED **PAST AGES**, BUT PERHAPS OUR EXPERIENCES OF **INDIVIDUAL FREEDOM** AND **SOCIAL RESPONSIBILITY** (OR **LACK** THEREOF) ARE THE **DREAM** OF...

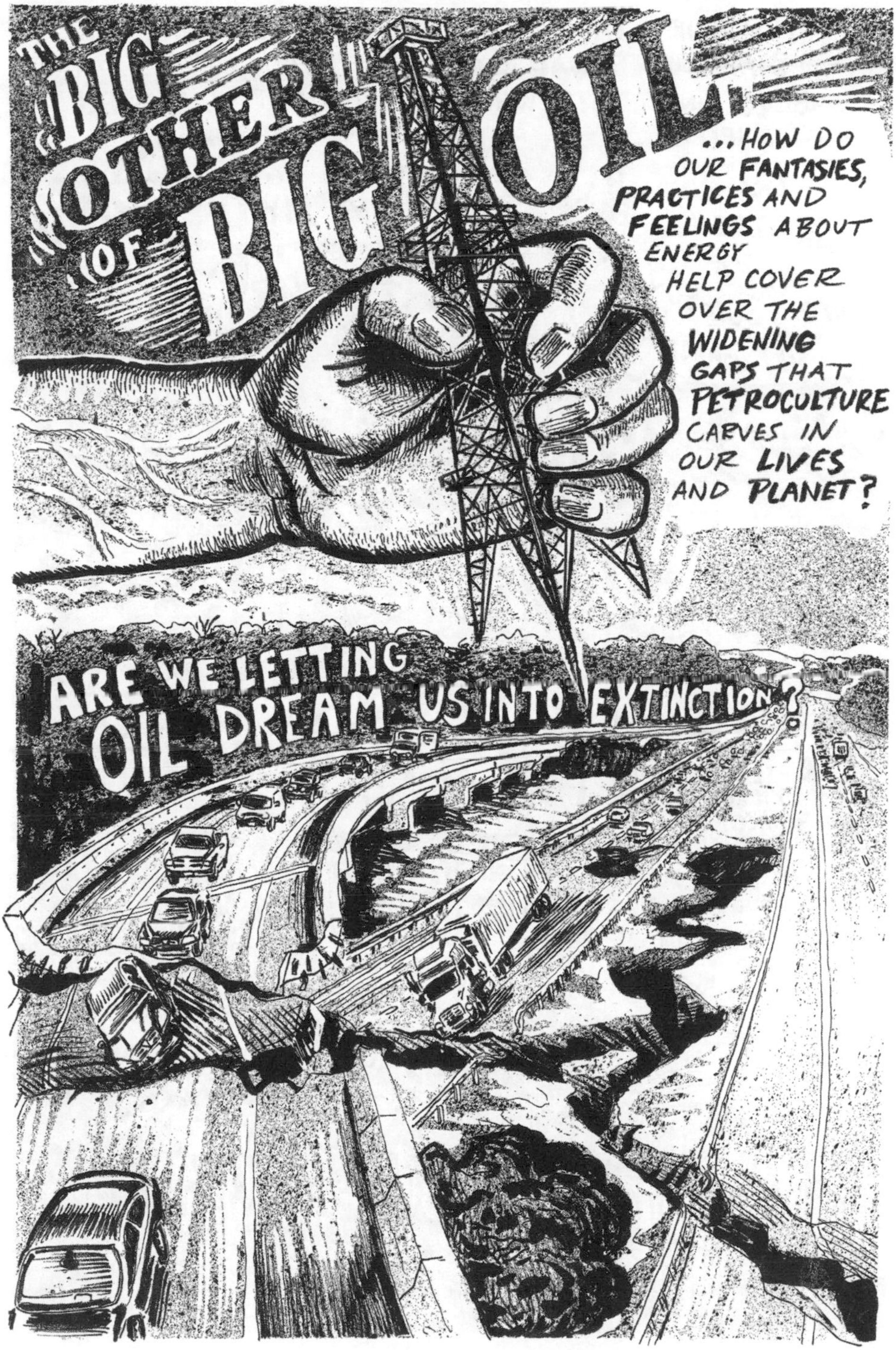
THE BIG OTHER OF BIG OIL
...HOW DO OUR FANTASIES, PRACTICES AND FEELINGS ABOUT ENERGY HELP COVER OVER THE WIDENING GAPS THAT PETROCULTURE CARVES IN OUR LIVES AND PLANET?
ARE WE LETTING OIL DREAM US INTO EXTINCTION?

AS THE SET OF RELATIONSHIPS, PRACTICES AND NARRATIVES THAT SHAPE OUR SOCIAL REALITY, PETROCULTURE BOTH ENABLES AND LIMITS WHAT WE THINK OF AS POSSIBLE ... OR EVEN AS REAL

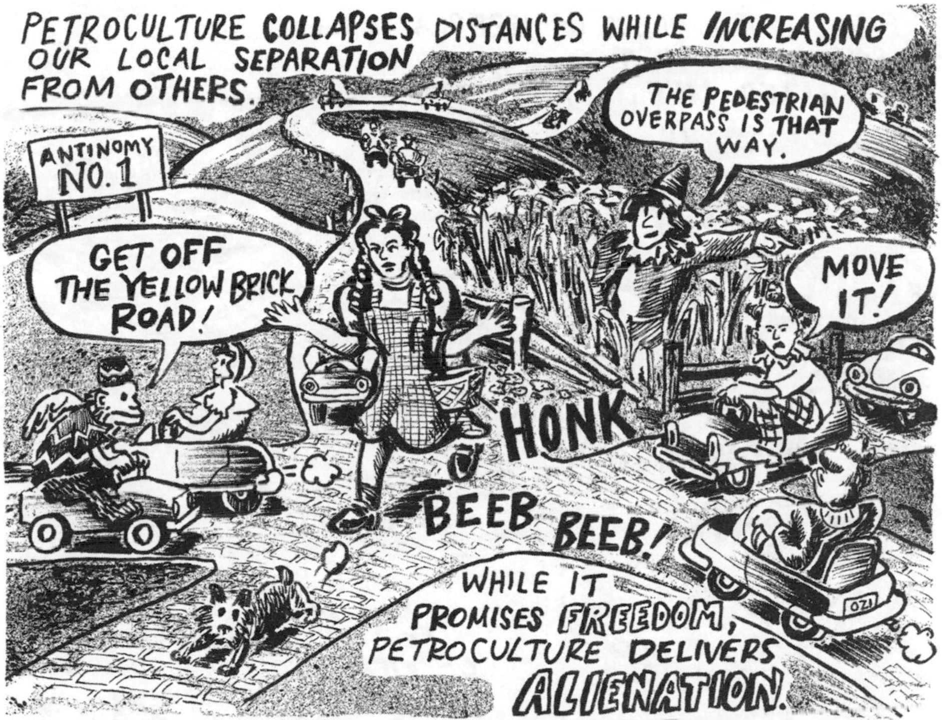
PETROCULTURE COLLAPSES DISTANCES WHILE INCREASING OUR LOCAL SEPARATION FROM OTHERS.
ANTINOMY NO. 1
THE PEDESTRIAN OVERPASS IS THAT WAY.
GET OFF THE YELLOW BRICK ROAD!
MOVE IT!
HONK
BEEB
BEEB!
OZ1
WHILE IT PROMISES FREEDOM, PETROCULTURE DELIVERS ALIENATION.

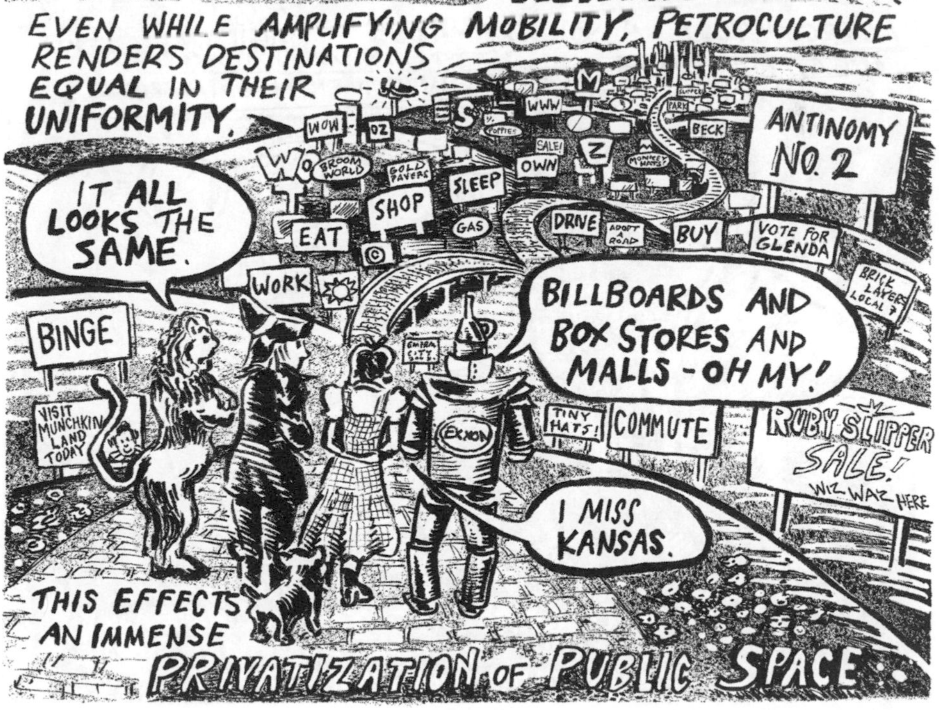
EVEN WHILE AMPLIFYING MOBILITY, PETROCULTURE RENDERS DESTINATIONS EQUAL IN THEIR UNIFORMITY.
ANTINOMY NO. 2
WOW
OZ
WWW
BECK
BROOM WORLD
GOLD PAVERS
OWN
Z
SLEEP
SHOP
EAT
GAS
DRIVE
BUY
VOTE FOR GLENDA
IT ALL LOOKS THE SAME.
WORK
BRICK LAYERS LOCAL 7
BINGE
BILLBOARDS AND BOX STORES AND MALLS - OH MY!
VISIT MUNCHKIN LAND TODAY
EXXON
TINY HATS!
COMMUTE
RUBY SLIPPER SALE!
WIZ WAZ HERE
I MISS KANSAS.
THIS EFFECTS AN IMMENSE PRIVATIZATION OF PUBLIC SPACE . . .

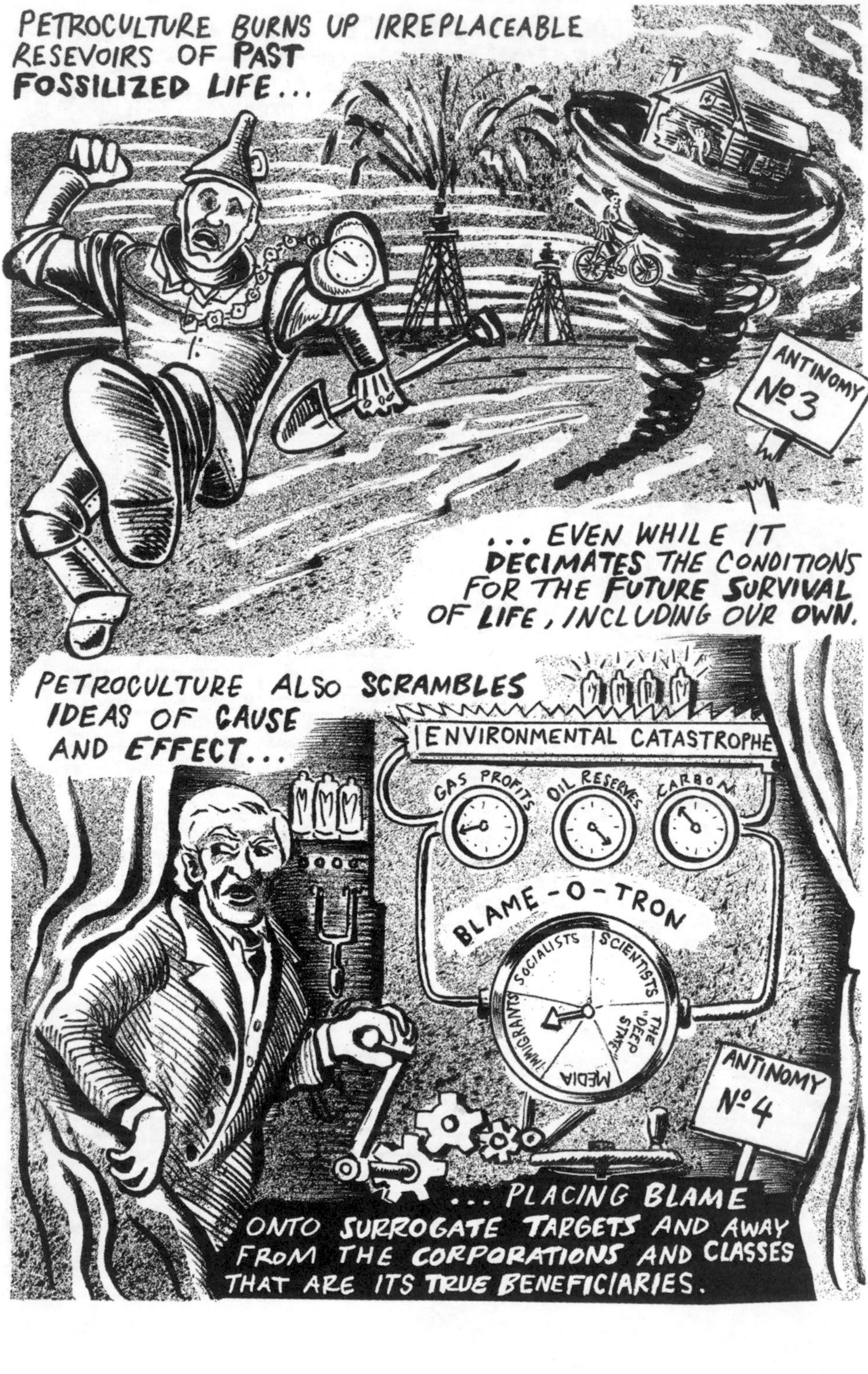
PETROCULTURE BURNS UP IRREPLACEABLE RESEVOIRS OF PAST FOSSILIZED LIFE...
ANTINOMY №3
... EVEN WHILE IT DECIMATES THE CONDITIONS FOR THE FUTURE SURVIVAL OF LIFE, INCLUDING OUR OWN.
PETROCULTURE ALSO SCRAMBLES IDEAS OF CAUSE AND EFFECT...
ENVIRONMENTAL CATASTROPHE
GAS PROFITS
OIL RESERVES
CARBON
BLAME-O-TRON
SOCIALISTS
SCIENTISTS
THE "DEEP STATE"
MEDIA
IMMIGRANTS
ANTINOMY №4
... PLACING BLAME ONTO SURROGATE TARGETS AND AWAY FROM THE CORPORATIONS AND CLASSES THAT ARE ITS TRUE BENEFICIARIES.

THESE ARE JUST A FEW OF THE WAYS PETROCULTURE **WARPS** OUR SENSE OF **SPACE, TIME RELATIONSHIPS** AND **CAUSALITY.** FOR **SALMINEN & VADÉN,** THE DISJUNCTION BETWEEN **MODERN** EXPERIENCES OF SHIFTING **VALUES** AND **SUBJECTIVITIES,** ON THE ONE HAND, AND **OIL'S** TECHNOLOGICAL AND **ECONOMIC** RE-ORGANIZING OF SOCIETY, ON THE OTHER, CREATES...

CON-DISTANCING

—OR THE WAY "FOSSIL FUELS **BIND THINGS TOGETHER** BY KEEPING THEM **SEPARATE,"** MUCH LIKE HOW THE DIVISION OF **LABOUR** INTO SEPARATE TASKS DE-SKILLS, DUMBS DOWN AND ATOMIZES OUR EXPERIENCES OF **WORK.** *

OBEY

"THE DEATH OF GOD AND THE BIRTH OF THE AGE OF OIL HAVE BEEN EXPERIENCED TOGETHER PRECISELY BY KEEPING THEM APART. THE DISTINCTION — THE SACRED AND MEANINGFUL HERE, THE ECONOMIC AND USEFUL THERE — IS ONE OF THE MOST ESSENTIAL CHARACTERISTICS OF THE AGE OF OIL." *

OIL HAS BECOME... "A SURROGATE GOD"

"EVERYTHING THAT SMACKS OF BEING SACRED IS BURNED IN THE BLACK MOTOR OF ECONOMIC GROWTH. A STRANGELY FAMILIAR ODOR HITS THE NOSE."

*QUOTES ON THIS PAGE: SALMINEN & VADÉN (2016) Pgs. 2-3.

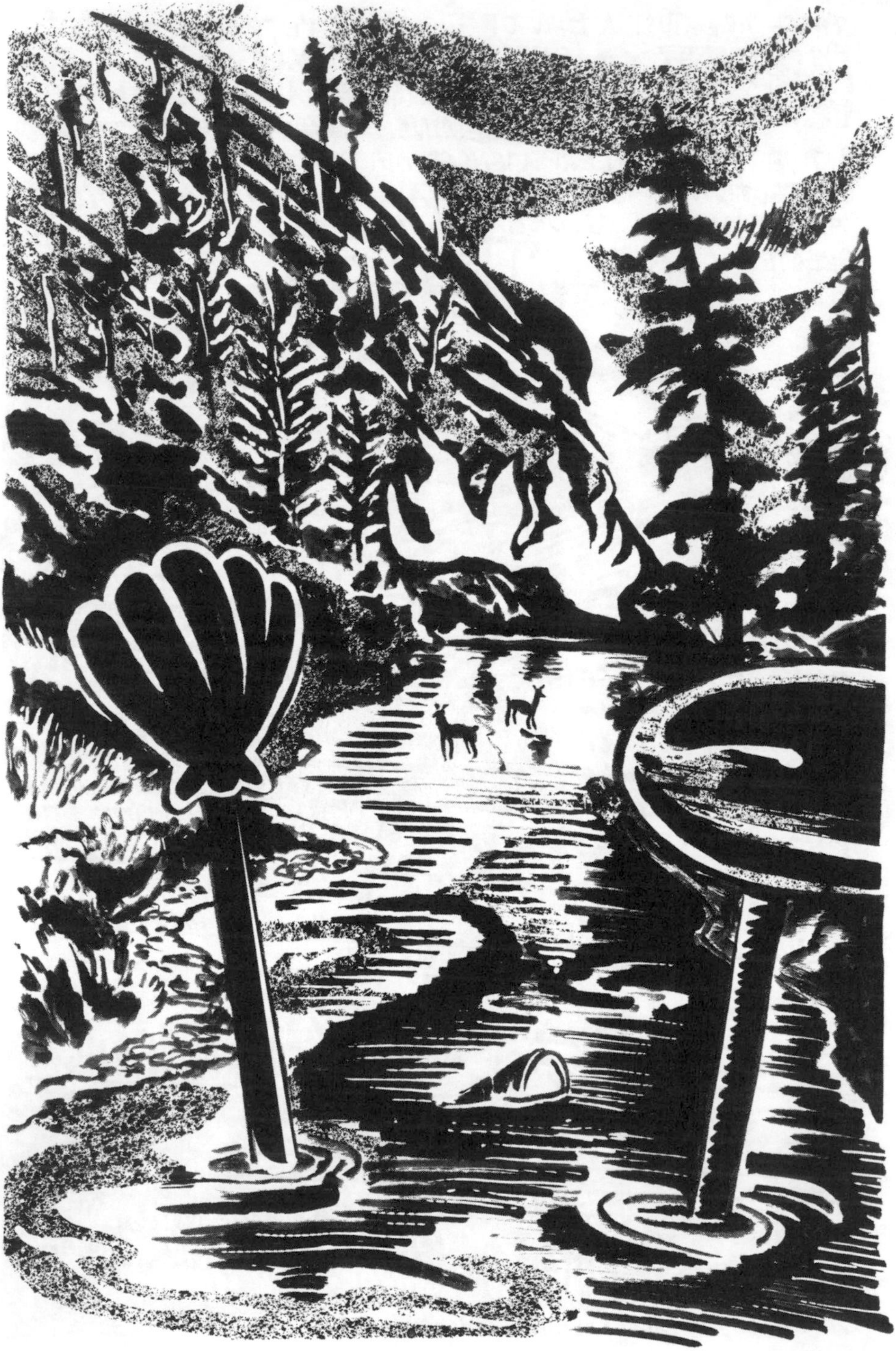

Chapter 3
Attachment

GIVEN THAT OUR **ATTACHMENT** TO PETROCULTURE IS DESTROYING THE BIOSPHERE AT AN ALARMING RATE, DO WE PERHAPS TAKE **PERVERSE ENJOYMENT** IN THE LEGACY OF SPECIES AND HABITAT LOSS THAT OUR USE OF FOSSIL FUELS IS EFFECTING?

ENJOYMENT IS THE **BARREL OF THE DANAIDES**...ONCE YOU GET INTO IT, YOU DON'T KNOW WHERE IT WILL **END UP**. IT BEGINS WITH A **TICKLE** AND ENDS WITH A **BLAZE OF PETROL**.*

*LACAN (2007) Pg.72.

PERHAPS OUR RELATIONSHIP TO PETROL GOES BEYOND PLEASURE INTO THE REALM OF WHAT **JACQUES LACAN** CALLED **JOUISSANCE**: OUR STUBBORN COMPULSION TO REPEAT THAT WHICH **HARMS** AND **ENDANGERS** US.

WHAT ARE THE **PSYCHOLOGICAL** AND **IDEOLOGICAL** DIMENSIONS OF THIS ATTACHMENT? SO MUCH OF CONTEMPORARY WORK, LIFE AND LEISURE IS CONDITIONED BY FOSSIL FUEL. BUT THE **ACT OF DRIVING** REMAINS ONE OF THE CENTRAL WAYS PETROCULTURE INTERPELLATES US AS SUBJECTS.

WHATEVER YOUR VIEWS ON CLIMATE CHANGE, ECONOMICS OR POLITICS, BEHIND THE WHEEL WE BECOME SUBJECTS OF THE **IDEOLOGICAL APPARATUSES OF PETROLEUM.**

IN A WORLD DESIGNED FOR CARS, PERHAPS WE ONLY TRULY EXIST WHILE DRIVING.

WE THINK OF CARS AS PRACTICAL MACHINES FOR GETTING PLACES, BUT THEY ARE ALSO VEHICLES OF **FANTASY, DESIRE** AND **ENJOYMENT.** TO DRIVE IS TO ENTER INTO AN **IMAGINARY RELATIONSHIP** WITH THE **REAL** CONDITIONS OF OUR EXISTENCE, AS **LOUIS ALTHUSSER** MIGHT SAY...

WHAT COULD BE MORE REAL THAN **DRIVING?**

BUT BY GETTING INTO A CAR WE **ABSTRACT OURSELVES** FROM THE IMMEDIATE ENVIRONMENT.

WARMER

UGLY AND ALIENATING SPACES BECOME PLEASURABLE AND EVEN STRANGELY BEAUTIFUL ONLY WHEN VIEWED IN PASSING.

MUCH OF OUR *PUBLIC SPACE*

IS REALLY ONLY BEARABLE WHEN EXPERIENCED FROM INSIDE A **VEHICLE.**

A SENSE OF *PLEASURE* COMES FROM THE EASE OF MOBILITY IT OFFERS THE **DRIVER.**

WALY MART

GIVEN THE MASSIVE ENCLOSURE OF PUBLIC SPACE BY COMMERCIAL AND AUTOMOTIVE PRIORITIES... WE TAKE REFUGE IN EITHER *VIRTUAL SPACE* OFFERED BY COMMUNICATION TECHNOLOGIES...

81

OR WE TAKE SOLACE IN ONE OF THE LAST PLACES OF SOLITUDE AND COMFORT LEFT TO US.

AND WITH SO MANY AVENUES OF SOCIALITY, AUTONOMY AND HOPE BLOCKED IN OUR CONTEMPORARY "SOCIETIES OF CONTROL," THE SIMPLE ACT OF PRESSING THE GAS PEDAL GIVES US AN IMMEDIATE SENSE OF RELIEF AND EMPOWERMENT.

EVEN WHEN THERE'S NOWHERE LEFT TO GO...

EXTINCTION

NOWHERE SLOW ↓

NORTH OBLIVION ↓

SOUTH OBLIVION ↓

NOWH FAST NEXT E

I DRIVE THEREFORE I AM

AT THE SAME TIME
AS DRIVING **ABSTRACTS** US
FROM THE **IMMEDIATE ENVIRONMENT**, REDUCING US TO
A SET OF **HABITUAL ACTIONS** FOCUSED ON THE
EVACUATED 'NOW,' THE **COLLECTIVE** EFFECT OF ALL
THIS MUTE, ANIMAL BEHAVIOUR INSCRIBES US INTO
THE **FUTURE** AS AN **ANONYMOUS CARBON FOOT-
PRINT** THAT WILL SHAPE THE **FATE OF EARTH**
LONG AFTER OUR **THOUGHTLESS**, BUSY ACTIVITY
HAS PASSED.

MANY CIVILIZATIONS HAVE MADE EXTRAVAGANT EXPENDITURES OF ENERGY, LIVES AND RESOURCES, MAKING MONUMENTS THAT HAVE OUTLIVED THE SOCIETIES THAT BUILT THEM

THIS IS ONE WAY OUR HUMAN AWARENESS OF MORTALITY IS ENTANGLED WITH CIRCUITS OF POWER AND INEQUALITY, BUT UNLIKE THE SLAVES OF OLD, WE MODERNS BARELY NOTICE THE COLLECTIVE EFFECTS OF OUR EVERYDAY LIFE ACTIVITIES.

WE MUST REPEAT... ♪ ARE WE NOT MEN? ♫

HOW COULD WE NOT BECOME DRUNK WITH THE POWER OF A THOUSAND SLAVES LITERALLY BENEATH OUR FOOT ON THE GAS PEDAL? AS WE BURN THROUGH MILLENNIA OF CONDENSED SUNLIGHT IN AN INSTANT, WE BECOME MOMENTARY LORDS OF SPACE AND MOTION, WE BECOME ....

PART OF THE MONUMENT

OIL IS A DREAMING SUBSTANCE WHOSE SIGNATURE INVOLVES THE **ERASURE** OF TIME, SPACE AND LOCALITY, ULTIMATELY LEADING TO THE **DECIMATION** OF THE CONDITIONS THAT SUPPORT **TERRESTRIAL LIFE** AS WE KNOW IT.

THE MORE OIL PURPORTS TO **LIBERATE** US AS **PETRO-SUBJECTS**, THE MORE WE FIND OURSELVES **ISOLATED** FROM AND **AT ODDS** WITH THE **SHRINKING HABITATS** THAT SUSTAIN US, AND WITH THE **POLITICAL** AND **ECONOMIC** SYSTEMS THAT ARE NO LONGER ABLE TO ADDRESS THE **CHALLENGES** FACING OUR **SPECIES**.

IT IS TIME TO WAKE UP FROM THE DREAM OF PETROL.

BUT PETROCULTURE WOULD ENCOURAGE US TO HIT 'SNOOZE' AND SLEEP A LITTLE LONGER.

400 PPM   +1.5° RISING   ALARMO

MAYBE IF WE CAN EXTEND THE FANTASY JUST A FEW DECADES MORE, THE CURRENT GENERATION CAN DIE COMFORTABLY, WITHOUT BEING WITNESS TO OR HELD ACCOUNTABLE FOR THE MASSIVE COLLAPSE OUR CHILDREN WILL EXPERIENCE FROM OUR INACTION.

FARM LANDS   HUMANS   OXYGEN   WETLANDS   BIRDS   MAMMALS   REPTILES   FLOWERS   LIFE   FISH   TREES   GRASSLANDS   PLANKTON   INSECTS   ALGAE   OCEANS   CORAL   GLACIERS

SO, WHAT PREVENTS THOSE OF US IN THE SUPPOSEDLY MOST ADVANCED AND PROSPEROUS PARTS OF THE WORLD FROM TRANSITIONING TO RENEWABLE ENERGY?

A 2019 REPORT BY THE ADVOCACY GROUP ENVIRONMENTAL DEFENSE CANADA NAMES THE OIL AND GAS LOBBY AS "THE SINGLE BIGGEST BARRIER TO CLIMATE ACTION IN CANADA."*

BUT WHAT CULTURAL AND SOCIAL FACTORS BUTTRESS THE ACCEPTANCE OF SUCH CORPORATE MEDDLING, BY EVERYDAY PEOPLE?

FOR EXAMPLE, ONE PERVASIVE SENTIMENT HOLDS THAT IT IS HYPOCRITICAL TO CRITIQUE BIG OIL, GIVEN OUR COLLECTIVE DEPENDENCE ON IT.

BUT, AS MALM ARGUES, THERE ARE CRUCIAL DIFFERENCES OF SCALE, MOTIVATION AND CULPABILITY BETWEEN THOSE WHO USE OIL FOR GENERATING SURPLUS PROFITS AND THE VAST MAJORITY OF US, WHOSE ENERGY CONSUMPTION IS BASED ON PRACTICAL, UTILITARIAN NEEDS**

**SEE CHAPTER 2.

PUBLIC OPINION PROCESSING PLANT

PRIVATIZED PROFITS

EXTINCTION

GENERALIZED GUILT

GOVERNMENTAL INERTIA

SOCIALIZED ENVIRONMENTAL IMPACT

AT THE SAME TIME, THERE IS AN EXCESSIVE ELEMENT OF ENJOYMENT THAT ACCOMPANIES OUR EVERYDAY OIL USE.

PERHAPS IT IS THIS FACTOR THAT LEADS US TO BLUR THE DISTINCTION BETWEEN THE CORPORATE BENEFICIARIES OF THE CARBON ECONOMY AND THE REST OF US...

* ENVIRONMENTALDEFENCE.CA/REPORT/OIL-BARRIER_CLIMATE_ACTION_CANADA

THE GAS CONSUMED BY *EVERYDAY* PEOPLE DRIVING HAS NOT HISTORICALLY BEEN THE LARGEST CONTRIBUTOR TO CO_2 EMISSIONS, THOUGH THE POPULARITY OF S.U.V.s IN THE PAST DECADE HAS MADE THEM THE SECOND-LARGEST SOURCE OF SUCH POLLUTION.

DRIVING ISN'T JUST A PRACTICAL SKILL — IT'S A SOCIAL RELATIONSHIP, AND IN MY S.U.V. I AM KING OF THE ROAD!

415 PPM

DESPITE S.U.V.s BEING MORE POLLUTING THAN CARS, THE ENERGY SECTOR ITSELF REMAINS THE LARGEST CO_2 EMITTER, BY ALMOST A *THREEFOLD* MARGIN.*

DRIVING'S MOST IMPORTANT AND *DESTRUCTIVE* ROLE IS NOT THE EMISSIONS IT PRODUCES, BUT THE CULTURAL AND PSYCHOLOGICAL WAYS IN WHICH IT INCULCATES OUR WILLING COMPLICITY WITH AN ENERGY REGIME.

COMMODITY FETISH

DRIVE THRU LFO

POWER

DENIAL

PERSONHOOD

MASCULINITY

FREEDOM

STATUS   DANGER

EASE   SPEED

DRIVING IS ONE OF THE *BRIBES* PETROCULTURE OFFERS IN EXCHANGE...

* THESE STATS ARE FOR 2019. SEE: OLIVER MILMAM, "HOW SUVs CONQURED THE WORLD," THE GUARDIAN, SEPT. 1, 2020.

... FOR SO MUCH OF OUR SPACE:

THE U.S. IS COVERED BY 2.6 MILLION MILES OF PAVED ROADS AND 1.8 BILLION TONNES OF ASPHALT. *

THE BILLION OR MORE PARKING SPACES ALONE ARE ENOUGH TO COVER MORE THAN THE STATE OF CONNECTICUT. **

CRUSH THE COMMONS

PUBLIC SPACE HAS BEEN COOPTED BY ALIENATED MOBILITIES WHERE "FULL" (I.E., WHITE & MASCULINE) PERSONHOOD IS PROMISED, BUT NEVER DELIVERED BY CAR OWNERSHIP.

...AND TIME:

IN 1974, ROMAN CATHOLIC PHILOSOPHER IVAN ILLICH WROTE:

THE TYPICAL AMERICAN MALE DEVOTES MORE THAN 16,000 HOURS A YEAR FOR HIS CAR... HE SPENDS FOUR OF HIS SIXTEEN WAKING HOURS ON THE ROAD OR GATHERING RESOURCES FOR IT... THE MODEL AMERICAN PUTS IN 16,000 HOURS AND GETS 75,000 MILES: LESS THAN FIVE MILES PER HOUR.

IN COUNTRIES DEPRIVED OF A TRANSPORTATION INDUSTRY, PEOPLE MANAGE TO DO THE SAME, WALKING WHEREVER THEY WANT TO GO, AND THEY ALLOCATE ONLY 3-8% OF THEIR SOCIETY'S TIME BUDGET TO TRAFFIC INSTEAD OF 28%. ***

* NATIONAL ASPHALT PAVEMENT ASSOCIATION, 2011.
** CLIVE THOMPSON, "NO PARKING HERE," MOTHER JONES, JAN/FEB 2016.
*** IVAN ILLICH, ENERGY AND EQUITY, 1974, PG. 19.

IF CARS ACTUALLY MONOPOLIZE *TIME* AND *SPACE* FOR ORDINARY FOLKS, THEY MUST SERVE OTHER, MORE SOCIAL AND POLITICAL ENDS.

IN NORTH AMERICA, DRIVING HAS BECOME BOTH A RITE OF PASSAGE AND A SIGNATURE OF AGENCY AND CITIZENSHIP.

CONVERSLEY, EXCLUSION FROM DRIVING BECOMES A MODE OF SOCIAL CONTROL — FULL PERSONHOOD IS SYSTEMICALLY DENIED CERTAIN POPULATIONS.

WELCOME TO LOVECRAFT COUNTRY

KEEP YOUR HANDS ON THE WHEEL WHERE HE CAN SEE THEM.

THE DIF-FERENTIAL POLICE HARASSMENT SUFFERED BY RACIALIZED DRIVERS MAINTAINS HIERARCHIES OF ACCESS TO THE ABILITY TO MOVE THROUGH PUBLIC SPACE WITHOUT FEAR

CAROL ANDERSON POINTS OUT HOW CLOSING DRIVER'S LICENCE OFFICES IN RURAL U.S.A. IS A STRATEGY FOR SUPPRESSING BLACK VOTING RIGHTS

...ALABAMA SHUT DOWN THE DEPT. OF MOTOR VEHICLES IN THE BLACK BELT COUNTIES. NOW YOU HAVE A 50-MILE TRIP IN ORDER TO GET A LICENCE. WELL, ALABAMA IS RANKED 48th IN THE NATION IN PUBLIC TRANSIT... SO HOW DO YOU GET TO THE LICENCE OFFICE?*

...AND WITHOUT A LICENCE, UNNECESSARILY HARSH VOTER I.D. LAWS MAKE IT DIFFICULT TO VOTE.

* DEMOCRACY NOW! OCT. 16, 2018.
ADAPTED FROM INTERVIEW.

ON A CONTINENT REDESIGNED FOR CARS, **FREEDOM** TAKES THE **HIGHLY CIRCUMSCRIBED** FORM OF DRIVING, BUT THIS SLIVER OF **AGENCY** IS RESERVED FOR CERTAIN SUBJECTS.

NOT ONLY ARE **IMPOVERISHED** AND **RACIALIZED** GROUPS SUBJECTED TO **POLICING** AND **DISENFRANCHISEMENT**, WOMEN ARE ALSO SUBJECTIFIED ACCORDING TO AN **ENTRENCHED** DIVISION OF SPACE BETWEEN **MASCULINIZED** PUBLIC SPACE AND **FEMINIZED** DOMESTIC SPACE.

DESPITE THE FACT THAT UPWARDS OF **70%** OF SERIOUS OR **FATAL** DRIVING ACCIDENTS IN THE U.S. ARE CAUSED BY **MEN**, PERSISTENT **STEREOTYPES** CAST WOMEN AS BAD DRIVERS *

THOUGH CARS PROVIDE A **PRIVATE ENVELOPE**, ALLOWING THE NAVIGATION OF PUBLIC SPACE WITH INCREASED **SECURITY**, PERVASIVE INSULTING DISCOURSES ATTEMPT TO RECLAIM THIS SPACE AS MASCULINE.

FURTHERMORE, WITH THE MALE PRIVILEGES OF DRIVING THREATENED BY THE **CLIMATE EMERGENCY**, POLITICAL THEORIST **CARA DAGGETT** IDENTIFIES THE EMERGENCE OF AN EXAGGERATED, FAR-RIGHT *PETRO-MASCULINITY*

AIN'T NO SNOWFLAKE COMMIES GONNA TAKE MY GOD-GIVEN RIGHT TO BURN RUBBER!

IT ARISES WHEN AGENTS OF HEGEMONIC MASCULINITY FEEL THREATENED OR UNDER-MINED, THEREBY NEEDING TO **INFLATE**, EXAGGERATE OR OTHERWISE DISTORT THEIR TRADITIONAL MASCULINITY. **

* SUNDERLAND (2017).

** DAGGETT (2018), P. 33.

FOR DAGGETT, PETROCULTURE HAS ALWAYS HARBOURED TOTALITARIAN TENDENCIES (AS TIMOTHY MITCHELL ALSO HIGHLIGHTS), SO IT IS NOT SURPRISING THAT PETRO-MASCULINITY...

...DISDAINS ANY VENEER OF HYBRIDITY OR CARE, AND IT ALSO HAS NO TRUCK WITH SUNNY CALIFORNIAN TECHNOSCIENTISM... AND WHILE PETRO-MASCULINITY IS BUILT UPON MID-20TH-C. FANTASIES, THERE IS NOTHING NOSTALGIC ABOUT ITS ORIENTATION TO FOSSIL FUELS [WHICH HAVE BECOME] A DEAD END, FOR BOTH THE PLANET AND THE GOAL OF MIDDLE-CLASS JOBS.

MOTOR CITY

IN THIS CONTEXT, BURNING FOSSIL FUELS CAN COME TO FUNCTION AS A KNOWINGLY VIOLENT EXPERIENCE, A REASSERTION OF WHITE MASCULINE POWER ON AN UNRULY PLANET THAT IS BELIEVED TO BE INCREASINGLY IN NEED OF VIOLENT, AUTHORITARIAN ORDER.*

THE VACANT, IMPASSIVE STARE OF RYAN GOSSLING'S CHARACTER, WHO IS ALSO PRONE TO ACTS OF BRUTAL VIOLENCE, IN THE 2011 FILM DRIVE, PROVIDES A FANTASY FIGURE FOR PETRO-MASCULINITY'S CONSTRAINED RANGE OF RELATIONALITY.

*DAGGETT (2018), PG. 34.

PETROCULTURE DOES NOT SIMPLY MIRROR OR AMPLIFY EXISTING SOCIAL DIVISIONS AND INEQUITIES, IT ACTIVELY FOSTERS THEM AS INHERENT ELEMENTS OF ITS REPRODUCTION, WHICH IS BASED ON AN IDEOLOGY OF MASTERY.

SO YOU SEE GRACHUS, IT IS NATURAL THAT SLAVES AND WOMEN EXIST, SO THAT MEN CAN PERSUE THE ARTS OF DEMOCRACY.

ACCORDING TO THIS NOTION, MAN IS BORN INTO PROTRACTED DEPENDENCE ON SLAVES WHICH HE MUST PAINFULLY LEARN TO MASTER.

IF HE DOES NOT USE PRISONERS, THEN HE NEEDS MOTORS TO DO MOST OF HIS WORK.

SCHOOL OF ATHENS

ACCORDING TO THIS DOCTRINE, THE WELL-BEING OF SOCIETY CAN BE MEASURED BY THE NUMBER OF YEARS ITS MEMBERS HAVE GONE TO SCHOOL AND BY THE NUMBER OF ENERGY SLAVES THEY HAVE THEREBY LEARNED TO COMMAND.

THIS BELIEF IS THREATENED BY THE OBVIOUS INEQUITY, HARRIEDNESS AND IMPOTENCE THAT APPEAR EVERYWHERE ONCE THE VORACIOUS HORDES OF ENERGY-SLAVES OUTNUMBER PEOPLE BY A CERTAIN PROPORTION.

THE ENERGY CRISIS FOCUSES CONCERN ON THE SCARCITY AND FODDER FOR THESE SLAVES. I PREFER TO ASK WHETHER FREE MEN NEED THEM.*

*IVAN ILLICH, ENERGY & EQUITY, 1974 P. 3-4.

93

THOUGH IVAN ILLICH'S CRITICAL LEGACY IS OVERSHADOWED BY HIS ESSENTIALIST AND REACTIONARY VIEWS ON GENDER, HIS IDEAS ABOUT ENERGY CAST HELPFUL LIGHT ON OUR CONTEMPORARY COLLECTIVE PARALYSIS IN ADDRESSING ENERGY TRANSITION...

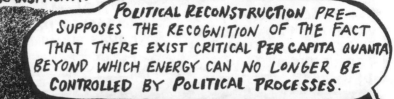

POLITICAL RECONSTRUCTION PRE-SUPPOSES THE RECOGNITION OF THE FACT THAT THERE EXIST CRITICAL PER CAPITA QUANTA BEYOND WHICH ENERGY CAN NO LONGER BE CONTROLLED BY POLITICAL PROCESSES.

IN HIGH-ENERGY-CONSUMING SOCIETIES, ARGUES ILLICH, PARTICIPATORY DEMOCRACY AND SOCIAL EQUITY BECOME IMPOSSIBLE, AND SOCIAL LIFE BECOMES MANAGED BY A TECHNOCRATIC ELITE. SOUND FAMILIAR?

HIGH SPEED IS THE CRITICAL FACTOR WHICH MAKES TRANSPORTATION [AS WELL AS COMMUNICATION & CONSUMPTION] SOCIALLY DESTRUCTIVE. A TRUE CHOICE AMONG POLITICAL SYSTEMS AND OF DESIRABLE SOCIAL RELATIONS IS POSSIBLE ONLY WHERE SPEED IS RESTRAINED. PARTICIPATORY DEMOCRACY DEMANDS LOW-ENERGY TECHNOLOGY, AND FREE PEOPLE MUST TRAVEL THE ROAD TO PRODUCTIVE SOCIAL RELATIONS AT THE SPEED OF A BICYCLE.*

*ILLICH, PG.18 (THE INSERTION ABOUT COMMUNICATION & CONSUMPTION IS FROM ILLICH'S FOOTNOTE, Pg.18.)

FOR ALL ITS SPEED AND SEEMING EFFICIENCY, PETROCULTURE HAS FAILED TO DELIVER MORE FREE TIME TO ORDINARY PEOPLE...

...AND, AS ILLICH PREDICTED, OUR HIGH-ENERGY-CONSUMING SOCIETIES HAVE EXPERIENCED INCREASING CRISES OF DEMOCRATIC INSTITUTIONS, MOUNTING DRAMATIC INEQUITY AND PARALYZING INERTIA.

I DO MY BEST THINKING ON THE BUS. THAT'S WHY I DON'T DRIVE, SEE?

YOU DON'T KNOW HOW TO DRIVE.

I DON'T WANT TO KNOW.

AT THE SAME TIME, THE MOUNTING CRISES ASSOCIATED WITH CLIMATE CHANGE MAKE THE LACK OF POLITICAL CHOICES AND AGENCY EVEN MORE POIGNANT AND DEVASTATING.

I DON'T WANT TO LEARN, SEE?

THE MORE YOU DRIVE, THE LESS INTELLIGENT YOU ARE.*

* FROM THE FILM REPOMAN (DIR. ALEX COX, 1984)

ADDICTED TO A VERY NARROWLY DEFINED AND INFRASTRUCTURALLY DETERMINED IDEAL OF FREEDOM, WE HAVE GIVEN UP SO MUCH OF OUR ABILITY TO SHAPE AND CARE FOR OUR COMMON LIVES AND WORLD.

SPEED IS ALSO CENTRAL TO THE ANALYSIS OF CULTURAL THEORIST **PAUL VIRILIO**, WHO ARTICULATES ITS POLITICAL DIMENSIONS AS AN EXTENSION OF WAR-TIME LOGICS INTO PEACE TIME, IN SERVICE OF A MILITARY-INDUSTRIAL COMPLEX THAT DEVELOPS IN TANDEM WITH MODERN MARKET ECONOMIES.

THE **BLINDNESS** OF THE SPEED OF MEANS OF **COMMUNICATING DESTRUCTION** IS NOT A LIBERATION FROM GEOPOLITICAL **SERVITUDE**, BUT THE **EXTERMINATION** OF SPACE AS THE FIELD OF **FREEDOM OF POLITICAL ACTION**. WE NEED ONLY REFER TO THE NECESSARY **CONTROLS** AND **CONSTRAINTS** OF THE RAILWAY, AIRWAY OR HIGHWAY TO SEE THE FATAL IMPULSE: THE MORE SPEED INCREASES, THE FASTER FREEDOM DECREASES.*

CHEER UP! IT'S ALL IN THE JOURNEY.

1987

WHAT ARE THE FORMS OF **AGENCY** AND **RELATIONSHIP**, THE POLITICAL AND SOCIAL **POTENTIALS**, THAT WE HAVE GIVEN UP IN EXCHANGE FOR THE SUPERHUMAN BUT HIGHLY CONSTRAINED AND INFRA-STRUCTURALLY DETERMINED CAPACITIES AFFORDED BY **PETROCULTURAL MOBILITY**?

WHAT POLITICAL, SOCIAL AND MORAL ABILITIES HAVE BECOME **INERT** AND DORMANT THROUGH LONG STUPOR AND **DISUSE**?

* PAUL VIRILIO (1977) Pg. 158.

WE SHOULD NOT INTERPRET THESE IDEAS AS CRUDELY DETERMINISTIC. LOWER ENERGY INPUTS DO NOT GUARANTEE GREATER EQUITY AND POLITICAL AGENCY.

NOR SHOULD WE DISCOUNT THE WAY ENERGY AND INDUSTRY HAVE IMPROVED BASIC LIVING CONDITIONS FOR MANY, THOUGH IN A HIGHLY UNEVEN WAY.

IF EVERYONE ON THE PLANET USED THE SAME ENERGY AS A CANADIAN, TOTAL PLANETARY CONSUMPTION WOULD BE 74 TERAWATTS PER YEAR - SIX TIMES AS MUCH ENERGY AS WE CURRENTLY CONSUME ACROSS THE GLOBE.*

* SZEMAN (2019) Pg. 18.

I'M EXHAUSTED ALREADY, PEOPLE.

ILLICH AND VIRILIO HELP US THINK ABOUT HOW PETROCULTURE, AND THE SPEED IT GENERATES, WHILE PROVIDING MANY PROMISES AND ENTICEMENTS, ALSO DRAMATICALLY CURTAILS OUR ABILITY TO RESPOND TO THE INEQUITIES AND CRISES THAT ARE DEEPENING WITH EACH PRESS OF THE ACCELERATOR.

WHAT IF WE HAVE CONFUSED SPEED WITH FREEDOM, EQUITY WITH EASE, SOCIALITY WITH TECHNOLOGY?

WHAT IF SLOWING DOWN WOULD NOT ONLY ALLOW US TO LIVE BETTER, BUT WOULD ALSO FREE UP THE WILL, TIME AND RESOURCES NEEDED TO PURSUE TRULY EQUITABLE AND DEMOCRATIC RELATIONSHIPS, BOTH WITHIN AND BETWEEN NATIONS?

THE 1969 FILM *EASY RIDER*, READ THROUGH AN ENERGY-SENSITIVE LENS, PROVIDES BITING CRITIQUE OF THE FALSE PROMISES AND SURROGATE FREEDOMS OF PETROCULTURE.

IN THE OPENING SCENES, WYATT (PETER FONDA) AND BILLY (DENNIS HOPPER) MAKE A FORTUNE SELLING COCAINE THEY HAVE SMUGGLED FROM MEXICO INSIDE OF EMPTY CAR BATTERIES.

THE SOUND OF PLANES FLYING OVERHEAD IS DEAFENING, AND WYATT IS FRAMED BY A PICKUP TRUCK WINDOW AS THE DEAL GOES DOWN.

(HE WILL MEET HIS END GUNNED DOWN FROM THE WINDOW OF A SIMILAR VEHICLE.)

THE DUO HIDE THE MONEY IN THE GAS TANK...

...OF WYATT'S MOTORBIKE. THE FIRST FEW MINUTES OF THE FILM THUS OFFER A STRIKING ASSEMBLAGE OF PETROCULTURAL SIGNIFIERS: DRUGS, MONEY, GAS, NATIONHOOD AND FREEDOM ARE CONDENSED INTO AN ELOQUENT GRAPHIC CODE THAT CAN HELP US DECIPHER THE FILM.

AS THE TWO COUNTERCULTURAL REBELS SET OUT ON A ROAD TRIP TO **MARDI GRAS** IN **NEW ORLEANS**, THE PEOPLE THEY MEET ALONG THE WAY OFFER GLIMPSES OF ALTERNATIVE POSSIBILITIES FOR 'THE GOOD LIFE.'

THEY VISIT A **FARMER'S** HOMESTEAD, WITH HIS LARGE FAMILY, DOING "HIS OWN THING IN HIS OWN TIME," AND A **HIPPIE COMMUNE** TRYING TO MAKE A GO OF IT IN THE DESERT.

BUT WHILE THE MORE **CONTEMPLATIVE WYATT** IS TEMPTED TO **LINGER** AND APPRECIATE THESE PLACES, THE **RESTLESS BILLY** DEMANDS THEY **PRESS ONWARDS** TOWARDS THEIR CHOSEN **DESTINATION**. IT IS AS IF THE **MONEY** STASHED IN THE **GAS TANK** KEEPS PROPELLING HIM TOWARDS THE ROAD AND AWAY FROM FORMING **LASTING RELATIONSHIPS**.

OR, PERHAPS IT IS PETROCULTURAL INFRASTRUCTURES OF HIGHWAYS AND GASOLINE THAT FUEL BILLY'S RESTLESSNESS.

THE FILM'S OPENING IMAGES OF THE GAS TANK SUGGEST THE PROTAGONISTS ARE IN THE GRIPS OF A POWERFUL COMPLEX OF HABITS AND ATTACHMENTS.

AS CULTURAL THEORIST STEPHANIE LeMENAGER ARGUES...

PETROLEUM INFRA-STRUCTURE HAS BECOME EMBODIED MEMORY AND HABITUS FOR MODERN HUMANS, INSOFAR AS EVERYDAY EVENTS SUCH AS DRIVING... ARE INCORPORATING PRACTICES, IN PAUL CONNERTON'S TERM FOR REPEATED PERFORM-ANCES THAT BECOME ENCODED IN THE BODY. *

LUKE ASKEW PLAYS A HITCHHIKER WHO IS TRYING TO CHALLENGE THIS HABITUS.

I'M FROM THE CITY...

*LEMENAGER (2014) Pg.104.

...A LONG WAY FROM THE CITY, AND THAT'S WHERE I WANT TO BE RIGHT NOW.

THE HITCHHIKER AND THE COMMUNE TO WHICH HE BELONGS ARE TRYING TO ENACT WHAT LeMENAGER DESCRIBES AS AN URGENT IMPERATIVE...

DECOUPLING HUMAN CORPOREAL MEMORY FROM THE INFRASTRUCTURES THAT HAVE SUSTAINED IT MAY BE THE PRIMARY CHALLENGE FOR ECOLOGICAL NARRATIVE IN THE SERVICE OF HUMAN SPECIES SURVIVAL BEYOND THE TWENTY-FIRST CENTURY. *

BUT EASY RIDER ACKNOWLEDGES THIS TASK IS MORE COMPLICATED THAN JUST HOPPING ON A MOTORCYCLE AND LEAVING TOWN. FOR INSTANCE, A CONTRAST IS DRAWN BETWEEN LOST INDIGENOUS CULTURE...

THE PEOPLE THIS PLACE BELONGS TO ARE BURIED RIGHT UNDER YOU... YOU COULD BE A TRIFLE POLITE.

* LEMENAGER (2014) Pg. 104.

... AND BURIED RESOURCES THAT A CONQUERING PEOPLE HAVE APPROPRIATED AND USED TO COMMODITIZE AND TRANSFORM THE LAND.

ENCO

SACRED MOUNTAIN

EVEN WHEN THE DUO FIND A FRIEND AND ALLY IN THE MAVERICK LAWYER GEORGE HANSON (JACK NICHOLSON) WE ARE LED TO WONDER WHETHER THE ENTICEMENTS OF THE ROAD CAN DELIVER ON THE PROMISES OF FREEDOM AND FULFILLMENT THE CHARACTERS SEEK.

AFTER HANSON IS MURDERED BY REDNECKS, A CLIMACTIC MONTAGE DEPICTS A BAD ACID TRIP THE PROTAGONISTS EXPERIENCE IN THE ST. LOUIS CEMETARY NO. 1 IN NEW ORLEANS.

HERE TOO, PETROCULTURAL INFRASTRUCTURE HAUNTS THE SCENE, THE SOUNDTRACK OF WHICH IS PUNCTUATED BY THE POUNDING OF A PILE DRIVER.

BOOM BAM BOOM BAM

IT IS PART OF THE FILMIC LORE SURROUNDING EASY RIDER THAT THE PILE DRIVER THE CHARACTERS PASS AT THE START OF THE CEMETERY SCENE WAS HAMMERING THE SUPPORT COLUMNS FOR AN INTERSTATE HIGHWAY OVER-PASS IN 1968.*

BIENVILLE

FORD

Bienville

Claiborne AVE.

THIS STREET USED TO BE SO VIBRANT.

A CAREFUL VIEWER WILL NOTE, HOWEVER, THAT THIS PLACES THE OPENING SHOTS OF THE SCENE AT A DIFFERENT CEMETERY, ST. LOUIS CEMETERY No. 2, SEVERAL BLOCKS NORTH-WEST FROM WHERE THE REST OF THE 'ACID TRIP' SCENE WAS SHOT.

FOR SOME REASON, EITHER DENNIS HOPPER OR DOCUMENTARY FILMMAKER LES BLANK (THE UNCREDITED DIRECTOR OF THE CEMETERY SEQUENCE) INCLUDED THIS DETAIL.

* SEE, FOR INSTANCE, KOLB (2013) Pg. 127.

LES BLANK RECIEVED HIS B.A. FROM TULANE UNIVERSITY IN NEW ORLEANS. HE WOULD HAVE KNOWN CLAIBORNE AVE'S IMPORTANCE TO THE AFRICAN AMERICAN COMMUNITY AND CULTURE.

WITH HUNDREDS OF BUSINESSES AND THE LONGEST STRAND OF OAK TREES IN THE COUNTRY, CLAIBORNE AVE. WAS A VITAL ARTERY OF BLACK CULTURE IN THE TREMÉ AND SEVENTH WARD NEIGHBOURHOODS. RESIDENTS WOULD CRAM THE TREE-LINED NEUTRAL GROUND TO WATCH THE MARDI GRAS PARADES.

IN 1968 THE TREES WERE REMOVED AND REPLACED BY THE CONCRETE PILLARS OF THE I-10. THE HIGHWAY DECIMATED THE COMMERCE AND CULTURE OF THE AVENUE, AND BY 2000 ONLY 44 BUSINESSES REMAINED.

IN 2002, NEW ORLEANS ARTISTS WERE COMMISSIONED TO PAINT MURALS COMMEMORATING THE SITE.

* SEE ENDNOTES FOR CITATIONS.

104

EASY RIDER IS OFTEN CHARACTERIZED AS AN ELEGY FOR THE VALUES AND LIFESTYLES OF THE 1960s' HIPPIE COUNTERCULTURE. BY PAYING ATTENTION TO PETROCULTURAL IMAGERY AND THEMES, WE ARE ABLE TO SEE A NEW DIMENSION OF THE FILM'S CRITIQUE.
AS BILLY SAYS...

EVERYTHING WE EVER DREAMED OF IS IN THAT **TEAR-DROP GAS TANK**, MAN.

THE FILM REVEALS THIS DREAMING TO BE A **VALE OF TEARS**...

...A VARIETY OF THE **CRUEL OPTIMISM** DESCRIBED BY **LAUREN BERLANT**.*

THIS MESSAGE IS REINFORCED WITH A **PILE DRIVER IN THE CEMETERY SCENE**, REMINDING US THAT THE SAME HIGHWAY SYSTEM THAT OFFERED WYATT & BILLY THE PROMISE OF **FREEDOM** IS A VEHICLE OF OPPRESSION AND DISPLACEMENT FOR MANY, SUCH AS **NEW ORLEAN'S AFRICAN AMERICAN** COMMUNITIES.

*SEE BERLANT (2011) AND CHAPTER 2 OF THIS BOOK.

ULTIMATELY, THE **MURDER OF BILLY** AND **WYATT BY REDNECKS IN A PICKUP TRUCK** ONLY REINFORCES THE FILM'S CRITIQUE, LEAVING LITTLE QUESTION AS TO THE KINDS OF RELATIONSHIPS AND VALUES FOSTERED BY A SOCIETY **ORGANIZED AROUND OIL**.

PETROCULTURAL COMPULSIONS, SO WELL ILLUSTRATED BY **EASY RIDER**, RESONATE BEHIND WYATT'S TACITURN WORDS..

WE BLEW IT.

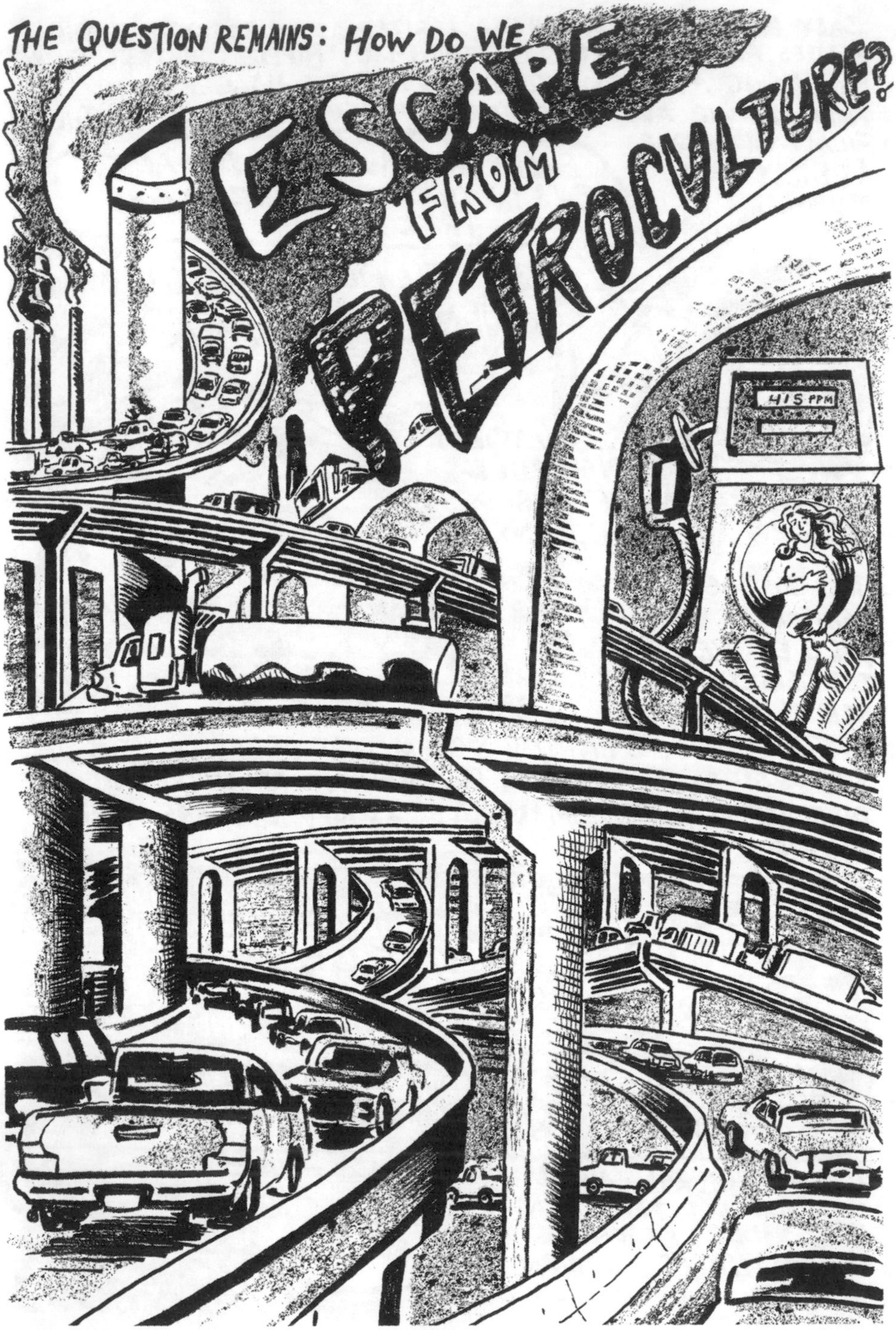
THE QUESTION REMAINS: HOW DO WE
ESCAPE FROM PETROCULTURE?
415 PPM

Chapter 4
Quilting Point

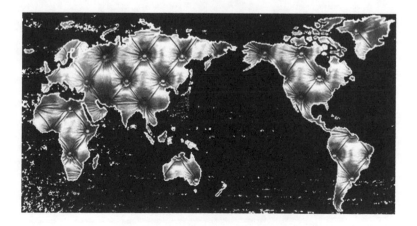

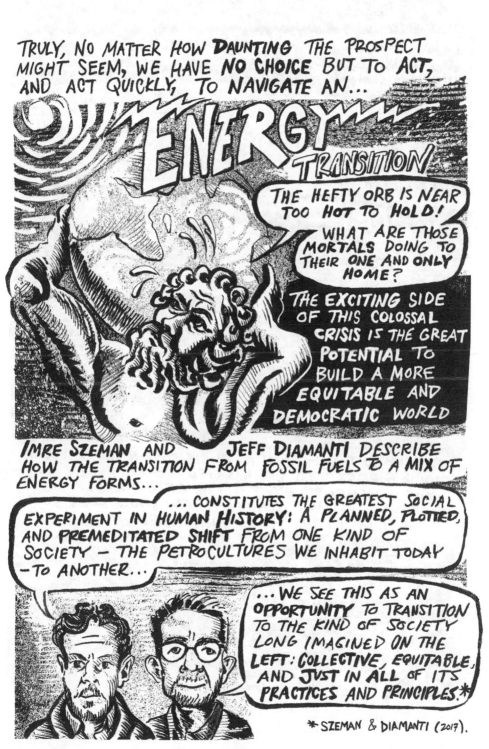

TRULY, NO MATTER HOW **DAUNTING** THE PROSPECT MIGHT SEEM, WE HAVE **NO CHOICE** BUT TO ACT, AND ACT QUICKLY, TO NAVIGATE AN...

ENERGY TRANSITION

THE HEFTY ORB IS NEAR TOO **HOT** TO **HOLD!**

WHAT ARE THOSE MORTALS DOING TO THEIR ONE AND **ONLY** HOME?

THE EXCITING SIDE OF THIS COLOSSAL CRISIS IS THE GREAT POTENTIAL TO BUILD A MORE EQUITABLE AND DEMOCRATIC WORLD

IMRE SZEMAN AND **JEFF DIAMANTI** DESCRIBE HOW THE TRANSITION FROM FOSSIL FUELS TO A MIX OF ENERGY FORMS...

... CONSTITUTES THE GREATEST SOCIAL EXPERIMENT IN HUMAN **HISTORY**: A PLANNED, PLOTTED, AND PREMEDITATED SHIFT FROM ONE KIND OF SOCIETY — THE PETROCULTURES WE INHABIT TODAY —TO ANOTHER...

... WE SEE THIS AS AN **OPPORTUNITY** TO TRANSITION TO THE KIND OF SOCIETY LONG IMAGINED ON THE LEFT: COLLECTIVE, EQUITABLE, AND JUST IN ALL OF ITS PRACTICES AND PRINCIPLES.*

* SZEMAN & DIAMANTI (2017).

THE GREAT, CURRENT DANGER IS THAT THE **MOUNTING CRISES** ASSOCIATED WITH A WARMING PLANET, COUPLED WITH ALREADY **THREADBARE** SOCIAL FABRICS, WILL BE USED AS OPPORTUNITIES FOR FURTHER CONSOLIDATIONS OF **AUTHORITARIAN POWER** BY THE SAME ELITES WHO HAVE PRODUCED THIS MESS.

THE CYNICAL STRATEGY OF BALDLY **DENYING** CLIMATE CHANGE WHILE MAKING PREPARATIONS TO **BENEFIT** FROM IT...

4TH NATIONAL CLIMATE CHANGE ASSESSMENT

PURE RUBBISH. WHERE'S MY WALL?

...MIGHT HAVE BEEN PIONEERED BY **EXXON** IN 1977, BUT IS NOW A CENTRAL STRATEGY OF THE RULING CLASSES. ...WHICH EXPLAINS THE **NERO SYNDROME** THAT SEEMS SO PREVALENT RECENTLY.

TO DENY IN THIS FASHION IS TO **LIE COLD-BLOODEDLY,** AND THEN TO **FORGET** THAT ONE HAS LIED — EVEN WHILE CONSTANTLY REMEMBERING THE LIE AFTER ALL, THIS IS **DRAINING.** WE MAY WONDER THEN: WHAT DOES SUCH A TANGLE DO TO THE PEOPLE ENTANGLED IN ITS NET?

IT DRIVES THEM CRAZY.*

*BRUNO LATOUR, "DOWN TO EARTH" (2018) P. 22.

110

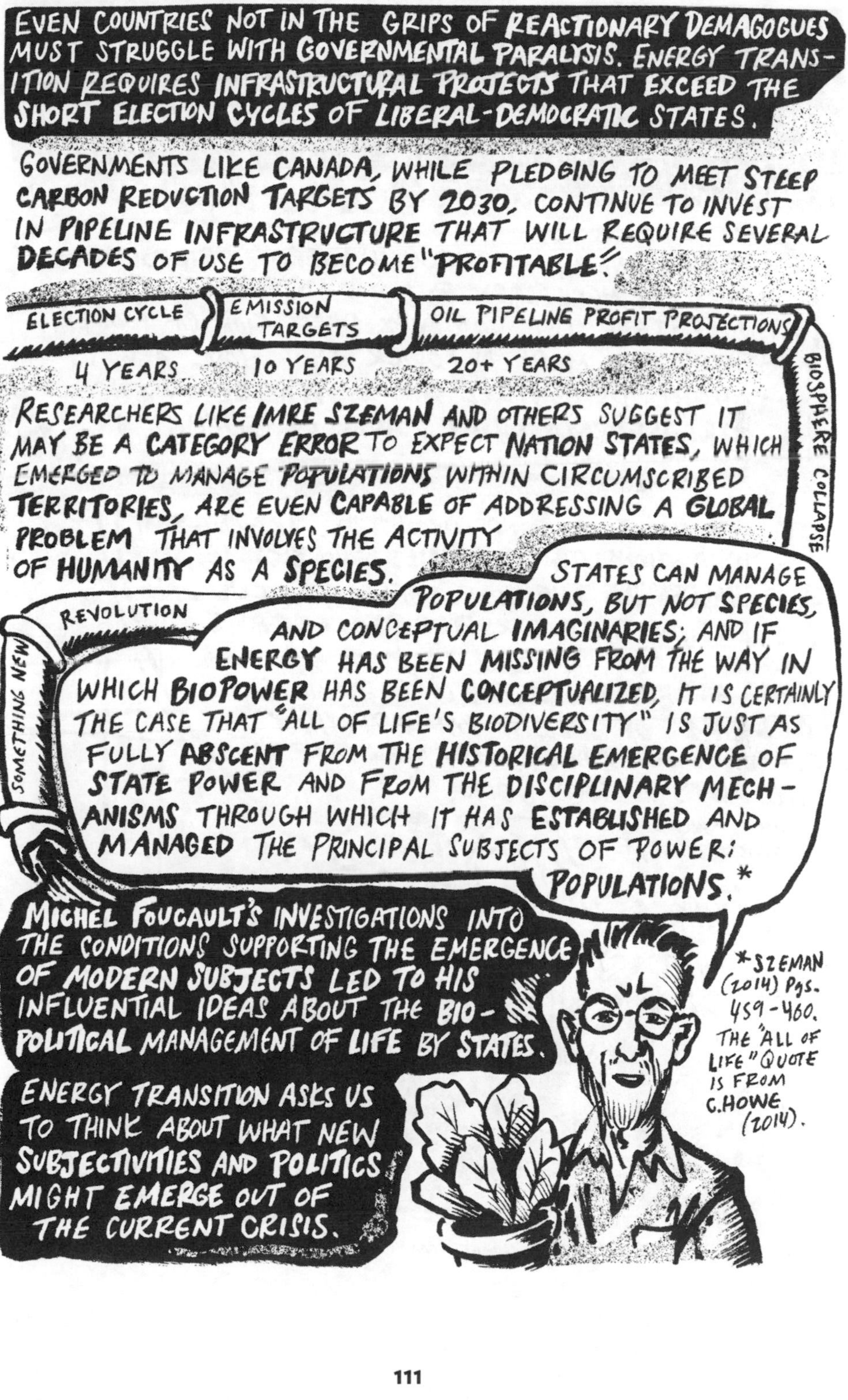
EVEN COUNTRIES NOT IN THE GRIPS OF REACTIONARY DEMAGOGUES MUST STRUGGLE WITH GOVERNMENTAL PARALYSIS. ENERGY TRANSITION REQUIRES INFRASTRUCTURAL PROJECTS THAT EXCEED THE SHORT ELECTION CYCLES OF LIBERAL-DEMOCRATIC STATES.
GOVERNMENTS LIKE CANADA, WHILE PLEDGING TO MEET STEEP CARBON REDUCTION TARGETS BY 2030, CONTINUE TO INVEST IN PIPELINE INFRASTRUCTURE THAT WILL REQUIRE SEVERAL DECADES OF USE TO BECOME "PROFITABLE."
ELECTION CYCLE
EMISSION TARGETS
OIL PIPELINE PROFIT PROJECTIONS
4 YEARS
10 YEARS
20+ YEARS
BIOSPHERE COLLAPSE
RESEARCHERS LIKE IMRE SZEMAN AND OTHERS SUGGEST IT MAY BE A CATEGORY ERROR TO EXPECT NATION STATES, WHICH EMERGED TO MANAGE POPULATIONS WITHIN CIRCUMSCRIBED TERRITORIES, ARE EVEN CAPABLE OF ADDRESSING A GLOBAL PROBLEM THAT INVOLVES THE ACTIVITY OF HUMANITY AS A SPECIES.
REVOLUTION
SOMETHING NEW
STATES CAN MANAGE POPULATIONS, BUT NOT SPECIES, AND CONCEPTUAL IMAGINARIES; AND IF ENERGY HAS BEEN MISSING FROM THE WAY IN WHICH BIOPOWER HAS BEEN CONCEPTUALIZED, IT IS CERTAINLY THE CASE THAT "ALL OF LIFE'S BIODIVERSITY" IS JUST AS FULLY ABSCENT FROM THE HISTORICAL EMERGENCE OF STATE POWER AND FROM THE DISCIPLINARY MECHANISMS THROUGH WHICH IT HAS ESTABLISHED AND MANAGED THE PRINCIPAL SUBJECTS OF POWER: POPULATIONS.*
MICHEL FOUCAULT'S INVESTIGATIONS INTO THE CONDITIONS SUPPORTING THE EMERGENCE OF MODERN SUBJECTS LED TO HIS INFLUENTIAL IDEAS ABOUT THE BIOPOLITICAL MANAGEMENT OF LIFE BY STATES.
*SZEMAN (2014) PGS. 459-460. THE "ALL OF LIFE" QUOTE IS FROM C. HOWE (2014).
ENERGY TRANSITION ASKS US TO THINK ABOUT WHAT NEW SUBJECTIVITIES AND POLITICS MIGHT EMERGE OUT OF THE CURRENT CRISIS.

IF BIOPOWER AS ARTICULATED BY FOUCAULT AND OTHERS INVOLVES POWER OVER **LIFE** AND **POPULATIONS**, AND IF CRITICAL ENGAGEMENT WITH ENERGY HAS BEEN LARGELY MISSING FROM THESE ANALYSES, OUR CURRENT, UNPRECEDENTED ENERGY CRISIS CALLS FOR NEW THINKING. ANTHROPOLOGIST **DOMINIC BOYER** COINED THE TERM *ENERGOPOLITICS*, DESCRIBING...

...POWER OVER (AND THROUGH) ENERGY... BIOPOLITICAL ANALYSIS IS **NECESSARY**, BUT NOT **SUFFICIENT**, TO UNDERSTAND THE COMPLEX OPERATION OF MODERN STATES AND MODERN POWER THAT HAVE ALWAYS SOUGHT TO **CONTROL** AND **CAPITALIZE** ON THE **TRANSFORMATIONAL** POWER OF ENERGY. *

CYMENE HOWE EXPANDS UPON THIS, ARGUING THAT CONSIDERATIONS ABOUT **SPECIES** AND **BIODIVERSITY** ARE **CHALLENGING** THE BIOPOLITICAL FOCUS ON POPULATION THAT OCCUPIES **STATECRAFT**.**

HOWE AND BOYER HOST THE LONG-RUNNING **CULTURES OF ENERGY** PODCAST THAT FEATURES INTERVIEWS WITH MANY OF THE THEORISTS IN THIS BOOK. ***

* BOYER, "ENERGO-POLITICS" (2011) Pg. 7.

** HOWE "ANTHROPOCENIC..." (2014) Pgs. 397-399.

(FOR MORE ON SPECIES, SEE CH. 5.)

*** SEE: CENHS, CULTURESOFENERGY.COM

OUR RECEIVED POLITICAL STRUCTURES MIGHT BE ILL-EQUIPPED TO GRAPPLE WITH ISSUES OF BIOME AND SPECIES SURVIVAL, BUT THESE THEMES ARE CERTAINLY PERCOLATING THROUGH POPULAR CULTURE...

THE 2020 HBO TV SERIES RAISED BY WOLVES INDULGES THE FANTASY THAT ARTIFICIALLY INTELLIGENT ANDROIDS MIGHT NURTURE AND SAVE THE REMNANTS OF HUMANITY WHO HAVE FLED AN EARTH LAID WASTE BY SECTARIAN CONFLICTS.

DISNEY'S STAR WARS SPINOFF SERIES THE MANDALORIAN LIKEWISE FEATURES ISSUES OF SPECIES SURVIVAL IN THE BABY YODA CREATURE AND HIS HUMAN AND ROBOT NURSEMAIDS.

THESE PARENTAL FIGURES SIGNIFY MODES OF SPECIES PROTECTION OUTSIDE OF EXISTING GOVERNMENTS AND ORGAN-IZATIONS, SKETCHING OUT A LIMIT TO WHAT OUR COLLECTIVE IMAGINATIONS ARE ABLE TO REPRESENT... AND POSSIBLY POINTING BEYOND.

JEDI JUMPER

IF THE **NATION FORM** IS INADEQUATE FOR ADDRESSING THE CRISIS OF GLOBAL CLIMATE CHANGE, SO TOO ARE THE **ECONOMIC PARADIGMS** THAT SUPPORT IT. OUR **IMAGINATIONS** ARE CULTURALLY CONDITIONED TO ACCEPT A VERSION OF **LIMITLESS GROWTH** AND **ACCUMULATION** AS "NATURAL."

HOWEVER, AS **JACOB LUND FISKER** POINTS OUT...

BEFORE THE **INDUSTRIAL REVOLUTION**, HUMAN SOCIETIES WERE NECESSARILY BASED ON 'STEADY-STATE ECONOMICS' DUE TO THE LIMITED **FLOW** OF THEIR **SOLAR-DERIVED** ENERGY SUPPLIES.

WITH THE ADVENT OF **FOSSIL ENERGY** SUPPLIES ECONOMIC GROWTH WAS ENABLED AND 'GROWTH ECONOMIES' REMAIN DEPENDENT ON A FRAMEWORK OF **CHEAP** AND **EASY ENERGY** SUPPLIES.*

MODERN ECONOMICS SIMPLY PRESUPPOSES ABUNDANT **FOSSIL ENERGY**.

KEYNES

FRIEDMAN

OUR MOST ADVANCED ECONOMIC MODELLING IS POWERLESS!

IT'S AS IF THE MONSTER FEEDS OFF COMPLACENT THEORIZING!

* FISKER (2005) Pg. 74.

114

FURTHERMORE, AS **TIMOTHY MITCHELL** POINTS OUT, "*THE ECONOMY*" ONLY CAME *INTO* EXISTENCE AS AN **OBJECT** OF TECHNICAL AND **GOVERNMENTAL EXPERTISE** IN THE *1930s* & *'40s.* BEFORE THAT, THE WORD MERELY DESCRIBED A **PROCESS** RATHER THAN A **DISCRETE TOOL** OF GOVERNANCE. *

IT'S CONSTANTLY GROWING, BUT WE CAN HARNESS ALL THAT POTENTIAL THROUGH SKILLED GOVERNMENTAL OVERSIGHT OF THE MARKET.

A KEY CHARACTERISTIC OF THIS NEW ENTITY, WHICH MEASURED **NOT ACCUMULATION** OF WEALTH BUT THE **SPEED** AND **FREQUENCY** BY WHICH MONEY TRADES HANDS, WAS ITS ABILITY TO **GROW** WITHOUT **PHYSICAL** OR **TERRITORIAL LIMITS.** *

BUT THIS IMAGE OF THE ECONOMY AS EVER EXPANDING, **LIMITLESS GROWTH** PRESUPPOSES A STEADY SUPPLY OF **LOW-COST ENERGY.** *

ITS CARBON FOOTPRINT IS **HUGE!**

* **MITCHELL** (2013) Pgs 124 - 143.

115

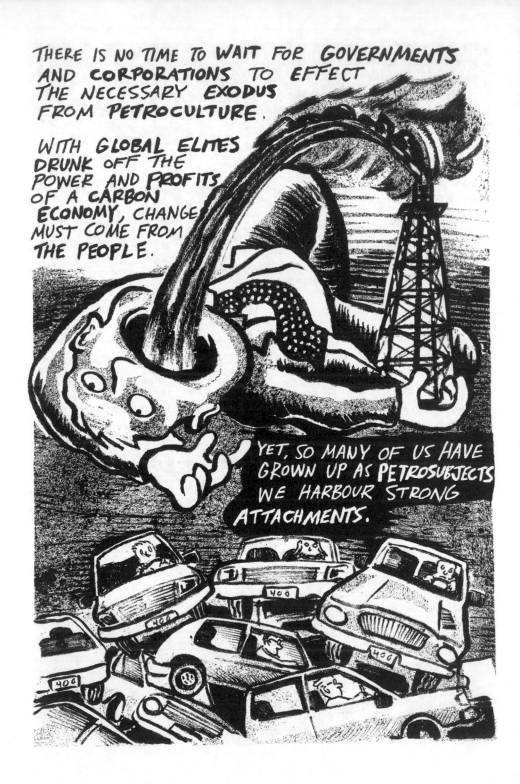

THERE IS NO TIME TO WAIT FOR GOVERNMENTS AND CORPORATIONS TO EFFECT THE NECESSARY EXODUS FROM PETROCULTURE.

WITH GLOBAL ELITES DRUNK OFF THE POWER AND PROFITS OF A CARBON ECONOMY, CHANGE MUST COME FROM THE PEOPLE.

YET, SO MANY OF US HAVE GROWN UP AS PETROSUBJECTS WE HARBOUR STRONG ATTACHMENTS.

IF FOSSIL FUELS WERE MERELY A SIMPLE SUBSTANCE, EXODUS FROM PETROCULTURE WOULD BE A RELATIVELY STRAIGHTFORWARD MATTER: A TECHNOLOGICAL SHIFT THAT MIGHT LEAVE MUCH OF OUR ECONOMIC AND CULTURAL SYSTEMS UNSHAKEN. BUT PETROLEUM IS A @QUILTING POINT.

ENERGY TRANSITION NECESSITATES WE RETHINK AND REIMAGINE OUR SHARED WORLD, EPISTEMOLOGIES, CULTURES AND VALUES. IT IS AN OPPORTUNITY TO REKINDLE SOLIDARITIES...

AND TO RECONNECT WITH A PLANET THAT MANY OF US HAVE LONG BEEN TREATING AS AN INERT BACKDROP — A COLLECTION OF RAW MATERIALS AT THE DISPOSAL OF HUMAN DESIRE.

THERE IS A VAST DIFFERENCE BETWEEN THE MIND AND THE BODY, IN RESPECT THAT BODY, FROM ITS NATURE, IS ALWAYS DIVISIBLE, AND THAT MIND IS ENTIRELY INDIVISIBLE... THIS WOULD BE ENOUGH TO TEACH ME THAT THE MIND OR SOUL OF MAN IS ENTIRELY DIFFERENT FROM THE BODY... *

COMBUSTION

Fig. E Pineal Gland

Fig. P Petrol Gland

Accelerator Nerve

Cover mighty distances in short times.

Rival four-footed machina in motion

Wheels upon wheels like the Great Music of the Spheres

Survey the Earth to make straight the King's pathways

THOUGH DESCARTES WAS WRITING MORE THAN TWO CENTURIES BEFORE THE AGE OF PETROCULTURE, WE MIGHT CHART A DIRECT LINEAGE FROM HIS POSITED NEXUS OF BODY AND SOUL IN THE PINEAL GLAND AND WHAT WE MIGHT IMAGINE AS...

The Petrol Gland

Fig. B. Brain in a Car

Accelerator Nerve

The Open Road

THOUGH MERELY A WHIMSICAL HYPOTHESIS, THE PETROL GLAND MAY BE THE SEAT OF THE FEELING OF FREEDOM FROM TERRESTRIAL LIMITS CAR CULTURE PROMISES.

*RENE DESCARTES, MEDITATIONS #VI, section 19, (1901), Pg. 276.

118

OF COURSE, X-RAYS AND AUTOPSIES WILL NEVER UNCOVER AN ACTUAL PETROL GLAND...

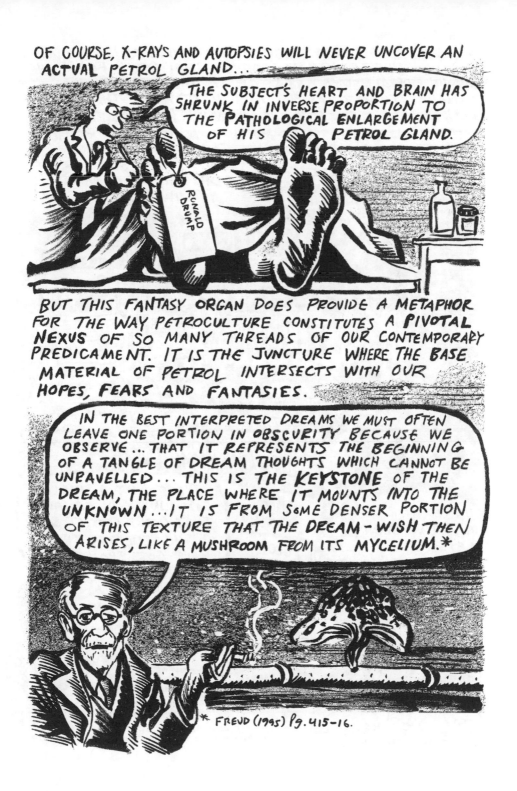

THE SUBJECT'S HEART AND BRAIN HAS SHRUNK IN INVERSE PROPORTION TO THE PATHOLOGICAL ENLARGEMENT OF HIS PETROL GLAND.

RONALD DRUMP

BUT THIS FANTASY ORGAN DOES PROVIDE A METAPHOR FOR THE WAY PETROCULTURE CONSTITUTES A PIVOTAL NEXUS OF SO MANY THREADS OF OUR CONTEMPORARY PREDICAMENT. IT IS THE JUNCTURE WHERE THE BASE MATERIAL OF PETROL INTERSECTS WITH OUR HOPES, FEARS AND FANTASIES.

IN THE BEST INTERPRETED DREAMS WE MUST OFTEN LEAVE ONE PORTION IN OBSCURITY BECAUSE WE OBSERVE... THAT IT REPRESENTS THE BEGINNING OF A TANGLE OF DREAM THOUGHTS WHICH CANNOT BE UNRAVELLED... THIS IS THE KEYSTONE OF THE DREAM, THE PLACE WHERE IT MOUNTS INTO THE UNKNOWN...IT IS FROM SOME DENSER PORTION OF THIS TEXTURE THAT THE DREAM-WISH THEN ARISES, LIKE A MUSHROOM FROM ITS MYCELIUM.*

* FREUD (1995) Pg. 415-16.

119

AN EXAMPLE OF SUCH A **TANGLE OF DREAM THOUGHTS** IS PROVIDED BY THE "**UNITED WE ROLL**" CONVOY THAT DROVE FROM THE PROVINCE OF ALBERTA, SEAT OF THE **OIL INDUSTRY** IN CANADA, TO PARLIAMENT HILL IN OTTAWA. THIS ADVOCACY PROTEST FOR THE OIL INDUSTRY WAS ENTANGLED WITH **XENOPHOBIC, ANTI-MUSLIM AND WHITE SUPREMACIST HATE SPEECH** ASSOCIATED WITH FAR-RIGHT GROUPS SUCH AS THE SOLDIERS OF ODIN AND THE CANADIAN YELLOW VEST MOVEMENT.

THE CONVOY WAS WELCOMED BY CONSERVATIVE PARTY LEADER ANDREW SCHEER AND ONTARIO PREMEIR DOUG FORD, WHO FOCUSED ON THE OIL MESSAGE WHILE IGNORING THE **RACIST** FORMS OF NATIONALISM BEING CHAMPIONED.

UNITED WE ROLL! UNITED WE STAND! LET'S BUILD SOME PIPELINES! *

NO

UN/GLOBALIS/

CARBON TAX

TANKER BAN

DIRTY FOREIGN OIL

OPEN BORDERS

THERE ISN'T A SINGLE COMMUNITY IN CANADA THAT CAN'T LOOK AT SOME OF THE BENEFITS THEY HAVE GOT FROM THE OIL AND GAS SECTOR. **

CHARGE TRUDEAU WITH TREASON

UNITED WE ROLL

FROM
* DOUG FORD'S FACEBOOK VIDEO. FORDNATION (2019).

**FROM ANDREW SCHEER'S SPEECH TO THE UNITED WE ROLL CONVOY. SCHEER (2019).

FAR-RIGHT WHITE NATIONALIST **FAITH GOLDY** SPOKE AT THE SAME RALLY AS NATIONAL CONSERVATIVE PARTY LEADER **ANDREW SHEER**.

NO MORE **OPEN BORDERS**! OUR BORDERS WILL BE PROTECTED! THERE IS SUCH A THING AS AN **ILLEGAL IMMIGRANT**! WE ARE TAKING OUR COUNTRY BACK AND ALL OF YOUR **GLOBALISM**, **COMMUNISM** AND **SOCIALISM** WILL BE **SQUASHED**! WE ARE **CANADIANS**. OUR PASSPORTS ARE VALID. OUR BORDERS WILL BE UPHELD AND YOUR **EVIL WORLD VIEW** WILL BE **DEFEATED**... MY ANCESTORS CAME HERE THE **RIGHT WAY**! YOU DON'T LIKE OUR BORDERS—**LEAVE THEM**!*

*FROM A VIDEO PUBLISED BY RiseCanada (2019).

THOUGH SOME OF THE MEDIA **AFTERMATH** OF THIS EVENT TRIED TO **DISASSOCIATE** THE "**LEGITIMATE**" CONCERNS OF OIL AND GAS WORKERS FROM THE **HATE SPEECH** OF **WHITE SETTLER** CONSERVATISM, THE TWO DISCOURSES ARE **UNITED** BY THE SAME **TANGLE** OF **DREAM THOUGHTS** ELICITED BY THE **FUMES OF PETROCULTURE**: A BELIEF THAT THE **CORROSIVE** EFFECTS OF GLOBALIZED PETRO-CAPITALISM CAN SOMEHOW BE **EXPUNGED** FROM A FORTIFIED, **RACIALLY DEFINED NATION STATE**.

IT SHOULD COME AS NO SURPRISE THAT PETROCULTURES WHICH PUBLICLY DISAVOW ANTHROPOGENIC CLIMATE CHANGE SHOULD ESPOUSE THE BIOPOLITICS OF RACE AND NATION.

NO CARBON TAX CANADA FIRST

OPEN BORDERS BREED CHAOS

MAGA MAKE ALBERTA GREAT AGAIN

SUCH A COUPLING INDICATES THAT BENEATH THE POSTURES OF DENIAL AND NOSTALGIA FOR A BYGONE ERA, BENEATH THE CONSPIRACY THEORIES AND SCRAMBLED COGNITIVE MAPPING, SUCH PROTESTS RECOGNIZE ALL TOO WELL THAT WE ARE ENTERING UNCERTAIN AND UNPRECEDENTED TIMES.

BUT IT WOULD BE A MISTAKE TO IDENTIFY SUCH POSITIONS WITH THE RACISMS OF THE PAST.

HAMILTON AGAINST FASCISM

NEVER AGAIN

Soldiers Of Odin

Canada

THE TRADITIONS OF ALL THE DEAD GENERATIONS WEIGHS LIKE A NIGHTMARE ON THE BRAINS OF THE LIVING. AND JUST WHEN THEY SEEM ENGAGED IN REVOLUTIONIZING THEMSELVES AND THINGS, IN CREATING SOMETHING THAT HAS NEVER YET EXISTED, PRECISELY IN SUCH PERIODS OF REVOLUTIONARY CRISIS THEY ANXIOUSLY CONJURE UP THE SPIRITS OF THE PAST TO THEIR SERVICE AND TO DRAW FROM THEM NAMES, BATTLE CRIES AND COSTUMES IN ORDER TO PRESENT THE NEW SCENE OF WORLD HISTORY IN THIS TIME-HONOURED DISGUISE AND THIS BORROWED LANGUAGE. *

*KARL MARX, "18TH BRUMAIRE," PG. 15

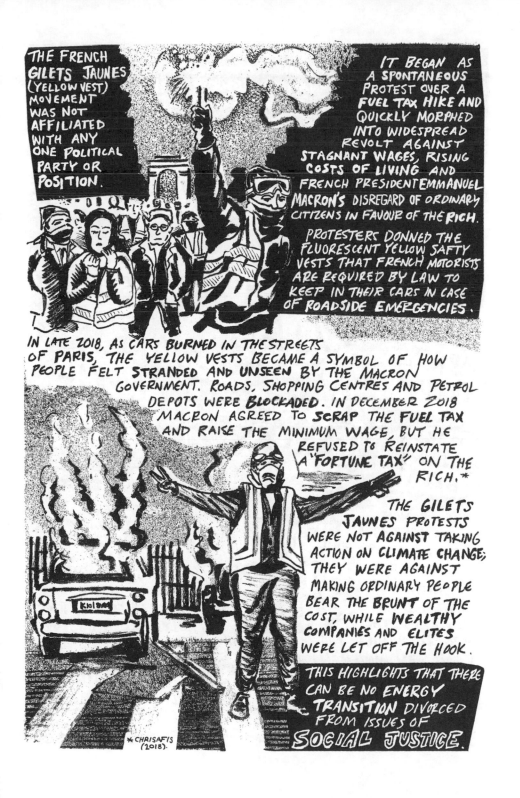

THE FRENCH GILETS JAUNES (YELLOW VEST) MOVEMENT WAS NOT AFFILIATED WITH ANY ONE POLITICAL PARTY OR POSITION.

IT BEGAN AS A SPONTANEOUS PROTEST OVER A FUEL TAX HIKE AND QUICKLY MORPHED INTO WIDESPREAD REVOLT AGAINST STAGNANT WAGES, RISING COSTS OF LIVING AND FRENCH PRESIDENT EMMANUEL MACRON'S DISREGARD OF ORDINARY CITIZENS IN FAVOUR OF THE RICH.

PROTESTERS DONNED THE FLUORESCENT YELLOW SAFTY VESTS THAT FRENCH MOTORISTS ARE REQUIRED BY LAW TO KEEP IN THEIR CARS IN CASE OF ROADSIDE EMERGENCIES.

IN LATE 2018, AS CARS BURNED IN THE STREETS OF PARIS, THE YELLOW VESTS BECAME A SYMBOL OF HOW PEOPLE FELT STRANDED AND UNSEEN BY THE MACRON GOVERNMENT. ROADS, SHOPPING CENTRES AND PETROL DEPOTS WERE BLOCKADED. IN DECEMBER 2018 MACRON AGREED TO SCRAP THE FUEL TAX AND RAISE THE MINIMUM WAGE, BUT HE REFUSED TO REINSTATE A "FORTUNE TAX" ON THE RICH.*

THE GILETS JAUNES PROTESTS WERE NOT AGAINST TAKING ACTION ON CLIMATE CHANGE; THEY WERE AGAINST MAKING ORDINARY PEOPLE BEAR THE BRUNT OF THE COST, WHILE WEALTHY COMPANIES AND ELITES WERE LET OFF THE HOOK.

THIS HIGHLIGHTS THAT THERE CAN BE NO ENERGY TRANSITION DIVORCED FROM ISSUES OF SOCIAL JUSTICE.

* CHRISAFIS (2018).

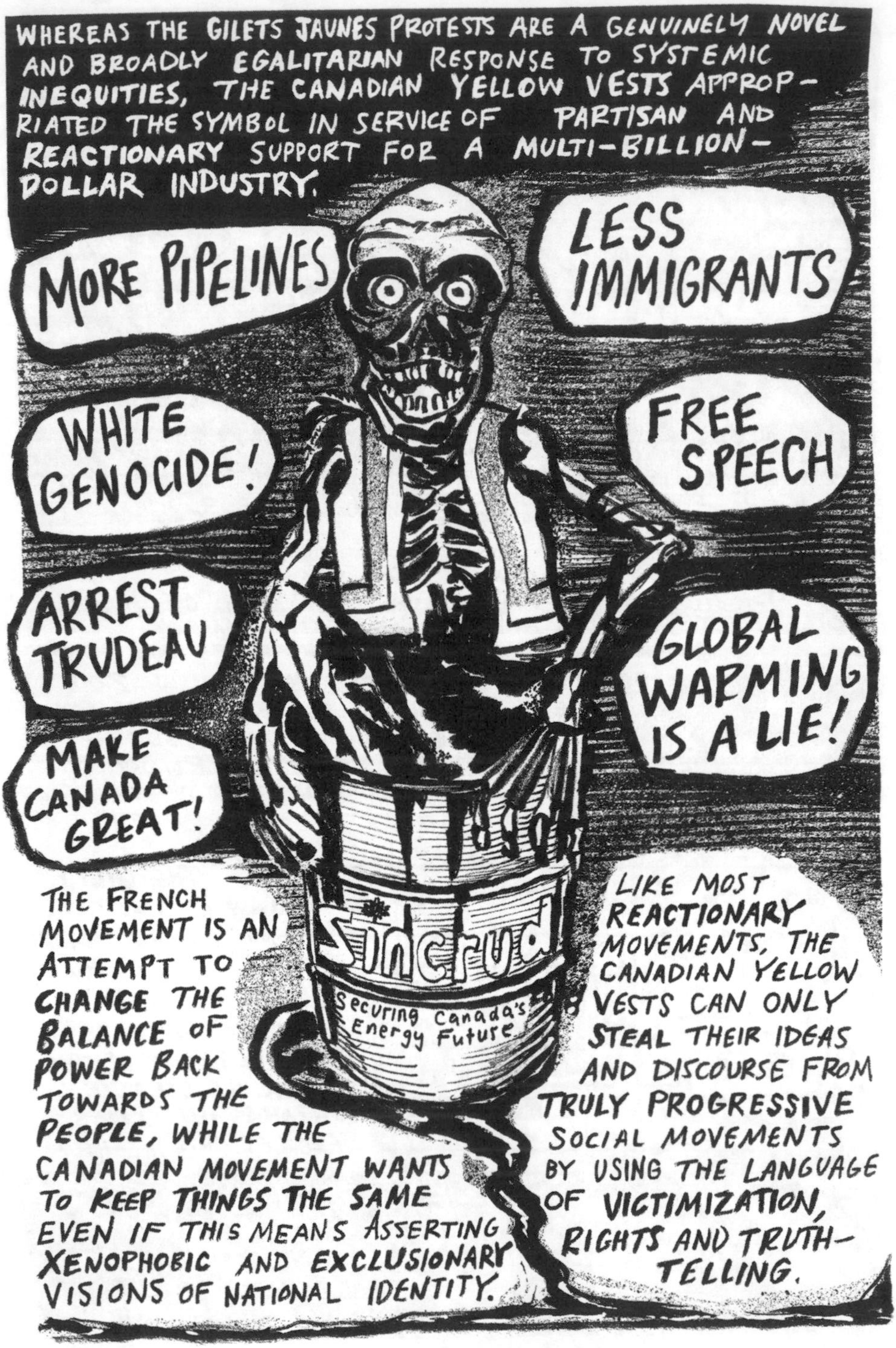
WHEREAS THE GILETS JAUNES PROTESTS ARE A GENUINELY NOVEL AND BROADLY EGALITARIAN RESPONSE TO SYSTEMIC INEQUITIES, THE CANADIAN YELLOW VESTS APPROPRIATED THE SYMBOL IN SERVICE OF PARTISAN AND REACTIONARY SUPPORT FOR A MULTI-BILLION-DOLLAR INDUSTRY.
MORE PIPELINES
LESS IMMIGRANTS
WHITE GENOCIDE!
FREE SPEECH
ARREST TRUDEAU
GLOBAL WARMING IS A LIE!
MAKE CANADA GREAT!
Sincrud
Securing Canada's Energy Future
THE FRENCH MOVEMENT IS AN ATTEMPT TO CHANGE THE BALANCE OF POWER BACK TOWARDS THE PEOPLE, WHILE THE CANADIAN MOVEMENT WANTS TO KEEP THINGS THE SAME EVEN IF THIS MEANS ASSERTING XENOPHOBIC AND EXCLUSIONARY VISIONS OF NATIONAL IDENTITY.
LIKE MOST REACTIONARY MOVEMENTS, THE CANADIAN YELLOW VESTS CAN ONLY STEAL THEIR IDEAS AND DISCOURSE FROM TRULY PROGRESSIVE SOCIAL MOVEMENTS BY USING THE LANGUAGE OF VICTIMIZATION, RIGHTS AND TRUTH-TELLING.

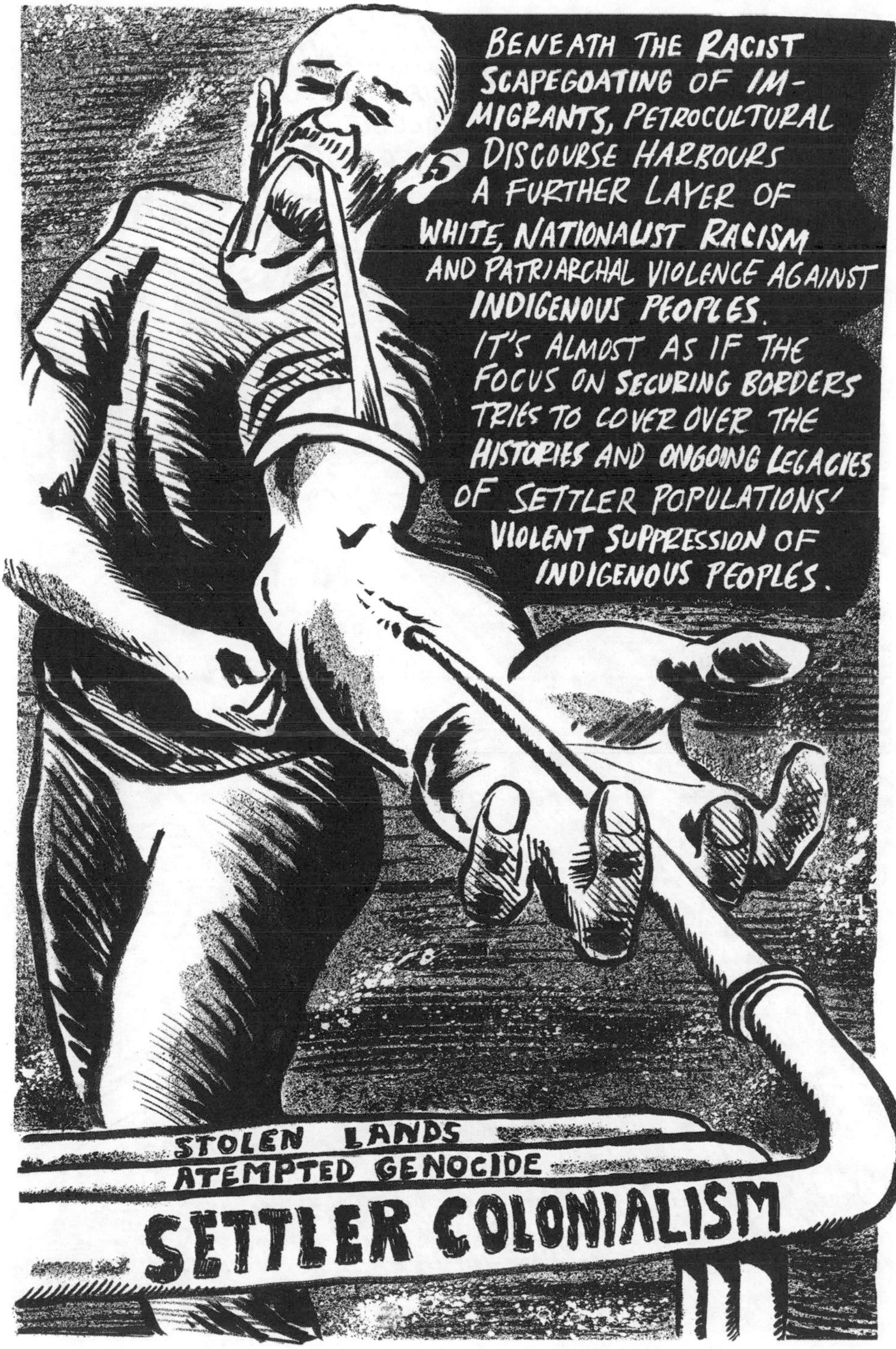
BENEATH THE RACIST SCAPEGOATING OF IMMIGRANTS, PETROCULTURAL DISCOURSE HARBOURS A FURTHER LAYER OF WHITE, NATIONALIST RACISM AND PATRIARCHAL VIOLENCE AGAINST INDIGENOUS PEOPLES.
IT'S ALMOST AS IF THE FOCUS ON SECURING BORDERS TRIES TO COVER OVER THE HISTORIES AND ONGOING LEGACIES OF SETTLER POPULATIONS' VIOLENT SUPPRESSION OF INDIGENOUS PEOPLES.
STOLEN LANDS
ATEMPTED GENOCIDE
SETTLER COLONIALISM

THE LINKS BETWEEN RACISM, NATIONALISM, SETTLER COLONIALISM AND PETROCULTURE ARE NOT ACCIDENTS OF HISTORY, BUT RATHER A HISTORICALLY SPECIFIC AND COHERENT MATRIX OF MUTUALLY REINFORCING IDEOLOGIES, PRACTICES, HABITS, FEELINGS AND CONDITIONED DISPOSITIONS.

PIONEERS

NOTHING WAS EVER HERE BUT ROADS

FOR INSTANCE, THE ERASURE OF PLACE EFFECTED BY DRIVING REITERATES AND IS STRANGELY CONTINUOUS WITH THE DOCTRINE OF TERRA NULLIUS BY WHICH EUROPEAN SETTLERS JUSTIFIED THE APPROPRIATION OF INDIGENOUS LANDS IN NORTH AMERICA AND ELSEWHERE.

AND THOUGH THE LAND WAS FAR FROM EMPTY WHEN THE COLONIZERS ARRIVED, THE VAST NETWORKS OF ROADS, PARKING LOTS AND GAS STATIONS WE HAVE BUILT SINCE HAVE MADE TERRA NULLIUS A SAD CONTEMPORARY REALITY.

THEFT IS NOT THE OPPOSITE OF OWNERSHIP; IT IS THE ORIGINARY ACT UPON WHICH PRIVATE PROPERTY IS FOUNDED, A VIOLENT IMPOSITION OF ACQUISITIVENESS THAT OBSCURES ALL OTHER MODES, TRADITIONS AND PRACTICES OF RELATING TO PLACE.

OUR ATTACHMENT TO THE ACT OF DRIVING IS AT ONCE A SYMPTOM OF OUR ALIENATION FROM PLACE, AN ATTEMPT TO FOSTER A SENSE OF CONNECTION TO THE WORLD AND ONE OF THE CENTRAL WAYS OF REPRODUCING AND LEGITIMATING THE SAME THEFT-PROPERTY COMPLEX THAT ENSURES OUR ALIENATION.

HAUDENOSAUNEE (SIX NATIONS, BEAR CLAN) AND ANISHNAABE SCHOLAR VANESSA WATTS CRITIQUES THE DOMINANT EUROPEAN-COLONIAL RELATIONSHIP TO LAND AS PROPERTY BASED ON POSSESSION, VIOLENCE AND ACCESS. IN CONTRAST, INDIGENOUS CULTURES RECOGNIZE LAND AS TEACHER AND GUIDE TO HUMAN ACTIVITY THAT IS NOT FUNDAMENTALLY SEPARATE FROM THE EARTH, WATER, PLANTS AND ANIMALS THAT SUPPORT US.

PLACE-THOUGHT

IS THE NON-DISTINCTIVE SPACE WHERE PLACE AND THOUGHT WERE NEVER SEPARATED BECAUSE THEY NEVER COULD OR CAN BE SEPARATED. PLACE-THOUGHT IS BASED ON THE PREMISE THAT LAND IS ALIVE AND THINKING AND NON-HUMANS DERIVE AGENCY THROUGH THE EXTENSIONS OF THESE THOUGHTS.*

WATTS RECOGNIZES THE COLONIAL ENTERPRISE AS AN ATTEMPT TO DELEGITIMATE AND DISRUPT INDIGENOUS PLACE-THOUGHT, REPLACING IT WITH AN ANDROCENTRIC AND EMPHATICALLY MASCULINIST VISION OF THE LAND AS AN INERT RESOURCE DEVOID OF AGENCY, WILL OR INTELLIGENCE.

HOWEVER, IF WE THINK OF AGENCY BEING TIED TO SPIRIT, AND SPIRIT EXISTS IN ALL THINGS, THEN ALL THINGS POSSESS AGENCY. IN THE WORDS OF (ANISHNAABE) ELDER FRED KELLY, OUR ORIGIN STORIES STATE THAT SKY WOMAN WAS ABLE TO COMMUNICATE WITH THE ANIMALS AND VICE VERSA. OUR ABILITY TO HAVE SOPH-ISTICATED GOVERNANCE SYSTEMS IS DIRECTLY RELATED TO NOT ONLY THE ANIMALS' ABILITY TO COM-MUNICATE WITH US, BUT THEIR WILLINGNESS TO DO SO.*

* WATTS (2013) PGS. 21, 30.

BY EXPLOITING ONE SPECIFIC AND NON-RENEWABLE FORM OF THE LAND'S SPIRIT — THE POTENT AND CONDENSED SOLAR ENERGY CONTAINED IN FOSSIL FUEL — PETROCULTURE HAS BEEN ABLE TO AMPLIFY THE SENSE OF HUMAN AGENCY WHILE REINFORCING THE ILLUSION OF THE LAND AND ANIMALS AS MERE RESOURCES AT OUR DISPOSAL. THE FANTASIES OF HUMAN SEPARATION AMPLIFIED BY PETROCULTURE REINFORCE THE COLONIAL SUPPRESSION OF PLACE-THOUGHT.

AND THE PRICE OF LIVING IN THIS DREAM WORLD IS NOT JUST THE DEVASTATION OF LAND, PLANTS AND ANIMALS, BUT THE ONGOING, VIOLENT SUPPRESSION OF INDIGENOUS PEOPLES WHO DEPEND ON THE LAND FOR THEIR MODES OF LIFE AND CULTURE.

FOR WATTS, HONOURING **PLACE-THOUGHT** ALLOWS INDIGENOUS PEOPLE TO RE-CONNECT WITH A **PRE-COLONIAL MINDSET** THAT IS CRUCIAL TO COUNTERACTING CENTURIES OF OVERT AND SYSTEMIC VIOLENCE AGAINST INDIGENOUS PEOPLE AND CULTURE.

COLONIZATION HAS DISRUPTED OUR ABILITY TO COMMUNICATE WITH PLACE AND HAS ENDANGERED AGENCY AMONGST INDIGENOUS PEOPLES... A DISRUPTION OF THIS ORIGINAL PROCESS GOES BEYOND LOSING A FORM OF INDIGENOUS **IDENTITY** OR **WORLDVIEW**... IT HAS BECOME A VIOLATION OF **SKY WOMAN'S INTENTIONALITY.** *

FOR SETTLER CULTURE TO RECOGNIZE **PLACE THOUGHT** AS PART OF THE **SOLUTION** TO AN ENVIRONMENTAL PREDICAMENT THAT IS, ITSELF, THE **DIRECT RESULT** OF SETTLER EPISTEMOLOGIES AND **PRACTICES**, WITHOUT ADDRESSING THE KEY ISSUES OF **INDIGENOUS SOVEREIGNTY** OVER **TRADITIONAL TERRITORIES**, ONLY PERPETUATES SETTLER-COLONIAL VIOLENCE IN THE GUISE OF **RECONCILLIATION** AND **TOLERANCE**.

SUCH STRATEGIES ARE ALL-TOO-COMMON IN SETTLER STATES LIKE CANADA.

25 YRS Nionwen KAHNASETAKE

STOP No Access WITHOUT CONSENT

* WATTS (2013) Pg. 23.

FOR EXAMPLE, IN 2010, MEMBERS OF THE WET'SUWET'EN NATION'S UNIST'OT'EN AND GIDUMDT'EN CLANS ERECTED GATED CHECKPOINTS ON AND NEAR THE MORICE RIVER BRIDGE IN NORTHERN BRITISH COLUMBIA TO BLOCK THE CONSTRUCTION OF THE COASTAL GASLINK PIPELINE THAT WOULD CARRY NATURAL GAS THROUGH TRADITIONAL WET'SUWET'EN TERRITORIES.

IN A HARD-WON 1997 SUPREME COURT RULING, INDIGENOUS TITLE TO THESE LANDS WAS RECOGNIZED, FORBIDDING USES OF LAND THAT ARE "IRRECONCILABLE WITH THE NATURE OF THE CLAIMANTS' ATTACHMENT TO THOSE LANDS."*

THE PROPOSED PIPELINE RECEIVED APPROVAL FROM THE FEDERAL AND B.C. GOVERNMENTS, AND FROM THE ELECTED TRIBAL CHIEFS OF THE WET'SUWET'EN NATION, BUT WAS REJECTED BY THE HEREDITARY CHIEFS, WHO CONSTITUTE THE NON-COLONIAL WET'SUWET'EN GOVERNANCE STRUCTURE. **

* DELGAMUUKW (1997)   ** "UNIST'OT'EN AND THE LIMITS" (2019)

131

DESPITE COURT RECOGNITION OF THE WET'SUWET'EN HEREDITARY CHIEF'S SOVEREIGNTY OVER 22000 KM² OF UNCEDED TERRITORY, CANADIAN R.C.M.P. AND GAS INDUSTRY WORKERS PERSISTENTLY ATTEMPTED TO BREACH THE CHECKPOINT.

DO YOU UNDERSTAND THAT THIS IS UNCEDED UNIST'OT'EN TERRITORY?

THAT'S WHAT'S CLAIMED. THAT'S CORRECT.

YOU DO NOT HAVE JURIS--DICTION TO WALK IN HERE.

YES I DO.

WHAT'S GOING ON?

FREDA HUSON IS THE CAMP'S SPOKESPERSON.

WE'RE HERE TO TALK.

LET'S GO BACK TO YOUR CAR BECAUSE YOU GUYS DON'T HAVE PERMISSION TO COME ACROSS HERE.

FROM A 2015 VIDEO: "RCMP BLOCKED FROM ENTER-ING UNISTOT'EN CAMP." WWW. STRAIGHT .COM BY CHARLIE SMITH.

132

THE UNIST'OT'EN CAMP IS MORE THAN JUST A PROTEST AGAINST PIPELINES; IT IS ALSO A HEALING CENTRE PROMOTING TRADITIONAL TEACHINGS AND LAND-BASED WELLNESS PRACTICES.

BOTH THE HEALING CAMP AND THE ASSERTION OF SOVEREIGNTY OVER TRADITIONAL LANDS REFLECT INDIGENOUS VALUES AND GOVERNANCE, AS HEREDITARY UNIST'OT'EN SPOKESPERSON FREDA HUSON EXPLAINS...

OUR PEOPLES' BELIEF IS THAT WE ARE PART OF THE LAND. THE LAND IS NOT SEPARATE FROM US., THE LAND SUSTAINS US. AND IF WE DON'T TAKE CARE OF HER, SHE WON'T BE ABLE TO SUSTAIN US, AND WE AS A GENERATION WILL DIE.*

RATHER THAN RELATING TO ENERGY AS A RESOURCE TO BE OWNED AND EX-TRACTED, TRADITIONAL INDIGENOUS CULTURES PRACTICE WHAT WARREN CARIOU CALLS **ENERGY INTIMACY**

*HUSON (2017).

THE LAND IS DEPICTED NOT AS A RESERVOIR OF RESOURCES TO BE EXPLOITED, BUT AS A SOURCE OF GIFTS THAT HUMANS MUST ACCEPT WITH **GRATITUDE** **

SPECTRA PIPELINE

GAS FRACKING

UNIST'OT'EN CAMP

PACIFIC TRAIL PIPELINE

SUMMIT LAKE

KITIMAT B.C.

THESE PRE-CAPITALIST, PRE-COLONIAL VALUES PUT INDIGENOUS KNOWLEDGE AT ODDS WITH EXTRACTIVIST STATES...

** CARIOU (2017) Pg. 18.

133

THE MATRILINEAL, HEREDITARY LEADERS OF THE WET'SUWET'EN NATION ACTED IN ACCORDANCE WITH PLACE-THOUGHT BY REFUSING TO ALLOW THE COSTAL GASLINK FRACKED GAS PIPELINE THROUGH THEIR TERRITORY.

THEY WERE ALSO ACTING IN ACCORD WITH CLIMATE SCIENCE, WHICH REINFORCES THE URGENT NEED TO KEEP FOSSIL FUELS IN THE GROUND AND OUT OF THE ATMOSPHERE.

BUT ON JAN. 7, 2019, HEAVILY ARMED R.C.M.P., ENFORCING A B.C. SUPREME COURT INJUNCTION, FORCIBLY BREACHED THE GIDIMT'EN CHECKPOINT, ARRESTING 14 PEOPLE AND ASSERTING RIGHT OF WAY FOR THE PIPELINE

POLICE

SUCH ACTS ARE CONSISTENT WITH 300 YEARS OF SETTLER VIOLENCE, AND DEMONSTRATE THAT STATE RHETORICS OF "TRUTH AND RECONCILIATION" STOP SHORT OF RECOGNIZING INDIGENOUS LAND SOVEREIGNTY.

WHILE PIPELINE PROJECTS THREATEN TO FURTHER POISON THE LAND THAT INDIGENOUS PEOPLES DEPEND UPON FOR PHYSICAL AND SPIRITUAL SURVIVAL, EXTRACTIVE INDUSTRIES USE LARGELY NON-INDIGENOUS, TRANSIENT, MALE WORKERS THAT REPRODUCE LONG LEGACIES OF SETTLER AGGRESSION

INDIGENOUS WOMEN AND GIRLS ALREADY SUFFER THE HIGHEST RATES OF GENDERED VIOLENCE IN CANADA AND SEVERAL STUDIES SHOW THAT MAN CAMPS CAN GREATLY AMPLIFY THIS.*

*SEE:
AMNESTY INERNATIONAL (2016);
GIBSON et al. (2017).

VIOLENCE AGAINST OUR EARTH AND WATER IS PERPETUATED ON A DAILY BASIS, AGAINST THOSE THINGS ABSOLUTELY VITAL TO OUR VERY EXISTENCE. WE CAN'T BE SURPRISED THAT PEOPLE WHO WOULD RAPE OUR LAND ARE ALSO RAPING OUR PEOPLE. WE MUST DO SOMETHING TO STOP THIS FROM CONTINUING.**

PATINA PARK, EXECUTIVE DIRECTOR OF THE MINNESOTA INDIAN WOMEN'S RESOURCE CENTRE, IS PART OF A COALITION WORKING TO DRAW ATTENTION TO THESE ISSUES.** ("SEXUAL VIOLENCE IN EXTRACTION ZONES," HONOREARTH.ORG.)

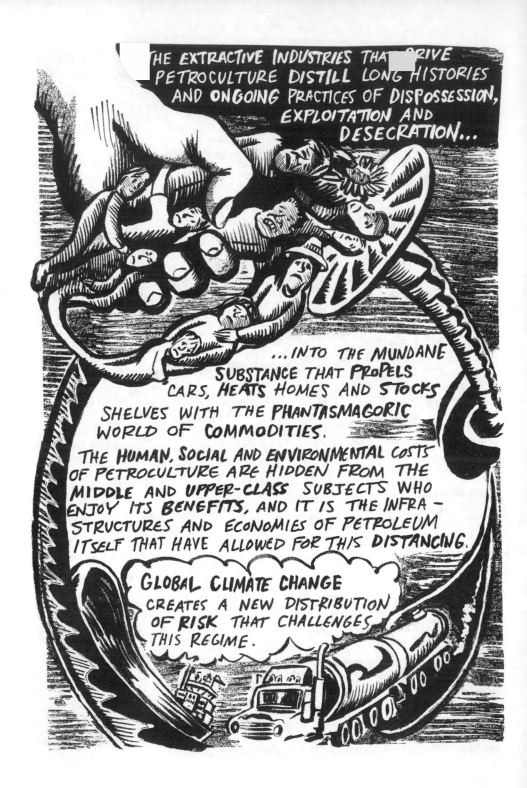

THE EXTRACTIVE INDUSTRIES THAT DRIVE PETROCULTURE DISTILL LONG HISTORIES AND ONGOING PRACTICES OF DISPOSSESSION, EXPLOITATION AND DESECRATION...

...INTO THE MUNDANE SUBSTANCE THAT PROPELS CARS, HEATS HOMES AND STOCKS SHELVES WITH THE PHANTASMAGORIC WORLD OF COMMODITIES.

THE HUMAN, SOCIAL AND ENVIRONMENTAL COSTS OF PETROCULTURE ARE HIDDEN FROM THE MIDDLE AND UPPER-CLASS SUBJECTS WHO ENJOY ITS BENEFITS, AND IT IS THE INFRA-STRUCTURES AND ECONOMIES OF PETROLEUM ITSELF THAT HAVE ALLOWED FOR THIS DISTANCING.

GLOBAL CLIMATE CHANGE CREATES A NEW DISTRIBUTION OF RISK THAT CHALLENGES THIS REGIME.

THE **SOPORIFIC** DRIVE TO **COMMODITIZE** THE **EARTH** ITSELF HAS COME UP AGAINST A SERIES OF **LIMITS** AS IT BECOMES INCREASINGLY CLEAR THAT THE **WORLD** THAT SUSTAINS US HAS A **WISDOM** AND **AGENCY** OF ITS OWN, OF WHICH HUMAN INTELLIGENCE IS BUT A PART.

MANY PEOPLE AND CULTURES THAT PETROL-COLONIAL SETTLER STATES HAVE LONG PERSECUTED HAVE NEVER FORGOTTEN THIS WISDOM.

DEFEND THE SACRED

TREATING THE WORLD AS AN **INERT** BACKDROP TO HUMAN **PRODUCTIVITY** AND **DESIRE** IS NO LONGER POSSIBLE IN THE AGE OF GLOBAL CLIMATE CHANGE, EVEN THOUGH SO MANY OF OUR INSTITUTIONS, **EPISTEMOLOGIES** AND **ECO**-NOMIC STRUCTURES ARE BASED UPON THIS ILLUSION. BUT PEOPLE ARE WAKING UP.

...AND MANY NEVER FELL ASLEEP.

Chapter 5
Petrotemporality

GEOLOGISTS CALL THE PERIOD DATING FROM THE END OF THE LAST ICE AGE ABOUT 11,700 YEARS AGO

THE HOLOCENE

VACANCY

DURING THIS ERA OF RELATIVE CLIMATE STABILITY, PRACTICES OF MASS AGRICULTURE, RESOURCE EXTRACTION, PRODUCTION AND MANAGEMENT OF SURPLUS WEALTH AND THE REFINEMENT OF COMPLEX HIERARCHICAL SOCIAL STRUCTURES ULTIMATELY LED TO THE WORLD WE INHABIT TODAY...

WHERE NOT A CORNER OF THE BIOSPHERE REMAINS UNMARKED BY HUMAN ACTIVITY.

THE REALIZATION THAT HUMAN CIVILIZATION HAS BECOME A GEOLOGIC FORCE HAS LED TO DEBATES OVER HOW TO PERIODIZE THE ERA OF HUMAN-DRIVEN CLIMATE CHANGE.

IN 2000, NOBEL PRIZE-WINNING ATMOSPHERIC CHEMIST **PAUL J. CRUTZEN** AND BIOLOGIST **EUGENE F. STOERMER** ARGUED THAT THE MAJOR AND GROWING **IMPACTS**...

...OF HUMAN ACTIVITIES ON **EARTH** AND **ATMOSPHERE** [MAKE IT] MORE THAN APPROPRIATE TO EMPHASIZE THE **CENTRAL ROLE** OF MANKIND IN **GEOLOGY** AND **ECOLOGY** BY PROPOSING TO **NAME** THE CURRENT, GEOLOGIC EPOCH...*

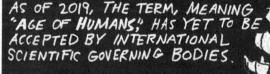

The **Anthropocene**

VACANCY?

DR. CRUTZEN OF EARTH

AS OF 2019, THE TERM, MEANING "**AGE OF HUMANS**," HAS YET TO BE ACCEPTED BY INTERNATIONAL SCIENTIFIC GOVERNING BODIES.

BUT IT HAS GAINED CONSIDERABLE **TRACTION** WITH SCHOLARS, ARTISTS AND THE GENERAL PUBLIC.

IT IS A CONCEPT FRAUGHT WITH **CONTRADICTIONS** AND SUBJECT TO SIGNIFICANT **CRITIQUES.**

* CRUTZEN & STOERMER (2000) P. 17.

IN 1990, A DECADE BEFORE CRUTZEN & STOERMER PROPOSED NAMING A NEW GEOLOGIC ERA, PHILOSOPHER MICHEL SERRES DESCRIBED HOW MODERN HUMAN ACTIVITY HAD BECOME A GEOLOGIC FORCE...

ON PLANET EARTH, HENCEFORTH, ACTION COMES NOT SO MUCH FROM MAN AS AN **INDIVIDUAL SUBJECT**, THE ANCIENT WARRIOR HERO OF PHILOSOPHY AND OLD-STYLE HISTORICAL CONSCIOUSNESS, NOT SO MUCH FROM THE CANONIZED **COMBAT** OF **MASTER** AND **SLAVE**, A RARE COUPLE IN QUICKSAND, NOT SO MUCH FROM GROUPS ANALYSED IN THE OLD SOCIAL SCIENCES — ASSEMBLIES, PARTIES, NATIONS, ARMIES, TINY VILLAGES...

NO, THE DECISIVE ACTIONS ARE NOW **MASSIVELY** THOSE OF **ENORMOUS** AND DENSE **TECHTONIC PLATES** OF **HUMANITY**. *

* SERRES (1990) Pg. 16.

SERRES DESCRIBES A **FIGURE-GROUND** SHIFT WHEREBY A **PROTRACTED** WAR AGAINST NON-HUMAN NATURE, PREVIOUSLY **OBSCURED** BY **HUMAN CONFLICT**, HAS NOW COME TO THE **FORE**.**

** (1990) Pgs 6-13.

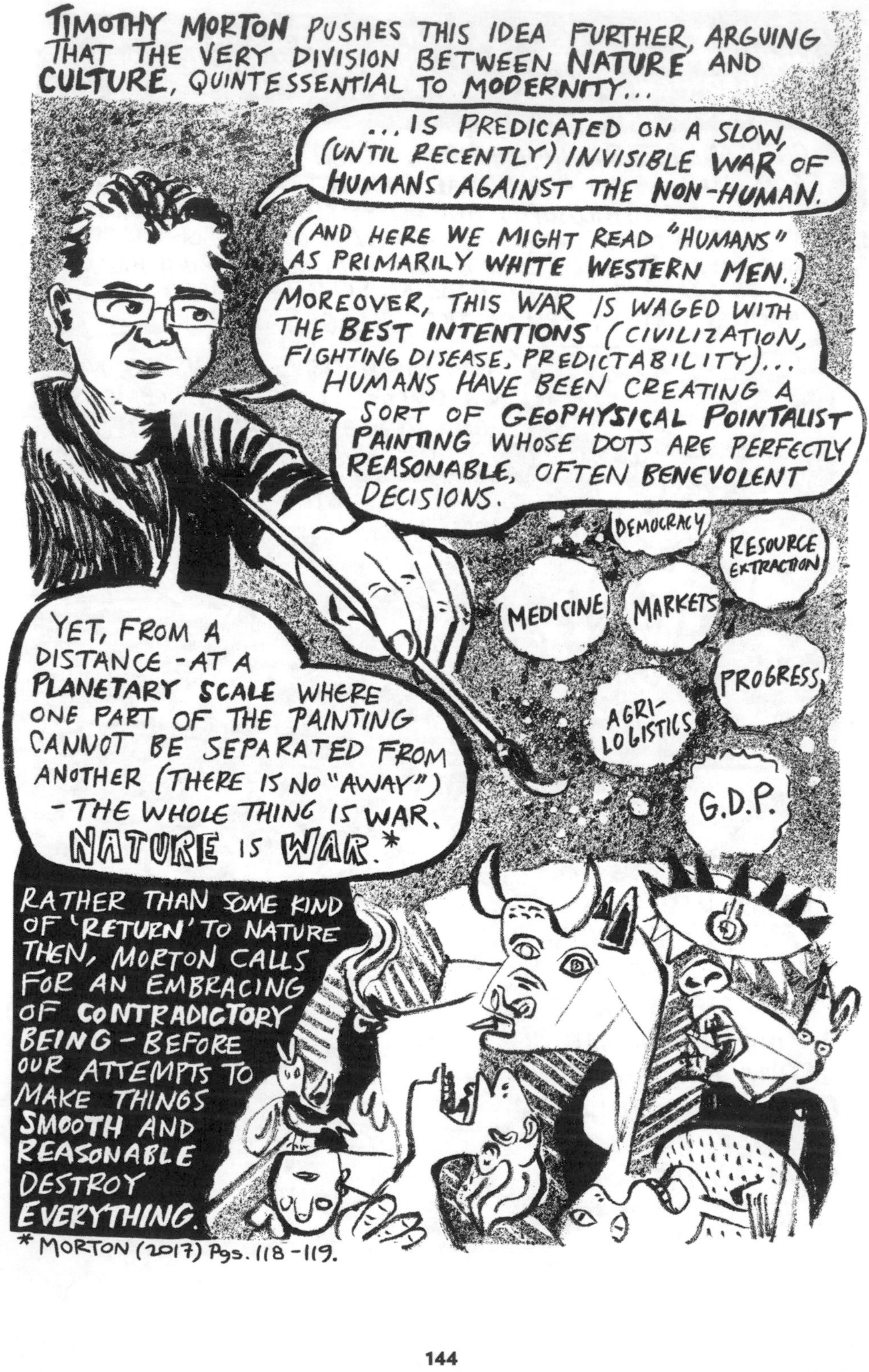
TIMOTHY MORTON PUSHES THIS IDEA FURTHER, ARGUING THAT THE VERY DIVISION BETWEEN NATURE AND CULTURE, QUINTESSENTIAL TO MODERNITY...
...IS PREDICATED ON A SLOW, (UNTIL RECENTLY) INVISIBLE WAR OF HUMANS AGAINST THE NON-HUMAN.
(AND HERE WE MIGHT READ "HUMANS" AS PRIMARILY WHITE WESTERN MEN.)
MOREOVER, THIS WAR IS WAGED WITH THE BEST INTENTIONS (CIVILIZATION, FIGHTING DISEASE, PREDICTABILITY)... HUMANS HAVE BEEN CREATING A SORT OF GEOPHYSICAL POINTALIST PAINTING WHOSE DOTS ARE PERFECTLY REASONABLE, OFTEN BENEVOLENT DECISIONS.
DEMOCRACY
RESOURCE EXTRACTION
MEDICINE
MARKETS
PROGRESS
AGRI-LOGISTICS
G.D.P.
YET, FROM A DISTANCE - AT A PLANETARY SCALE WHERE ONE PART OF THE PAINTING CANNOT BE SEPARATED FROM ANOTHER (THERE IS NO "AWAY") - THE WHOLE THING IS WAR. NATURE IS WAR.*
RATHER THAN SOME KIND OF 'RETURN' TO NATURE THEN, MORTON CALLS FOR AN EMBRACING OF CONTRADICTORY BEING - BEFORE OUR ATTEMPTS TO MAKE THINGS SMOOTH AND REASONABLE DESTROY EVERYTHING.
* MORTON (2017) Pgs. 118-119.

HOWEVER, AT A JUNCTURE THAT CALLS FOR **RADICAL CRITIQUE** OF **HUMAN EXCEPTIONALISM** AND THE **NATURE/CULTURE BINARY**, THE IDEA OF ANTHROPOCENE RISKS OBSCURING AND PERPETUATING OTHER IMPORTANT ISSUES.

FIRST, BY SMOOTHING OVER WHAT ARE ACTUALLY SPECIFIC **HISTORICAL MODES OF SOCIETAL ORGANIZATION**, SUCH AS **CAPITALISM**, THE TERM HELPS **NATURALIZE** ECONOMIC SYSTEMS THAT BENEFIT ONLY A **PORTION** OF HUMANITY, BUT BLAMES THE WHOLE SPECIES FOR ITS OUTCOMES. THIS HAS LED SOME TO SUGGEST A MORE APT TERM WOULD

BE THE **CAPITALOCENE*** THE AGE WHEN CAPITALISM MEETS ITS TERRESTRIAL LIMITS.

GLOBAL MARKETS

CLIMATE CHANGE

* SEE, FOR INSTANCE: JASON W. MOORE, "NAME THE SYSTEM! ANTHROPOCENES & THE CAPITALOGENE ALTERNATIVE" (2016) ONLINE.

HISTORIAN **DIPESH CHAKRABARTY** FURTHER COMPLICATES THIS ANALYSIS BY POINTING OUT THAT, EVEN THOUGH THE CURRENT CLIMATE CRISIS IS THE DIRECT RESULT OF **CAPITALIST** MODES **OF PRODUCTION** AND ENERGY USE, OUR UNDERSTANDING OF AND RESPONSE TO THE PROBLEM REQUIRES CONVERSATIONS BETWEEN **FIELDS OF KNOWLEDGE** THAT LIE BEYOND TRADITIONAL, HUMANIST **POLITICAL ECONOMY** AND **HISTORY**. IT REQUIRES ENGAGING WITH THE IDEA OF **SPECIES**

IT IS A WORD THAT WILL **NEVER** OCCUR IN ANY STANDARD HISTORY OR POLITICAL-ECONOMY ANALYSIS OF **GLOBALIZATION** [WHICH REFERS] ONLY TO THE RECENT AND RECORDED HISTORY OF HUMANS. **SPECIES THINKING**, ON THE OTHER HAND, IS CONNECTED TO THE ENTERPISE OF **DEEP HISTORY**.

PLIOCENE | 2 MIL. YbP PLEISTOCENE | 500 000 YbP | 50 000 YbP | HOLOCENE 10 000 YbP

HOMO HABILIS

HOMO ERECTUS

HOMO SAPIENS

THE **TASK** OF PLACING **HISTORICALLY** THE CRISIS OF CLIMATE CHANGE THUS REQUIRES US TO BRING TOGETHER INTELLECTUAL FORMATIONS THAT ARE SOMEWHAT IN **TENSION** WITH EACH OTHER: THE PLANETARY AND THE **GLOBAL**, DEEP AND RECORDED HISTORIES; **SPECIES THINKING** AND **CRITIQUES** OF **CAPITAL**.*

*CHAKRABARTY (2009) P. 213.

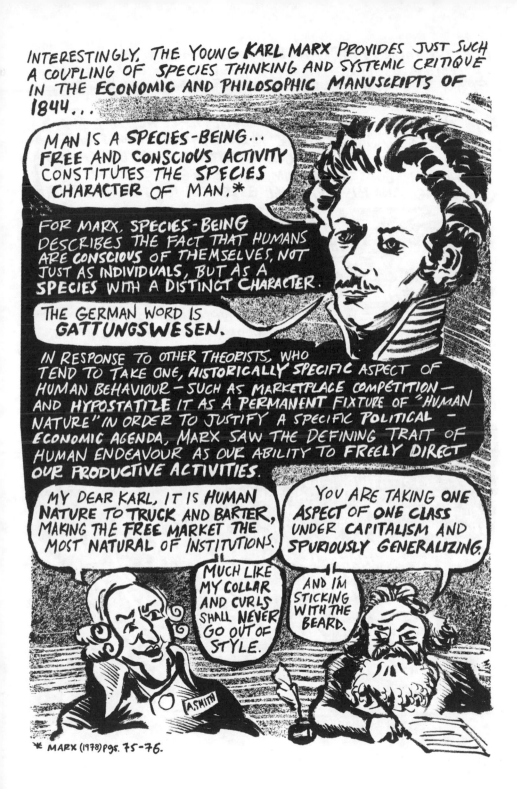

INTERESTINGLY, THE YOUNG **KARL MARX** PROVIDES JUST SUCH A COUPLING OF **SPECIES THINKING** AND **SYSTEMIC CRITIQUE** IN THE **ECONOMIC AND PHILOSOPHIC MANUSCRIPTS OF 1844**...

MAN IS A **SPECIES-BEING**... FREE AND **CONSCIOUS** ACTIVITY CONSTITUTES THE **SPECIES CHARACTER** OF MAN. ✱

FOR MARX, **SPECIES-BEING** DESCRIBES THE FACT THAT HUMANS ARE **CONSCIOUS** OF THEMSELVES, NOT JUST AS INDIVIDUALS, BUT AS A **SPECIES** WITH A **DISTINCT CHARACTER**.

THE GERMAN WORD IS **GATTUNGSWESEN**.

IN RESPONSE TO OTHER THEORISTS, WHO TEND TO TAKE ONE, **HISTORICALLY SPECIFIC** ASPECT OF HUMAN BEHAVIOUR — SUCH AS MARKETPLACE COMPETITION — AND **HYPOSTATIZE IT AS A PERMANENT FIXTURE** OF "HUMAN NATURE" IN ORDER TO JUSTIFY A SPECIFIC **POLITICAL - ECONOMIC AGENDA**, MARX SAW THE DEFINING TRAIT OF HUMAN ENDEAVOUR AS OUR ABILITY TO **FREELY DIRECT** OUR **PRODUCTIVE ACTIVITIES**.

MY DEAR KARL, IT IS **HUMAN NATURE** TO TRUCK AND BARTER, MAKING THE **FREE MARKET** THE MOST NATURAL OF INSTITUTIONS.

MUCH LIKE MY COLLAR AND CURLS SHALL **NEVER** GO OUT OF STYLE.

YOU ARE TAKING **ONE** ASPECT OF **ONE CLASS** UNDER CAPITALISM AND SPURIOUSLY GENERALIZING.

AND I'M STICKING WITH THE BEARD.

A. SMITH

✱ MARX (1978) PGS. 75-76.

FOR THE YOUNG MARX, A CENTRAL PROBLEM WITH CAPITALISM IS THAT IT ESTRANGES OR ALIENATES US FROM OUR SPECIES-BEING:

IN DEGRADING SPONTANEOUS ACTIVITY, FREE ACTIVITY, TO A MEANS, ESTRANGED LABOUR MAKES MAN'S SPECIES LIFE A A MEANS TO HIS PHYSICAL EXISTENCE... IT ESTRANGES MAN'S OWN BODY FROM HIM, AS IT DOES EXTERNAL NATURE AND HIS SPIRITUAL ESSENCE, HIS HUMAN BEING.

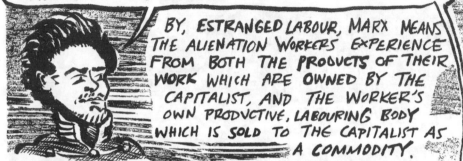

BY, ESTRANGED LABOUR, MARX MEANS THE ALIENATION WORKERS EXPERIENCE FROM BOTH THE PRODUCTS OF THEIR WORK WHICH ARE OWNED BY THE CAPITALIST, AND THE WORKER'S OWN PRODUCTIVE, LABOURING BODY WHICH IS SOLD TO THE CAPITALIST AS A COMMODITY.

THIS SITUATION TAKES THE LIBERATORY NATURE OF WORK, OUR HUMAN ABILITY TO DIRECT OUR PRODUCTIVE ACTIVITY, AND TURNS IT INTO A BEING **ALIEN** TO HIM.*

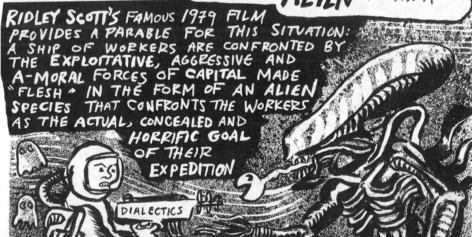

RIDLEY SCOTT'S FAMOUS 1979 FILM PROVIDES A PARABLE FOR THIS SITUATION: A SHIP OF WORKERS ARE CONFRONTED BY THE EXPLOITATIVE, AGGRESSIVE AND A-MORAL FORCES OF CAPITAL MADE "FLESH" IN THE FORM OF AN ALIEN SPECIES THAT CONFRONTS THE WORKERS AS THE ACTUAL, CONCEALED AND **HORRIFIC GOAL OF THEIR EXPEDITION**

DIALECTICS

* MARX (1978) Pg. 77.

CAPITALISM BLOCKS OUR ABILITY TO THINK AT THE LEVEL OF SPECIES. A CENTRAL PRINCIPLE OF ECONOMIC LIBERALISM IS THAT EACH INDIVIDUAL, ACTING IN HIS OR HER OWN SELF-INTEREST, WILL INADVERTANTLY CONTRIBUTE TO THE PROSPERITY OF THE WHOLE THROUGH WHAT ADAM SMITH CALLED THE INVISIBLE HAND of the Market

BUT THOUGH THE GLOBALIZED MARKET IS NOW THE PRIMARY STRUCTURE ORGANIZING HUMAN PRODUCTIVITY AT THE LEVEL OF SPECIES, IT HAS FAILED TO DISTRIBUTE ITS BENEFITS TO THE NEARLY EIGHT BILLION SOULS SHARING THE PLANET. WHAT IT HAS PRODUCED AND SHARED IS AN UNPRECEDENTED GLOBAL CLIMATE CRISIS, THOUGH EVEN THIS IS NOT SHARED EQUALLY.

EARTH OVERSHOOT DAY IS THE MOMENT IN A GIVEN YEAR WHEN A COUNTRY USES UP ITS NATURAL CAPITAL AND BEGINS ACCRUING DEBT AGAINST THE EARTH.

IN 2019, E.O.D. WAS IN MID-MARCH FOR CANADA AND THE U.S. AND AUGUST FOR MEXICO AND THAILAND. *

THE NUMBER OF VIRTUAL EARTHS IT WOULD TAKE FOR ALL OF EARTH'S HUMAN INHABITANTS TO ACHIEVE THE IDEALS OF "MODERNITY" ENJOYED IN THE WEST WOULD BE FROM TWO TO FIVE EXTRA PLANETS. MEANWHILE, THE ONE WE ACTUALLY HAVE IS NOT DOING VERY WELL... **

* "COUNTRY OVERSHOOT DAYS 2019."   ** LATOUR. (2008) Pg. 2.

149

AS MARX PREDICTED, AN ECONOMIC SYSTEM BASED ON THE PRIVATIZED, (SEEMINGLY) LIMITLESS PURSUIT OF WEALTH ESTRANGED US FROM OUR ABILITY TO THINK AND ACT AS A SPECIES CAPABLE OF FREELY DIRECTING OUR ACTIVITY.

IN TANDEM WITH AN ENERGY SOURCE THAT HAS ENABLED THE FANTASY OF LIMITLESS GROWTH ON A FINITE GLOBE, PETRO-CAPITALISM HAS INADVERTANTLY PRODUCED A CRISIS THAT NOW REQUIRES MODES OF COLLECTIVE COOPERATION WHICH EXCEED THE PURSUIT OF INDIVIDUAL SELF-INTEREST.

BUT AS THE PETROL-SOAKED FICTION OF A MODERNITY TO WHICH THE ENTIRE PLANET CAN ASPIRE DISSOLVES, PEOPLE TAKE REFUGE IN REACTIONARY FORMATIONS AND NOSTALGIA.

COMMON HORIZON

FEAR

NATIONALISM

SECURE BORDERS

RACISM PATRIARCHY

THOUGH MANY OF THESE FACTIONS WERE SUPPORTED AND EXPLOITED BY THE NOW THREATENED ENERGY REGIME OF PETROCULTURE, THEY CANNOT INSULATE US FROM OR NAVIGATE IN ISOLATION OUR CURRENT PREDICAMENT, WHICH REQUIRES THINKING AND ACTING AT THE LEVEL OF SPECIES AND BEYOND THE KINDS OF DISTRIBUTIVE NETWORKS GOVERNED BY MARKET THINKING.

THE TENSION BETWEEN A BLOCKED **SPECIES** BEING, DEFINED AS OUR ABILITY TO FREELY AND CONSCIOUSLY DIRECT OUR COLLECTIVE ACTIVITY AND THE LARGELY **UNCONSCIOUS** ORCHESTRATION OF **INDIVIDUAL WILLS** VIA "THE INVISIBLE HAND" OF GLOBAL MARKETS IS DEVELOPING INTO THE CENTRAL, COLLECTIVE **PATHOLOGY OF OUR AGE**, ONE WHOSE

SYMPTOMS ARE EVERYWHERE MOUNTING.

FOR INSTANCE...

THE RENEWED SPECTRE OF OLD BUGBEARS LIKE THE **NUCLEAR ARMS RACE** PROVIDE A STRANGELY COMFORTING **DISTRACTION** FROM THE ACTUAL AND UNPRECEDENTED APOCALYPTIC SITUATION WE FACE.

MAGA

HELLO DARKNESS MY OLD FRIEND...

LIKE ANY EFFECTIVE SYMPTOM, NUCLEAR RE-ARMAMENT TAKES A REAL ANXIETY — ABOUT GLOBAL HUMAN EXTINCTION — AND DISGUISES ITS CAUSE, PROVIDING AN **IMAGINARY** FORM OF **AGENCY** AND INDULGING A HIDDEN WISH **FULFILLMENT**.

THE CRISIS WE REFUSE TO ADDRESS (**GLOBAL WARMING**) IS SUBSTITUTED FOR ONE THAT HAS A FULLY HUMAN ARCHITECT, CREATING DESTABILIZING DRAMA THAT COVERS OVER OUR BLOCKED AGENCY.

THIS ALLOWS FOR THE WISH FULFILLMENT — THE PERPETUATION OF **PETROCULTURE** — WHILE SIMULTANEOUSLY RE-INFORCING THE VERY CAUSE OF THE **BLOCKAGE** (PURSUING BUSINESS AS USUAL) THAT **FEEDS** THE **SYMPTOM**.

ANOTHER END OF THE WORLD IS POSSIBLE

151

RENEWED NUCLEAR DRAMAS ARE JUST ONE OF THE COLLECTIVE ANXIETY DREAMS THAT PLAY OUT ON OUR TV SETS AND MEDIA FEEDS, ALLOWING US TO PROLONG THE SLEEP OF PETROL JUST A LITTLE LONGER.

INTENSIFYING NATIONALISM, DEEPENING BORDERS, POLARIZED IDENTITARIAN STRUGGLES, BATTLES OVER AUTHENTICITY, BELONGING, REPRESENTATION, MOUNTING HATE SPEECH AND SCAPEGOATING, THE RETRENCHMENT OF OLD DOGMATISMS, BINARIES, ESSENTIALISMS AND DIVISIONS, ALL PROVIDE FOREGROUND DISTRACTIONS FROM THE TRUE SCENE OF OUR DISQUIET.

SURELY OUR UNREST IS ANCHORED IN THE FACT THAT THE ENERGY SOURCE FUELLING MODERN FANTASIES OF SUBJECTIVITY, MOBILITY, PROGRESS, PRODUCTIVITY, FREEDOM, WORK, POLITICS, MASCULINITY, ECONOMICS AND PERSONHOOD HAS BEEN REVEALED AS UNSUSTAINABLE DUE TO A CRISIS THAT CALLS INTO QUESTION AN ENTIRE WAY OF LIFE. BUT DESPITE OUR GREAT ATTACHMENT TO THIS MODE OF BEING, PERHAPS A SUPPRESSED PART OF OURSELVES WANTS PETROCULTURE TO END.

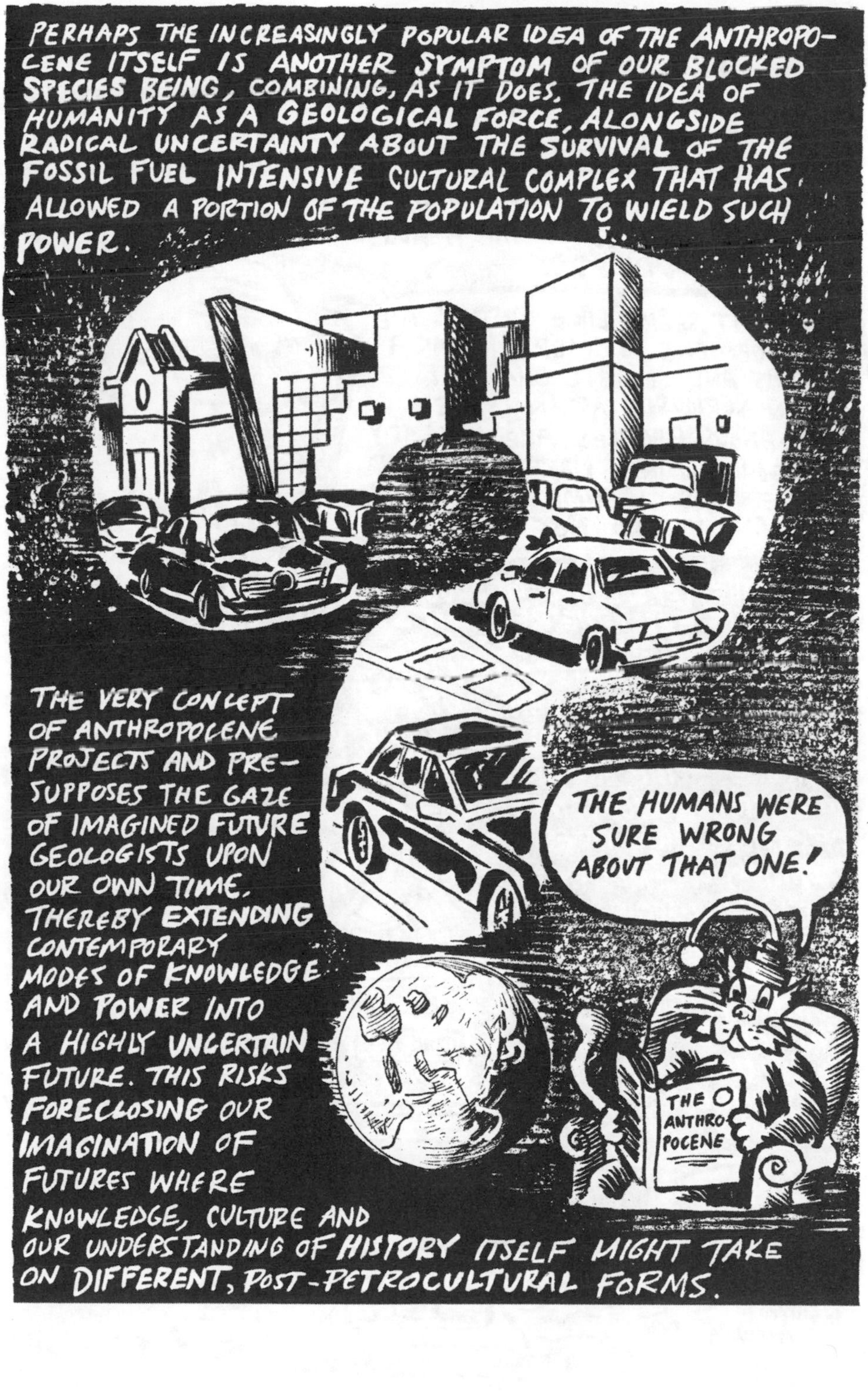
PERHAPS THE INCREASINGLY POPULAR IDEA OF THE ANTHROPOCENE ITSELF IS ANOTHER SYMPTOM OF OUR BLOCKED SPECIES BEING, COMBINING, AS IT DOES, THE IDEA OF HUMANITY AS A GEOLOGICAL FORCE, ALONGSIDE RADICAL UNCERTAINTY ABOUT THE SURVIVAL OF THE FOSSIL FUEL INTENSIVE CULTURAL COMPLEX THAT HAS ALLOWED A PORTION OF THE POPULATION TO WIELD SUCH POWER.
THE VERY CONCEPT OF ANTHROPOCENE PROJECTS AND PRESUPPOSES THE GAZE OF IMAGINED FUTURE GEOLOGISTS UPON OUR OWN TIME, THEREBY EXTENDING CONTEMPORARY MODES OF KNOWLEDGE AND POWER INTO A HIGHLY UNCERTAIN FUTURE. THIS RISKS FORECLOSING OUR IMAGINATION OF FUTURES WHERE KNOWLEDGE, CULTURE AND OUR UNDERSTANDING OF HISTORY ITSELF MIGHT TAKE ON DIFFERENT, POST-PETROCULTURAL FORMS.
THE HUMANS WERE SURE WRONG ABOUT THAT ONE!
THE ANTHROPOCENE

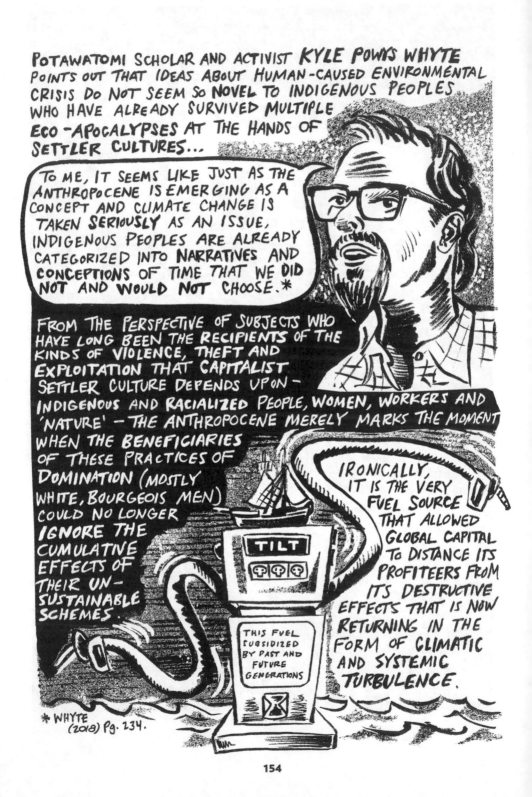

POTAWATOMI SCHOLAR AND ACTIVIST KYLE POWYS WHYTE POINTS OUT THAT IDEAS ABOUT HUMAN-CAUSED ENVIRONMENTAL CRISIS DO NOT SEEM SO NOVEL TO INDIGENOUS PEOPLES WHO HAVE ALREADY SURVIVED MULTIPLE ECO-APOCALYPSES AT THE HANDS OF SETTLER CULTURES...

TO ME, IT SEEMS LIKE JUST AS THE ANTHROPOCENE IS EMERGING AS A CONCEPT AND CLIMATE CHANGE IS TAKEN SERIOUSLY AS AN ISSUE, INDIGENOUS PEOPLES ARE ALREADY CATEGORIZED INTO NARRATIVES AND CONCEPTIONS OF TIME THAT WE DID NOT AND WOULD NOT CHOOSE.*

FROM THE PERSPECTIVE OF SUBJECTS WHO HAVE LONG BEEN THE RECIPIENTS OF THE KINDS OF VIOLENCE, THEFT AND EXPLOITATION THAT CAPITALIST SETTLER CULTURE DEPENDS UPON— INDIGENOUS AND RACIALIZED PEOPLE, WOMEN, WORKERS AND 'NATURE'— THE ANTHROPOCENE MERELY MARKS THE MOMENT WHEN THE BENEFICIARIES OF THESE PRACTICES OF DOMINATION (MOSTLY WHITE, BOURGEOIS MEN) COULD NO LONGER IGNORE THE CUMULATIVE EFFECTS OF THEIR UN-SUSTAINABLE SCHEMES.

IRONICALLY, IT IS THE VERY FUEL SOURCE THAT ALLOWED GLOBAL CAPITAL TO DISTANCE ITS PROFITEERS FROM ITS DESTRUCTIVE EFFECTS THAT IS NOW RETURNING IN THE FORM OF CLIMATIC AND SYSTEMIC TURBULENCE.

TILT

THIS FUEL SUBSIDIZED BY PAST AND FUTURE GENERATIONS

* WHYTE (2018) Pg. 234.

154

BY COVERING OVER THE TENSIONS BETWEEN A SPURIOUS UNIVERSALISM ("HUMANITY") AND MORE PARTICULAR HISTORICAL AND CLASS INTERESTS, THE ANTHROPOCENE AS A CONCEPT REVEALS A COLLECTIVE YEARNING FOR SOMETHING LIKE **SPECIES BEING.**

CAUGHT IN THE MAGNETIC FEILD OF PETROCULTURE, HOWEVER, "ANTHROPO-CENE" HELPS COVER OVER THE CONTRADICTIONS OF...

PETROTEMPORALITY

FUTURE EARTHS

DEEP PAST

WHICH BURNS UP BOTH PAST AND FUTURE RESOURCES AND LIVES IN THE REPRODUCTION OF A **RESTLESS NOW...**

450

DDN:2000

.. ONE THAT DESPERATELY TRIES TO ESCAPE ITS OWN SUFFOCATING CONDITIONS OF POSSIBILITY.

THOUGH PETROCULTURE AND ITS UNIQUE TEMPORALITIES ARE SCARCELY 150 YEARS OLD, IT IS ENTANGLED WITH LONGER HISTORIES OF EXTRACTIVISM AND EXCAVATION.

THE BEGINNING OF THE MODERN OIL INDUSTRY IS USUALLY CREDITED TO EDWIN L. DRAKE'S 1859 WELL IN TITUSVILLE, PENNSYLVANIA, BUT THE FIRST NORTH AMERICAN OIL WELL WAS ACTUALLY DRILLED IN OIL SPRINGS, ONTARIO IN 1858 BY JAMES MILLER WILLIAMS OF HAMILTON, ONTARIO. *

1858   150th ANNIVERSARY   2008
BIRTH OF THE OIL INDUSTRY OIL SPRINGS

EVEN AS PROSPECTORS LIKE WILLIAMS WERE DIGGING FOSSIL FUEL OUT OF THE EARTH ARCHEOLOGISTS WERE DIGGING UP FOSSILS THAT WOULD RADICALLY CHANGE HOW MODERN SCIENCE UNDERSTANDS OUR PLACE IN THE LONG HISTORY OF LIFE ON THE PLANET.

THE WORLD WAS CREATED BY OUR LORD ON SUNDAY, OCT. 23 RD 4004 BEFORE CHRIST.

AND EVEN AS THE VAST DIMENSIONS OF DEEP TIME WERE BEING UNCOVERED...

THE WORLD HAS BEEN SWARMING WITH LIVING CREATURES FOR VAST YET STILL QUITE UNKNOWN PERIODS OF TIME.

HOLY BIBLE

...VAST DEPOSITS OF FOSSILIZED CARBON WERE BEING UNEARTHED TO FUEL THE TRANSFORMATION OF VICTORIAN SOCIETY.

* CANADIAN PETROLEUM HALL OF FAME (2019).

"IN ENDLESS SPACE, COUNTLESS LUMINOUS SPHERES ROUND EACH OF WHICH SOME DOZEN SMALLER ILLUMINATED ONES REVOLVE...

...HOT AT THE CORE AND COVERED OVER WITH A HARD, COLD CRUST, ON THIS CRUST A MOULDY FILM HAS PRODUCED LIVING AND KNOWING BEINGS...

...YET FOR A BEING WHO THINKS, IT IS A PRECARIOUS POSITION TO STAND ON ONE OF THOSE NUMBERLESS SPHERES...

...FREELY FLOATING IN BOUNDLESS SPACE WITHOUT KNOWING WHENCE OR WHITHER...

...AND ONLY TO BE ONE OF INNUMERABLE SIMILAR BEINGS THAT THRONG, PRESS AND TOIL, RESTLESSLY AND RAPIDLY ARISING AND PASSING AWAY IN BEGINNINGLESS AND ENDLESS TIME." *

*ARTHUR SCHOPENHAUER (1958) Pg. 3

157

AT THE SAME TIME AS EUROPEAN CULTURE WAS CONFRONTING THE DIZZYING DIMENSIONS OF THE EXTERNAL UNIVERSE, REVOLUTIONARY THINKERS WERE AWAKENING TO THE VAST, DARK REGIONS OF THE HUMAN PSYCHE AND HISTORY.

IN MENTAL LIFE NOTHING WHICH HAS ONCE BEEN FORMED CAN PERISH... NOTHING THAT HAS COME INTO EXISTENCE WILL HAVE PASSED AWAY AND ALL THE EARLIER PHASES OF DEVELOPMENT CONTINUE TO EXIST ALONGSIDE THE LATEST ONE.*

WHILE FREUD AND OTHERS LOOKED WITHIN, THINKERS LIKE MARX AND ENGELS WERE DECIPHERING THE HIDDEN DIMENSIONS OF SYSTEMIC EXPLOITATION AND OPPRESSION.

MODERN BOURGEOIS SOCIETY WITH ITS RELATIONS OF PRODUCTION OF EXCHANGE AND OF PROPERTY, A SOCIETY THAT HAS CONJURED UP SUCH GIGANTIC MEANS OF PRODUCTION AND OF EXCHANGE, IS LIKE THE SORCERER WHO IS NO LONGER ABLE TO CONTROL THE POWERS OF THE NETHER WORLD WHOM HE HAS CALLED UP BY HIS SPELLS.**

* FREUD (1961) Pgs. 16-18.
** MARX AND ENGELS (1978) Pg. 478.

158

AT THE SAME TIME AS MODERN WESTERN CULTURE WAS WAKING UP TO BOTH THE VAST SWEEP OF GEOLOGIC TIME AND THE HISTORICAL REALITIES OF INEQUALITY, EXPLOITATION AND TRAUMA, THE USE OF FOSSIL FUELS WAS CREATING THE CONDITIONS THAT NOW PLACE FUTURE HUMAN TENANCY ON THE GLOBE IN QUESTION.

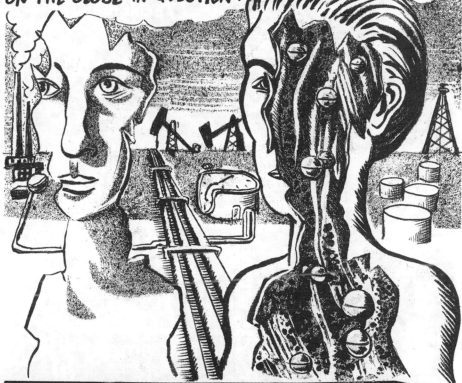

AND IT IS THIS SAME FUEL SOURCE, WITH ITS UNIQUE CHARACTERISTICS OF PORTABILITY AND EXTREMELY HIGH EROEI,* THAT HAS ALLOWED A SOCIO-ECONOMIC SYSTEM BASED NOT ON EQUALITY OR SHARING, BUT RATHER ON THE PRIVATIZED APPROPRIATION OF COLLECTIVELY GENERATED WEALTH, TO MANAGE, DISPLACE AND DEFER THE DEMANDS FOR JUSTICE AND EQUITY THAT HAVE BEEN STEADILY MOUNTING FOR THE PAST SEVERAL CENTURIES.

*ENERGY RETURNED ON ENERGY INVESTED

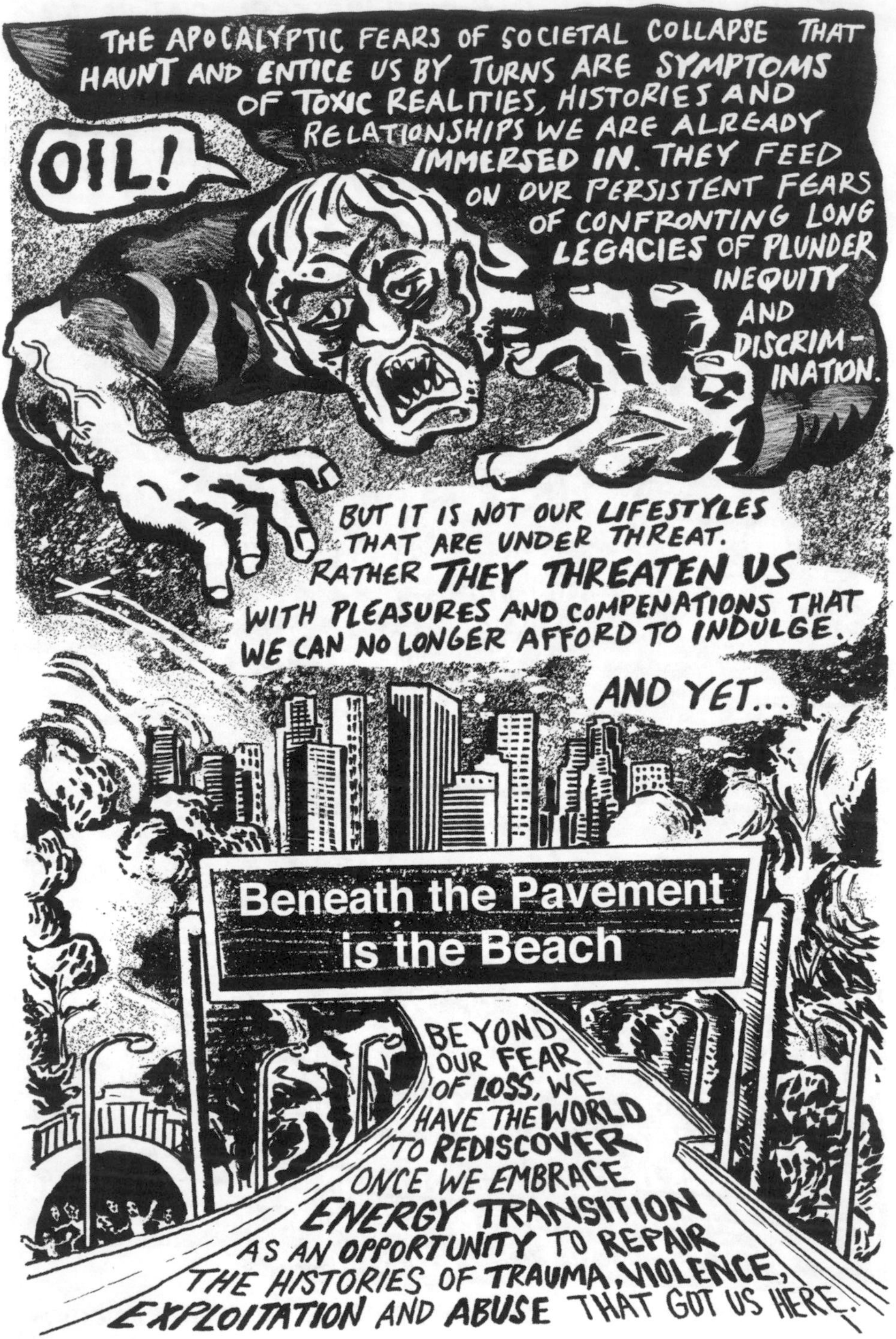
THE APOCALYPTIC FEARS OF SOCIETAL COLLAPSE THAT HAUNT AND ENTICE US BY TURNS ARE SYMPTOMS OF TOXIC REALITIES, HISTORIES AND RELATIONSHIPS WE ARE ALREADY IMMERSED IN. THEY FEED ON OUR PERSISTENT FEARS OF CONFRONTING LONG LEGACIES OF PLUNDER INEQUITY AND DISCRIM-INATION.
OIL!
BUT IT IS NOT OUR LIFESTYLES THAT ARE UNDER THREAT. RATHER THEY THREATEN US WITH PLEASURES AND COMPENATIONS THAT WE CAN NO LONGER AFFORD TO INDULGE.
AND YET...
Beneath the Pavement is the Beach
BEYOND OUR FEAR OF LOSS, WE HAVE THE WORLD TO REDISCOVER ONCE WE EMBRACE ENERGY TRANSITION AS AN OPPORTUNITY TO REPAIR THE HISTORIES OF TRAUMA, VIOLENCE, EXPLOITATION AND ABUSE THAT GOT US HERE.

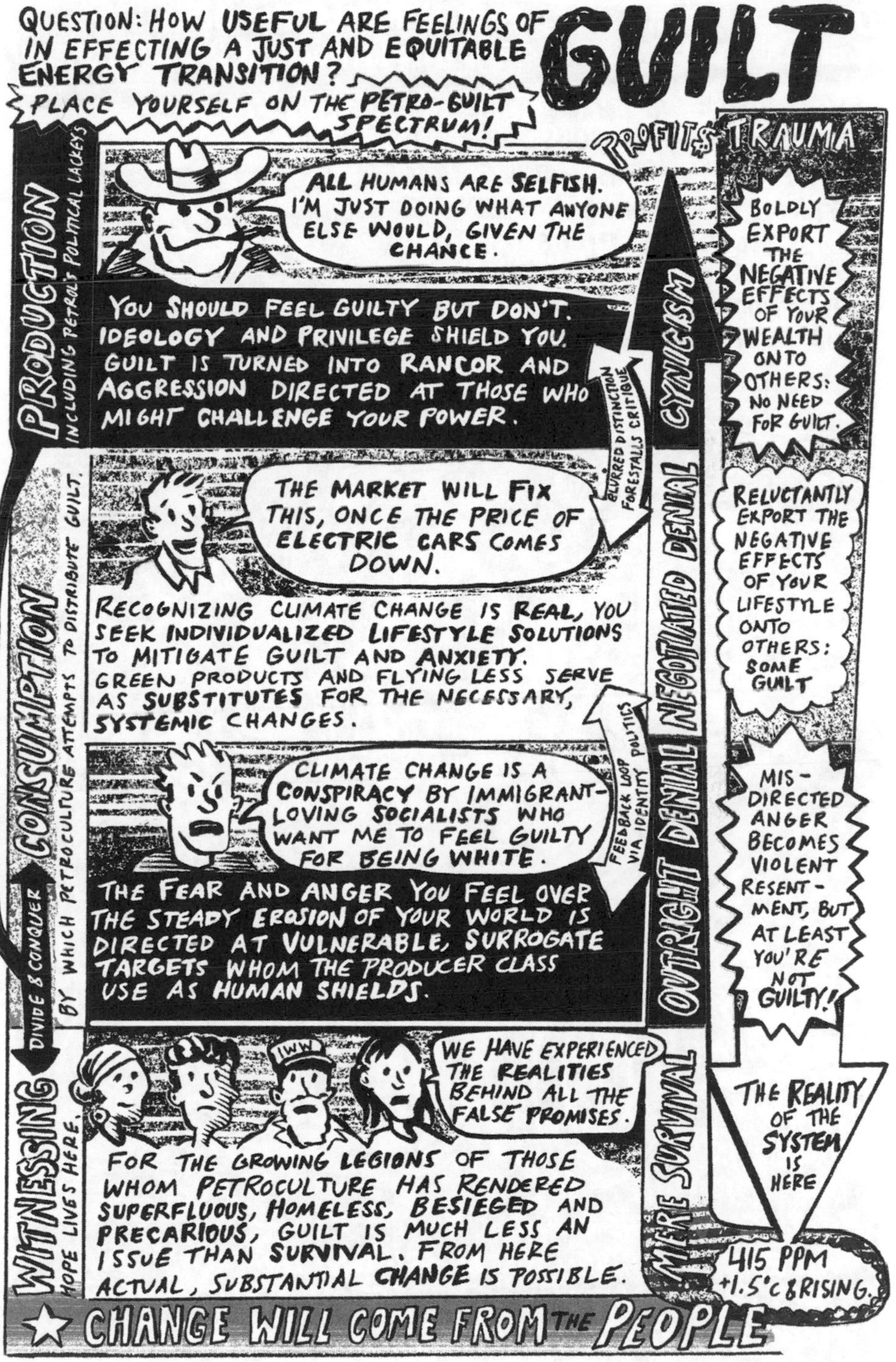
QUESTION: HOW USEFUL ARE FEELINGS OF GUILT IN EFFECTING A JUST AND EQUITABLE ENERGY TRANSITION?
PLACE YOURSELF ON THE PETRO-GUILT SPECTRUM!
PROFITS
TRAUMA
PRODUCTION
INCLUDING PETROL'S POLITICAL LACKEYS
ALL HUMANS ARE SELFISH. I'M JUST DOING WHAT ANYONE ELSE WOULD, GIVEN THE CHANCE.
YOU SHOULD FEEL GUILTY BUT DON'T. IDEOLOGY AND PRIVILEGE SHIELD YOU. GUILT IS TURNED INTO RANCOR AND AGGRESSION DIRECTED AT THOSE WHO MIGHT CHALLENGE YOUR POWER.
CYNICISM
BLURRED DISTINCTION FORESTALLS CRITIQUE
BOLDLY EXPORT THE NEGATIVE EFFECTS OF YOUR WEALTH ONTO OTHERS: NO NEED FOR GUILT.
CONSUMPTION
BY WHICH PETROCULTURE ATTEMPTS TO DISTRIBUTE GUILT.
THE MARKET WILL FIX THIS, ONCE THE PRICE OF ELECTRIC CARS COMES DOWN.
RECOGNIZING CLIMATE CHANGE IS REAL, YOU SEEK INDIVIDUALIZED LIFESTYLE SOLUTIONS TO MITIGATE GUILT AND ANXIETY. GREEN PRODUCTS AND FLYING LESS SERVE AS SUBSTITUTES FOR THE NECESSARY, SYSTEMIC CHANGES.
NEGOTIATED DENIAL
RELUCTANTLY EXPORT THE NEGATIVE EFFECTS OF YOUR LIFESTYLE ONTO OTHERS: SOME GUILT
FEEDBACK LOOP VIA IDENTITY POLITICS
CLIMATE CHANGE IS A CONSPIRACY BY IMMIGRANT-LOVING SOCIALISTS WHO WANT ME TO FEEL GUILTY FOR BEING WHITE.
THE FEAR AND ANGER YOU FEEL OVER THE STEADY EROSION OF YOUR WORLD IS DIRECTED AT VULNERABLE, SURROGATE TARGETS WHOM THE PRODUCER CLASS USE AS HUMAN SHIELDS.
OUTRIGHT DENIAL
MIS-DIRECTED ANGER BECOMES VIOLENT RESENT-MENT, BUT AT LEAST YOU'RE NOT GUILTY!
DIVIDE & CONQUER
WITNESSING
HOPE LIVES HERE.
IWW
WE HAVE EXPERIENCED THE REALITIES BEHIND ALL THE FALSE PROMISES.
FOR THE GROWING LEGIONS OF THOSE WHOM PETROCULTURE HAS RENDERED SUPERFLUOUS, HOMELESS, BESIEGED AND PRECARIOUS, GUILT IS MUCH LESS AN ISSUE THAN SURVIVAL. FROM HERE ACTUAL, SUBSTANTIAL CHANGE IS POSSIBLE.
MERE SURVIVAL
THE REALITY OF THE SYSTEM IS HERE
415 PPM +1.5°C & RISING.
★ CHANGE WILL COME FROM THE PEOPLE

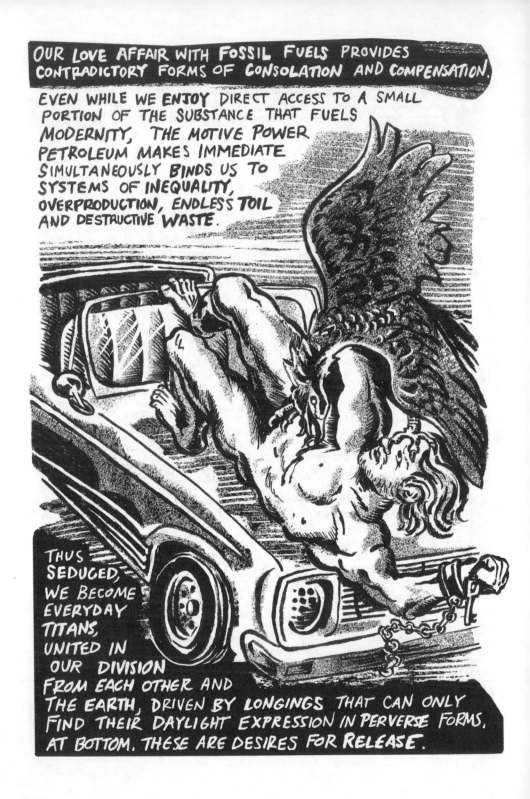

OUR LOVE AFFAIR WITH FOSSIL FUELS PROVIDES CONTRADICTORY FORMS OF CONSOLATION AND COMPENSATION.

EVEN WHILE WE ENJOY DIRECT ACCESS TO A SMALL PORTION OF THE SUBSTANCE THAT FUELS MODERNITY, THE MOTIVE POWER PETROLEUM MAKES IMMEDIATE SIMULTANEOUSLY BINDS US TO SYSTEMS OF INEQUALITY, OVERPRODUCTION, ENDLESS TOIL AND DESTRUCTIVE WASTE.

THUS SEDUCED, WE BECOME EVERYDAY TITANS, UNITED IN OUR DIVISION FROM EACH OTHER AND THE EARTH, DRIVEN BY LONGINGS THAT CAN ONLY FIND THEIR DAYLIGHT EXPRESSION IN PERVERSE FORMS. AT BOTTOM, THESE ARE DESIRES FOR RELEASE.

162

KYLE P. WHYTE ASKS US TO CONSIDER THE PERNICIOUS ANCESTRAL FANTASIES THAT OFTEN INFORM EVEN THE WELL-INTENTIONED ALLYSHIP OF SOME LEFTIST ACTIVISM, ONE SUCH FANTASY POSITS INDIGENOUS CULTURES AS ANTIQUATED HOLDOVERS IN NEED OF SAVING, OR HOLOCENE SURVIVORS.

LET'S ACKNOWLEDGE THAT INDIGENOUS PEOPLE HAVE BEEN THE CARETAKERS OF THE LAND FOR THOUSANDS OF YEARS, AND THEY NOW HAVE A GREAT GIFT TO SHARE WITH US IN THIS ERA OF GLOBAL CLIMATE CHANGE.

"NO MONEY IN THE WORLD IS WORTH DESTROYING OUR LAND AND OUR WATER"
SHELLY A. YOUNG

PURSUED UNREFLECTIVELY, THE DISCOURSE OF CLIMATE EMERGENCY RISKS PERPETUATING THE VERY SAME SETTLER-COLONIAL POWER AND RELATIONSHIPS THAT HAVED HELPED PRODUCE THE CRISIS.

PERHAPS IT IS ALL PART OF ALLIES' ANCESTRAL FANTASIES THAT THEIR DESCENDANTS WOULD HAVE THE PRIVILEGE OF UNLIMITED INDIVIDUAL AND COLLECTIVE AGENCY TO EXPLOIT INDIGENOUS PEOPLE AND THE PRIVILEGE OF CLAIMING MORAL HIGH GROUND AS SAVIORS.*

HELP US SURVIVE THE WINTER AND WE WILL SHARE THIS LAND AS EQUALS.

HELP US OUT OF THIS CLIMATE MESS AND WE WILL SAVE YOU FROM EXTINCTION.

* WHYTE, (2018) P. 238.

163

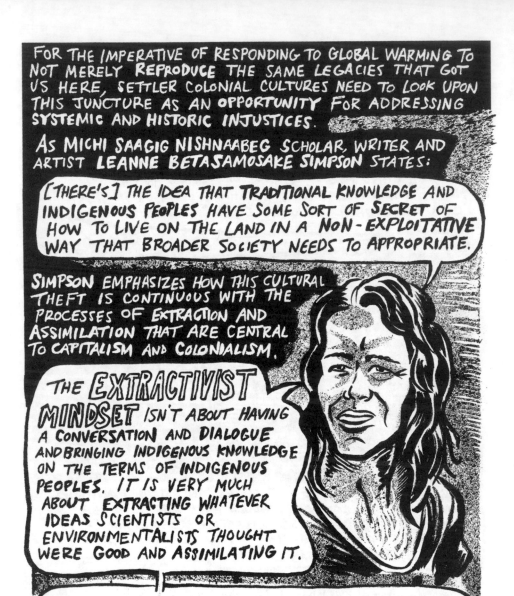

FOR THE IMPERATIVE OF RESPONDING TO GLOBAL WARMING TO NOT MERELY **REPRODUCE** THE SAME LEGACIES THAT GOT US HERE, SETTLER COLONIAL CULTURES NEED TO LOOK UPON THIS JUNCTURE AS AN **OPPORTUNITY** FOR ADDRESSING SYSTEMIC AND HISTORIC INJUSTICES.

AS MICHI SAAGIG **NISHNAABEG** SCHOLAR, WRITER AND ARTIST **LEANNE BETASAMOSAKE SIMPSON** STATES:

[THERE'S] THE IDEA THAT **TRADITIONAL KNOWLEDGE AND INDIGENOUS PEOPLES** HAVE SOME SORT OF **SECRET** OF HOW TO LIVE ON THE LAND IN A **NON-EXPLOITATIVE** WAY THAT BROADER SOCIETY NEEDS TO APPROPRIATE.

SIMPSON EMPHASIZES HOW THIS CULTURAL THEFT IS CONTINUOUS WITH THE PROCESSES OF **EXTRACTION AND ASSIMILATION** THAT ARE CENTRAL TO **CAPITALISM** AND **COLONIALISM.**

THE **EXTRACTIVIST MINDSET** ISN'T ABOUT HAVING A **CONVERSATION** AND **DIALOGUE** AND BRINGING INDIGENOUS KNOWLEDGE ON THE **TERMS OF INDIGENOUS PEOPLES.** IT IS VERY MUCH ABOUT **EXTRACTING WHATEVER IDEAS** SCIENTISTS OR ENVIRONMENTALISTS THOUGHT WERE GOOD AND ASSIMILATING IT.

THE ALTERNATIVE IS DEEP RECIPROCITY. IT'S RESPECT, IT'S A **RELATIONSHIP,** AND IT'S LOCAL. IF YOU'RE FORCED TO STAY IN YOUR **50-MILE RADIUS,** THEN YOU VERY MUCH ARE GOING TO **EXPERIENCE** THE IMPACTS OF YOUR **EXTRACTIVIST BEHAVIOUR.** *

* NAOMI KLEIN, "DANCING THE WORLD INTO BEING: A CONVERSATION WITH IDLE NO MORE'S LEANNE SIMPSON." YESMAGAZINE.ORG. MARCH, 2013.

SINCE A DEFINING TENDENCY OF EXTRACTIVIST, CAPITALIST CULTURE IS TO TURN IMMEDIATE RELATIONSHIPS INTO ABSTRACT THINGS WHICH CAN BE EXCHANGED ON THE MARKET, IT IS NO SURPRISE THAT SETTLER SOCIETY SHOULD MISPERCEIVE INDIGENOUS KNOWLEDGE AND CULTURE AS A SET OF DISCRETE IDEAS THAT CAN BE COMMODITIZED AND SOLD.

PETROCULTURE EXACERBATES THESE TENDENCIES, AND ALSO SEDUCES SOME ENVIRONMENTALISTS INTO VIEWING INDIGENOUS CULTURE AS JUST ANOTHER SET OF TOOLS AT THE DISPOSAL OF A SETTLER CULTURE IN CRISIS.

BUT AS LEANNE SIMPSON POINTS OUT, THE STRENGTH AND WISDOM OF INDIGENOUS WAYS OF KNOWING RESIDES FOREMOST IN RELATIONALITY

IF I LOOK AT HOW MY ANCESTORS LIVED EVEN 200 YEARS AGO, THEY DIDN'T SPEND A LOT OF TIME BANKING CAPITAL, THEY DIDN'T RELY ON MATERIAL WEALTH FOR THEIR WELL-BEING AND ECONOMIC STABILITY

THEY PUT THEIR ENERGY INTO MEANINGFUL AND AUTHENTIC RELATIONSHIPS. SO THEIR FOOD SECURITY AND THEIR ECONOMIC SECURITY WAS BASED ON HOW GOOD AND RESILIENT THEIR RELATIONSHIPS WERE... NOT THE MONEY THEY SAVED IN THE BANK... IT WAS THE QUALITY OF THESE RELATIONSHIPS – NOT HOW MUCH THEY HAD OR CONSUMED – THAT WAS THE BASIS OF THEIR HAPPINESS.*

*KLEIN, 2013.

165

KYLE P. WHYTE MAKES A SIMILAR POINT IN HIS ARTICULATION OF ANISHINAABE UNDERSTANDINGS OF TIME WHICH WERE INFORMED BY SEASONAL MIGRATION PRACTICES.

SEASONAL CHANGE IS ALWAYS ASSOCIATED WITH A SOCIAL ACTIVITY, THE COORDINATION OF WHICH ENSURES THAT AS A SOCIETY WE ARE ABLE TO HAVE THE BEST STEWARDSHIP RELATIONSHIPS TO THE ENVIRONMENT.

WHAT'S INTERESTING ABOUT ANISHINAABE THOUGHT IS THAT THE WAY YOU COORDINATE TIME IS BY ENSURING THAT YOU HAVE MORAL RELATIONSHIPS IN YOUR SOCIETY AT A CULTURAL LEVEL THAT WILL SUPPORT THE BEST POSSIBLE COORDINATION.

AND THESE MORAL RELATIONSHIPS ARE ACTUALLY NOT RIGHTS OR CONTRACTS, BUT ARE BASED ON CONSENT, TRUST, RECIPROCITY AND ACCOUNTABILITY. SO FOR US, ONE EXPERIENCES TIME NOT AS A CALENDAR OR AS AN HOUR OR TWO OR THREE. *

RIGHT ON!

* BOYER, DOMINIC AND CYMENE HOWE, CULTURES OF ENERGY PODCAST, #166 FEB. 28, 2019

SUCH EXPERIENCES OF TIME ARE GROUNDED IN *INTIMATE RELATIONSHIPS* BETWEEN HUMAN *SOCIETIES* AND THE *RENEWABLE ENERGIES* OF THE *PLANET* AND *COSMOS.*

PETROCULTURE'S RELATIONSHIPS TO TIME ARE ALSO GROUNDED IN PRODUCTIVITY BUT ARE IMPOSED AND ABSTRACTED FROM IMMEDIATE RELATIONS TO THE EARTH. THEY ARE THE PRODUCT OF *EXPLOITATIVE* SOCIAL RELATIONSHIPS IN SERVICE OF PRODUCING EVER-EXPANDING, *PRIVATIZED PROFITS.*

ENDLESS EXPANSION ON A FINITE GLOBE IS A FICTION PETROCULTURE HAS ALLOWED MODERNITY TO INDULGE.

AND THOUGH IT HAS BROUGHT THE ENVIRONMENTS AND RELATIONSHIPS THAT SUSTAIN HUMAN (AND ALL) LIFE TO THE POINT OF COLLAPSE, PETROCULTURE CONTINUES TO TELL US STORIES THAT KEEP A DARK, VISCOUS SUBSTANCE AT THE CENTRE OF OUR TROUBLED WORLD AND DREAMS.

Chapter 6
Scenarios

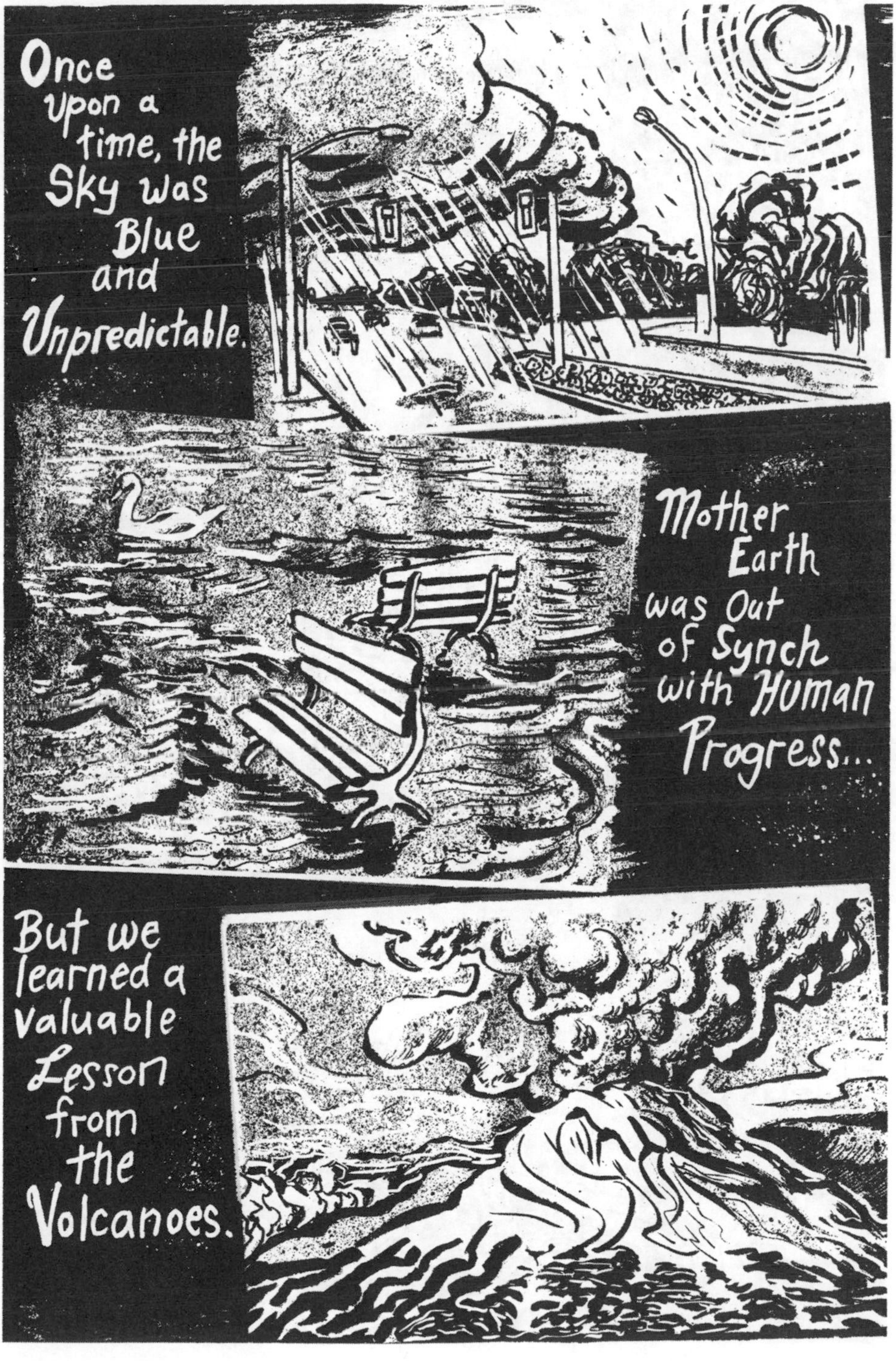
Once upon a time, the Sky was Blue and Unpredictable.
Mother Earth was Out of Synch with Human Progress...
But we learned a valuable Lesson from the Volcanoes.

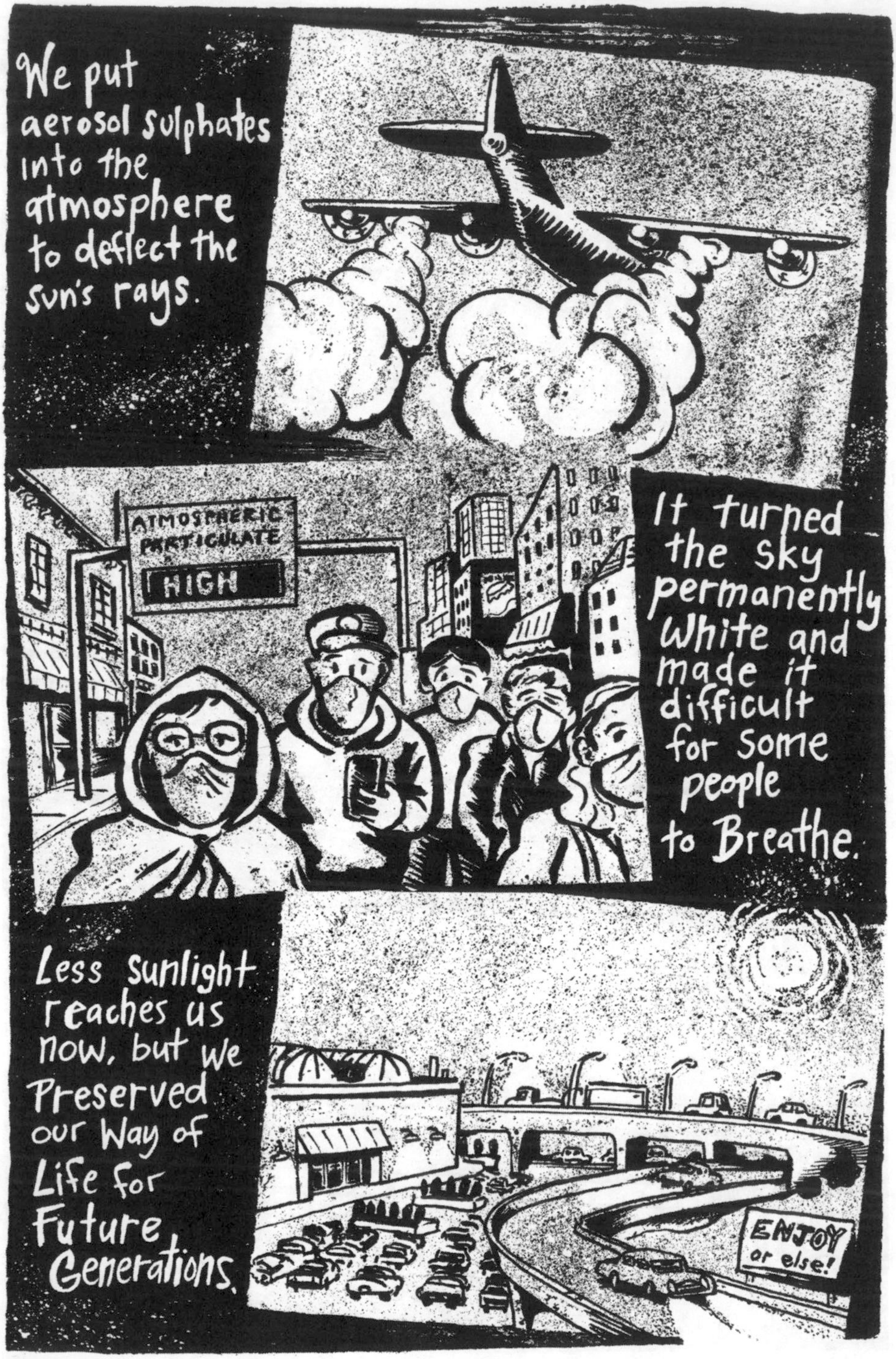
We put aerosol sulphates into the atmosphere to deflect the sun's rays.
ATMOSPHERIC PARTICULATE
HIGH
It turned the sky permanently White and made it difficult for some people to Breathe.
Less sunlight reaches us now, but we Preserved our Way of Life for Future Generations.
ENJOY or else!

But the Free World still must struggle with those who don't share our values...

DRONE STRIKES AGAINST THE TERRORIST GROUP WARRIORS OF KALI INTENSIFIED TODAY IN RESPONSE TO LAST WEEK'S SHOOTING DOWN OF A GLOBAL ALLIANCE SALTING PLANE OVER THE INDIA-PAKISTAN BORDER.

POPULIST SUPPORT FOR FUND-AMENTALIST GROUPS IS GROWING IN SOUTH ASIA, WHERE SKY SALTING HAS DISRUPTED PACIFIC WEATHER PATTERNS AND CAUSED HAVOCK TO LOCAL ECOSYSTEMS. SOME WESTERN ACTIVISTS LAY BLAME ON ALLIANCE POLICIES, CLAIMING THEY REINFORCE LEGACIES OF COLONIAL VIOLENCE.

MAKE LOVE NOT CO2

CHANGE THE SYSTEM NOT THE CLIMATE

ONE PLANET ONE HUMANITY

WE HAVE SUFFERED THE COST OF IGNORING CLIMATE SCIENCE IN THE PAST, WE CANNOT AFFORD TO MAKE THIS MISTAKE AGAIN.

BUT PRESIDENT BAKER HAS DEFENDED THE U.S.-LED DRONE ATTACKS, CLAIMING THAT ONGOING EFFORTS AT PEACEKEEPING ARE NEEDED TO AVOID THE RUNAWAY WARMING THAT WOULD RESULT FROM INTERRUPTIONS TO THE AEROSOL SULPHATE SKY-SALTING PROGRAM.

173

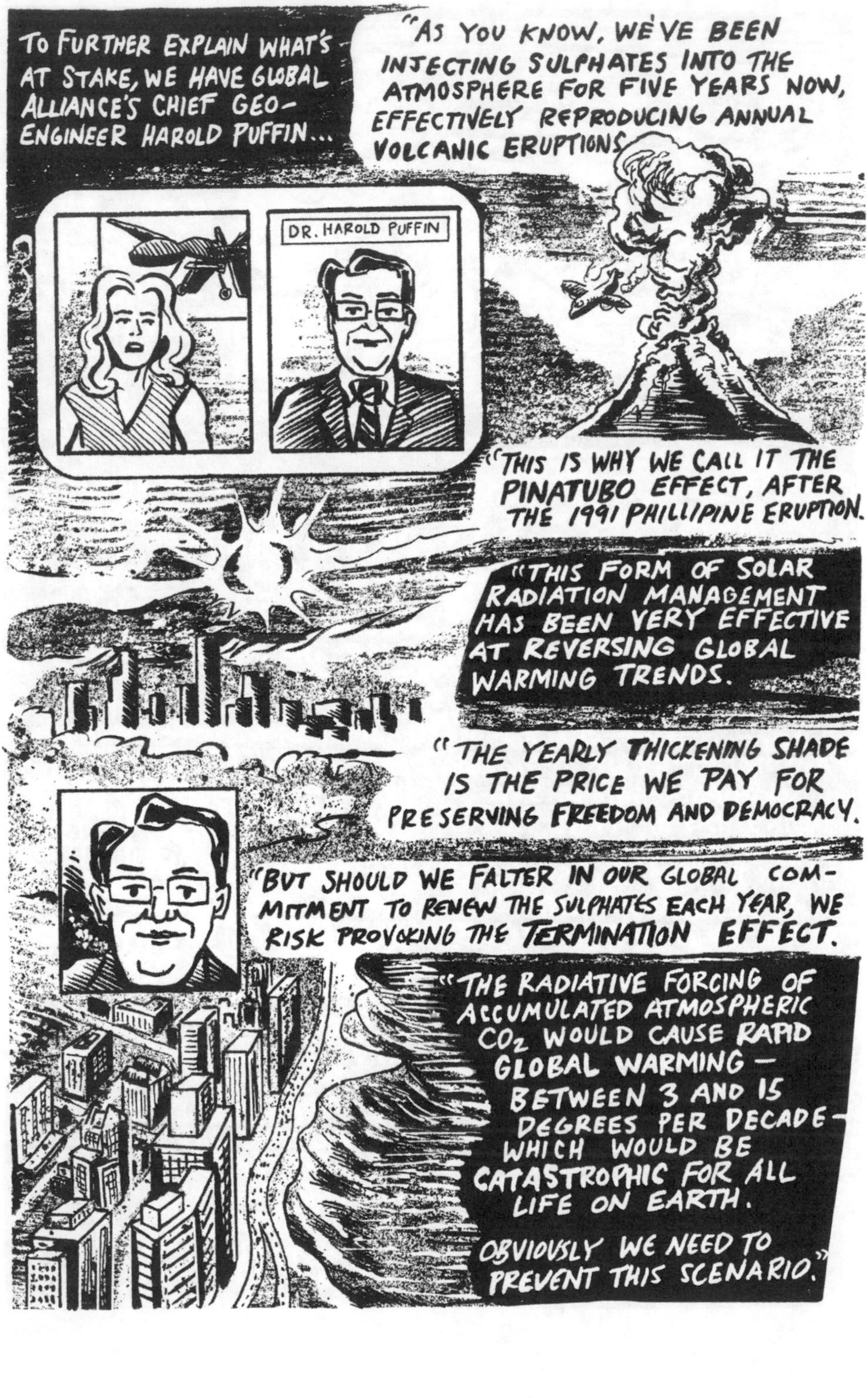

TO FURTHER EXPLAIN WHAT'S AT STAKE, WE HAVE GLOBAL ALLIANCE'S CHIEF GEO-ENGINEER HAROLD PUFFIN...
"AS YOU KNOW, WE'VE BEEN INJECTING SULPHATES INTO THE ATMOSPHERE FOR FIVE YEARS NOW, EFFECTIVELY REPRODUCING ANNUAL VOLCANIC ERUPTIONS.
DR. HAROLD PUFFIN
"THIS IS WHY WE CALL IT THE PINATUBO EFFECT, AFTER THE 1991 PHILLIPINE ERUPTION.
"THIS FORM OF SOLAR RADIATION MANAGEMENT HAS BEEN VERY EFFECTIVE AT REVERSING GLOBAL WARMING TRENDS.
"THE YEARLY THICKENING SHADE IS THE PRICE WE PAY FOR PRESERVING FREEDOM AND DEMOCRACY.
"BUT SHOULD WE FALTER IN OUR GLOBAL COMMITMENT TO RENEW THE SULPHATES EACH YEAR, WE RISK PROVOKING THE TERMINATION EFFECT.
"THE RADIATIVE FORCING OF ACCUMULATED ATMOSPHERIC CO2 WOULD CAUSE RAPID GLOBAL WARMING—BETWEEN 3 AND 15 DEGREES PER DECADE—WHICH WOULD BE CATASTROPHIC FOR ALL LIFE ON EARTH.
OBVIOUSLY WE NEED TO PREVENT THIS SCENARIO."

"WE HAVE NO CHOICE IN THE FREE WORLD BUT TO STAND UNITED AGAINST THE MOUNTING THREAT OF ECO-TERRORISTS."

DESPITE ITS SEMBLANCE TO SCIENCE FICTION, STRATOSPHERIC SULPHUR RELEASE IS ONE OF THE PROPOSED RESPONSES TO GLOBAL CLIMATE CHANGE, SUPPORTED BY SUCH FIGURES AS BILL GATES AND CANADIAN OIL MAGNATE N. MURRAY EDWARDS.*

WHILE RELATIVELY CHEAP AND EASY TO IMPLEMENT, S.S.R. WOULD LIKELY REQUIRE INCREASED GLOBAL POLICING MEASURES TO MAINTAIN.

IT WOULD ALSO ALMOST CERTAINLY REINFORCE THE HEGEMONY OF THE SAME TECHNOCRATIC AND CORPORATE ELITES WHO STEERED US INTO THE CURRENT CRISIS.

IT'S AN ENGINEERING PROBLEM AND THERE WILL BE AN ENGINEERING SOLUTION.**

THE DISCOURSE OF A **TECHNOLOGICAL FIX** ESCHEWS THE POLITICAL, ECONOMIC AND CULTURAL DIMENSIONS OF ENERGY TRANSITION.

* MALM (2016) Pg. 387.

** REX TILLERSON, QUOTED IN MALM (2016) PG. 387.

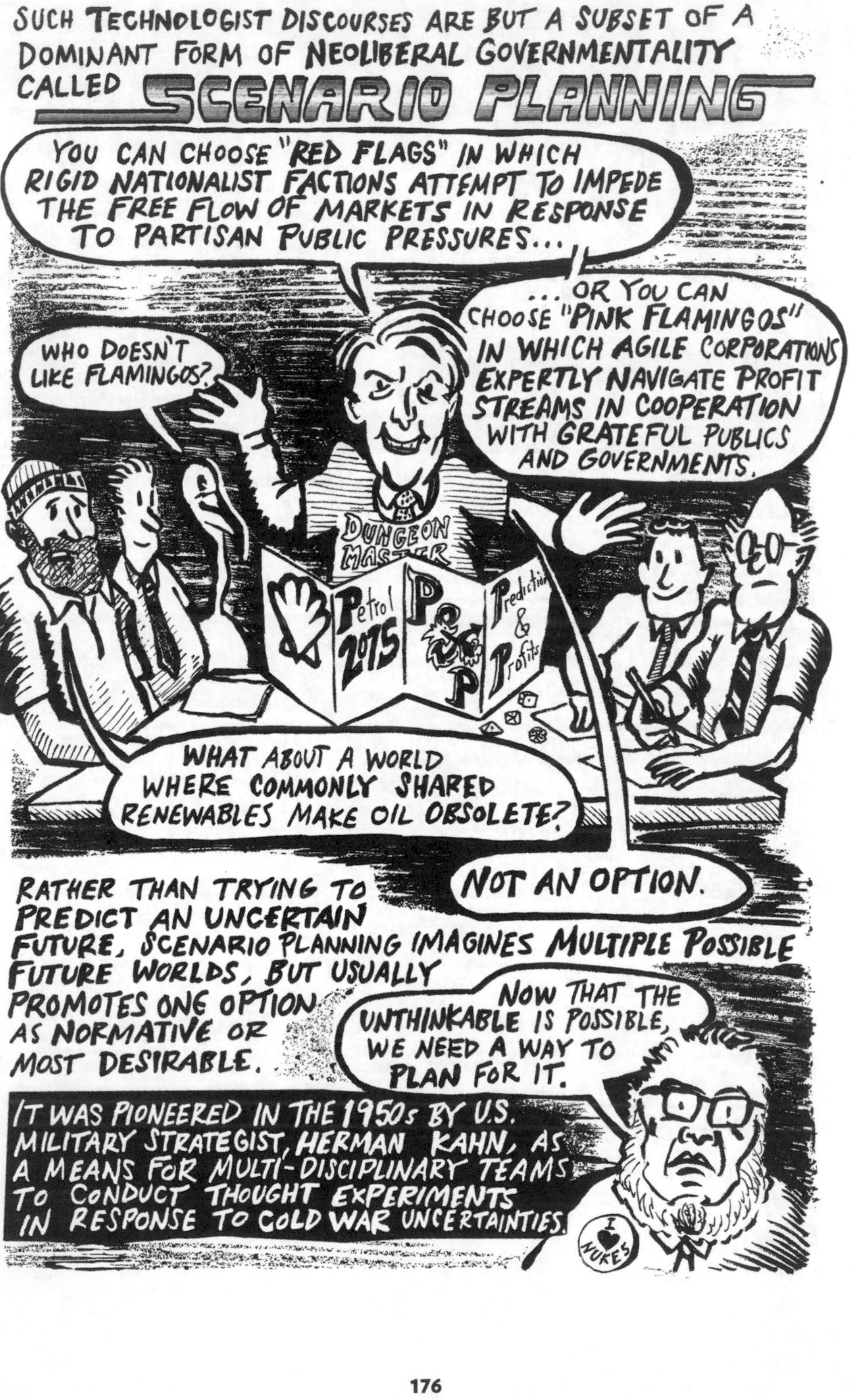
SUCH TECHNOLOGIST DISCOURSES ARE BUT A SUBSET OF A DOMINANT FORM OF NEOLIBERAL GOVERNMENTALITY CALLED SCENARIO PLANNING
YOU CAN CHOOSE "RED FLAGS" IN WHICH RIGID NATIONALIST FACTIONS ATTEMPT TO IMPEDE THE FREE FLOW OF MARKETS IN RESPONSE TO PARTISAN PUBLIC PRESSURES...
...OR YOU CAN CHOOSE "PINK FLAMINGOS" IN WHICH AGILE CORPORATIONS EXPERTLY NAVIGATE PROFIT STREAMS IN COOPERATION WITH GRATEFUL PUBLICS AND GOVERNMENTS.
WHO DOESN'T LIKE FLAMINGOS?
DUNGEON MASTER
Petrol 2075
P & P
Prediction & Profits
WHAT ABOUT A WORLD WHERE COMMONLY SHARED RENEWABLES MAKE OIL OBSOLETE?
NOT AN OPTION.
RATHER THAN TRYING TO PREDICT AN UNCERTAIN FUTURE, SCENARIO PLANNING IMAGINES MULTIPLE POSSIBLE FUTURE WORLDS, BUT USUALLY PROMOTES ONE OPTION AS NORMATIVE OR MOST DESIRABLE.
NOW THAT THE UNTHINKABLE IS POSSIBLE, WE NEED A WAY TO PLAN FOR IT.
IT WAS PIONEERED IN THE 1950s BY U.S. MILITARY STRATEGIST, HERMAN KAHN, AS A MEANS FOR MULTI-DISCIPLINARY TEAMS TO CONDUCT THOUGHT EXPERIMENTS IN RESPONSE TO COLD WAR UNCERTAINTIES.
I ♥ NUKES

THE OIL COMPANY ROYAL DUTCH SHELL WAS AN EARLY ADOPTER OF SCENARIO PLANNING (S.P.), WHICH IT USED TO ANTICIPATE AND NAVIGATE THE 1970s OPEC CRISIS.

THE STRATEGY ALLOWED COMPANIES LIKE SHELL TO

SHOOT THE RAPIDS!

AS FRENCH OIL EXECUTIVE PIERRE WACK FAMOUSLY STATED.*

THESE 'RAPIDS' INCLUDED THE NEWLY VOLATILE CURRENCY AND COMMODITY MARKETS AFTER U.S.A. AND BRITAIN ABANDONED THE BRETTON WOODS GOLD STANDARD.

SCENARIO PLANNING CAN BRING DIVERSE GROUPS TOGETHER TO FORM CONSENSUS IN AN AGE THAT IS SUSPICIOUS OF BIG GOVERNMENT.

BUT THEY ALSO MEANT POLITICAL AND SOCIAL TURBULENCE, SUCH AS THE OPEC OIL EMBARGO OF 1973-4.

AN OFTEN CITED USE OF S.P. CAME IN 1992-3 WHEN SHELL EXEC. ADAM KAHNE FACILITATED THE 'MOUNT FLEUR' SCENARIO EXERCISE THAT FOSTERED THE RESTRUCTURING OF POST-APARTHEID SOUTH AFRICA.

THE SCENARIOS MAPPED OUT INCLUDED "OSTRICH" (DENIAL), "ICARUS" (TOO AMBITIOUS), AND "FLAMINGO" (COOPERATION & ASCENT).

* WACK (1985).

S.P. RESPONDS TO CONTEMPORARY MISTRUST OF GOVERNMENT AUTHORITY BY OFFERING A SEEMINGLY COLLABORATIVE AND OPEN-ENDED PROCESS OF IMAGINED **POSSIBILITIES**.

BUT WHILE IT PURPORTS TO DESCRIBE POTENTIAL **FUTURES**, THE NARRATIVE STRUCTURE OF S.P. ALSO WORKS TO SHAPE THE **UNCERTAIN WORLD** TO WHICH IT CLAIMS TO BE MERELY RESPONDING.

FOR INSTANCE, SOCIOLOGIST **ANNA ZALIK** HIGHLIGHTS THE WAY SHELL'S SCENARIO EXERCISES REINFORCE **NEOLIBERAL VALUES**, SUCH AS **MARKET DEREGULATION**, THROUGH SHIFTING **NARRATIVES** THAT INCORPORATE AND **OBFUSCATE DISSENT**.*

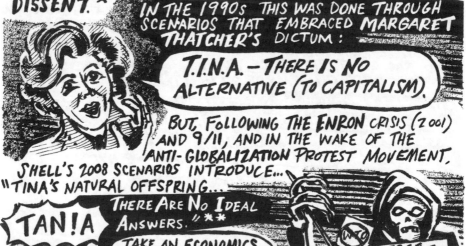

IN THE 1990s THIS WAS DONE THROUGH SCENARIOS THAT EMBRACED **MARGARET THATCHER'S** DICTUM:

T.I.N.A. – THERE IS NO ALTERNATIVE (TO CAPITALISM).

BUT, FOLLOWING **THE ENRON** CRISIS (2001) AND 9/11, AND IN THE WAKE OF THE ANTI-GLOBALIZATION PROTEST MOVEMENT,

SHELL'S 2008 SCENARIOS INTRODUCE... "TINA'S NATURAL OFFSPRING...

TAN!A

THERE ARE NO IDEAL ANSWERS."**

TAKE AN ECONOMICS CLASS, YOU IDEALIST HIPPIES!

CAPITALISM ISN'T WORKING
ANOTHER WORLD IS POSSIBLE

FREE TO EXPLOIT PEOPLE & NATURE TRADE

* ANNA ZALIK (2010) Pgs. 556–7.
** SHELL INTERNATIONAL (2008) Pgs. 6–7.

AFTER DISCREDITING ANY ALTERNATIVES TO GLOBALIZED NEOLIBERAL CAPITALISM AS IDEALISTIC, SHELL'S "SCENARIOS TO 2050" OFFER TWO ALTERNATIVE VISIONS, BOTH OF WHICH ASSUME THE EXPANSION OF OIL PRODUCTION AS A GIVEN. *

YOU ARE FREE TO CHOOSE EITHER DOOR! WHICH WILL IT BE?

BLUEPRINT

SCRAMBLE

AS ZALIK POINTS OUT, NOT ONLY DOES 'SCENARIOS 2050' FORECLOSE OPPOSITION TO THE PETROL INDUSTRY, IT USES A SIMPLISTIC MODEL OF SUPPLY AND DEMAND TO OBFUSCATE THE CENTRAL ROLE PLAYED BY THE FUTURES MARKET IN DETERMINING GAS PRICING. * *

GLOBAL WARMING

UNDER CONDITIONS OF VOLATILITY, THE OIL MARKET ENTERS 'CONTAGIO' IN WHICH THE VALUE OF A FUTURE BARREL OF OIL WILL SURPASS ITS CURRENT PRICING. * * *

WHEN DEMAND FOR OIL DROPS, AS IT DID FOLLOWING THE FINANCIAL CRISIS OF 2008, FUTURE PRICES SURPASS CURRENT (SPOT) PRICES, ENCOURAGING THE STORAGE OF OIL COUPLED WITH PURCHASING FUTURES CONTRACTS THAT WILL DELIVER PROFITS AT A LATER DATE.

THE FORTUNES OF FINANCIERS THUS DEPEND ON THE CONTINUED USE OF OIL, A DYNAMIC IGNORED AND THUS FURTHERED BY SHELL'S 2050 SCENARIOS.

* ZALIK (2010) Pgs. 557, * * 560-62, * * * 662.

179

ZALIK'S ANALYSIS HELPS US SEE HOW SHELL'S 2050 SCENARIOS' DISCURSIVE STRATEGIES USE MISREPRESENTATION TO STIFLE OPPOSITION TO PETROCULTURE, TO THE BENEFIT OF AN UNACKNOWLEDGED CLASS OF FINANCIERS POSITIONED TO PROFIT FROM THE GLOBAL TURBULENCES OF CLIMATE CHANGE.

CULTURAL THEORIST MELINDA COOPER EMPHASIZES HOW S.P.'s REFLEXIVITY - THE ABILITY OF SCENARIOS TO ACTUALLY BRING ABOUT THE CONDITIONS OF TURBULENCE THEY PREDICT- MIRRORS THE WORKINGS OF SPECULATIVE FINANCE WHERE...

WEATHER DERIVATIVES

END OF WORLD INSURANCE!

THE LEVERAGABLE EVENT MAY BE OF ANY KIND - FINANCIAL, POLITICAL OR BIOSPERIC ...YET WHILE DERIVATIVES ABSTRACT FROM THE SUBSTANTIVE NATURE OF THINGS AND FORCES THEY SIMULTANEOUSLY OPERATE AT THE MOST INTIMATE OF MATERIAL LEVELS, INVESTING TRANSVERSAL RELATIONS THAT CONNECT AND COMBINE THE ENTIRE WORLD OF PRICEABLE RISK.

THIS IS A POWER THAT OPERATES IN THE FUTURE SUBJUNCTIVE... *

..BUT HAS THE EFFECT OF CRUCIALLY SHAPING EVERYDAY LIFE.

LATER THIS WEEK YOU CAN EXPECT TO SEE A SHARP RISE IN THE VALUES OF WILD FIRE RE-INSURANCE SWAPS THANKS TO EARLY ARRIVAL OF THE SANTA ANA WINDS.

DRY STORMS
FIRE RISK
INVESTMENT OPPORTUNITIES
HOT!

HOWEVER, HOME OWNERS IN THE AREA ARE STILL SCREWED.

THROUGH THE BUYING AND SELLING OF FUTURE RISK PROJECTIONS, THE CLASS OF FINANCIERS CAN MAKE PROFITS FROM ANY MANNER OF DISASTER.

* Melinda Cooper (2010) Pg.18.

THE NARRATIVE STRUCTURES OF SCENARIO PLANNING, AND THE FINANCIALIZED PROFIT STREAMS IT SUPPORTS, EXHIBIT A DREAM-LOGIC THAT WE SHOULD NOW BE ABLE TO RECOGNIZE...

...SCENARIO PLANNING'S SEEMINGLY COLLABORATIVE AND OPEN-ENDED FORM OF STORYTELLING HELPS CONTAIN, DISGUISE AND DISCIPLINE DISCORDANT VOICES THAT MIGHT OTHERWISE DISTURB THE STATUS-QUO OF PETROCULTURE.

IT ACCOMPLISHES THIS BY PROVIDING WHAT SEEMS LIKE A SERIES OF PLAUSIBLE FUTURES THAT ALL POSTPONE ANY DECISIVE RECKONING WITH THE CIRCUITS OF FINANCE AND PETROL THAT SHAPE THE WORLD.

WHY IS THE PRICE OF GAS SO HIGH?

IT'S THE INTERNATIONAL RING OF PEDOPHILE BILLIONAIRES.

GIVEN THAT OUR WORLD, FROM GAS PRICES TO GOVERNMENTAL INACTION ON CLIMATE CHANGE, IS SHAPED BY ABSTRACTED SYSTEMS OF COMMODITIZED RISK, IS IT ANY WONDER THAT INCREASINGLY BIZARRE CONSPIRACY THEORIES SHOULD EMERGE TO "MAKE SENSE" OF AND REPRESENT THESE REALITIES?

PERHAPS THESE NARRATIVES ARE BUT THE POPULIST TWIN OF SCENARIO PLANNING?

POST-COLONIAL AND GLOBALIZATION SCHOLAR SUSIE O'BRIEN EMPHASIZES THAT ONE OF THE THINGS THAT MAKES S.P. SO EFFECTIVE IS HOW IT HARNESSES THE POWER OF STORYTELLING TO DELIVER...

...AN ODD MIX OF ECONOMIC THEORY AND MYTHOLOGY, WHOSE METAPHORICAL FORM IS THOUGHT TO MAKE THE STORIES BOTH COMPELLING AND UNIVERSALLY INTELLIGIBLE. CONCEPTS LOOSELY BORROWED FROM EVOLUTION SCIENCE HELP TO SUTURE THE ELEMENTS OF MYTH AND NEOLIBERAL ECONOMICS INTO A FRAMEWORK OF PROGRESS BASED ON THE LOGIC: ADAPT OR DIE. *

BE A FLAMINGO, NOT AN OSTRICH!

TANYA

PETROCULTURE IS DESTROYING MY HABITATS.

* O'BRIEN (2016) Pg. 335.
** IBID., Pg. 340.

IN CONTRAST TO S.P.'s SPURIOUS AND NATURALIZED UNIVERSALISMS, O'BRIEN CELEBRATES MODES OF STORYTELLING THAT REFLECT THE FRACTURED AND UNEVEN TEMPORALITIES AND TOPOGRAPHIES THAT CONTEMPORARY GLOBALIZATION PRODUCES...

WITHOUT RECOURSE TO A (FICTIONAL) PAST, FROM WHICH "THE WORLD WAS MAKEABLE" AND THE FUTURE APPARENTLY SECURE, THE POSTCOLONIAL SUBJECT GRASPS THE EFFECTS OF CHAOS AND CONTINGENCY ON A VISCERAL AS WELL AS AN INTELLECTUAL LEVEL... THE ABSENCE OF ANY SOLID STAKE IN CONTEMPORARY CONSTRUCTIONS OF FUTURITY MAKE IT POSSIBLE TO SEE ITS LIMITS, AND MIGHT CREATE SPACE FOR RADICAL POSSIBILITIES. **

PETROCULTURAL SCENARIO PLANNING BOTH EXACERBATES AND RICHLY PROFITS FROM TURBULENCE AND VOLATILITY, WHILE SIMULTANEOUSLY CASTING OPPOSITION TO THIS SCHEME AS DESTRUCTIVE, IDEALISTIC, ATTAVISTIC AND MISGUIDED...

...AND WHILE THE MOUNTING RISKS PROVIDED BY THIS RECKLESS CONFIDENCE GAME REMAIN UNEVENLY DISTRIBUTED ACROSS SOCIETIES AND CONTINENTS, MORE AND MORE OF US ARE "VISERALLY" AND "INTELLECTVALLY" AFFECTED BY THESE REALITIES

AND, CONTRARY TO PARANOID SEDUCTIONS OFFERED BY CONSPIRACY THEORIES...

...IT IS ACTUALLY THE INHUMAN LOGIC OF FINANCE AND PETROL DRIVING THESE CATASTROPHIES.

RATHER THAN SUBSCRIBING TO THESE MURKY DREAMS, PERHAPS WE CAN BEGIN TO IDENTIFY TRULY NEW POSSIBILITIES (AND REINVIGORATE OLD ONES) IN A PROCESS OF ACTUAL COLLABORATION AMONGST THE GROWING LEGIONS OF WILLFULL AND RELUCTANT EXILES FROM PETROCULTURE.

Chapter 7
Excess

AT THE HEART OF **FANTASIES** OF A **TECHNOLOGICAL FIX**, WHETHER THESE BE GEO-ENGINEERING OR COLONIZING DISTANT PLANETS, IS THE BELIEF THAT THE VERY SAME TOOLS AND TENDENCIES THAT CREATED ANTHROPOGENIC CLIMATE CHANGE WILL ALSO SOMEHOW SAVE US FROM IT, ALLOWING US TO KEEP PETROCULTURAL MODES OF LIVING INTACT INDEFINITELY.

THOU SHALT HAVE NO OTHER GODS

PROFITS • PROGRESS • PETROLEUM

SPEED • INSTRUMENTAL REASON • DESIRE

OUR STAIN ENDURETH IN THE FIRMAMENT

TECHNOLOGIST THINKING IS OFTEN COUPLED WITH A FAITH IN MARKET-BASED SOLUTIONS, DESPITE THE FACT THAT THE MODERN MARKET'S IMPERATIVE TO CONSTANT EXPANSION OF PROFITS GAURANTEES ITS FEVERISH DEPENDENCE ON OIL.

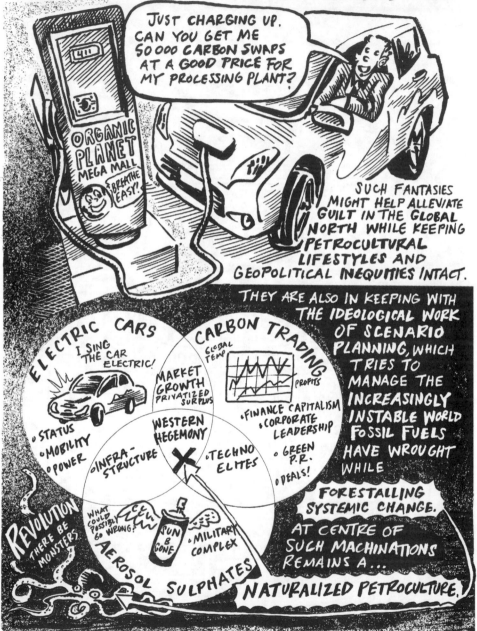

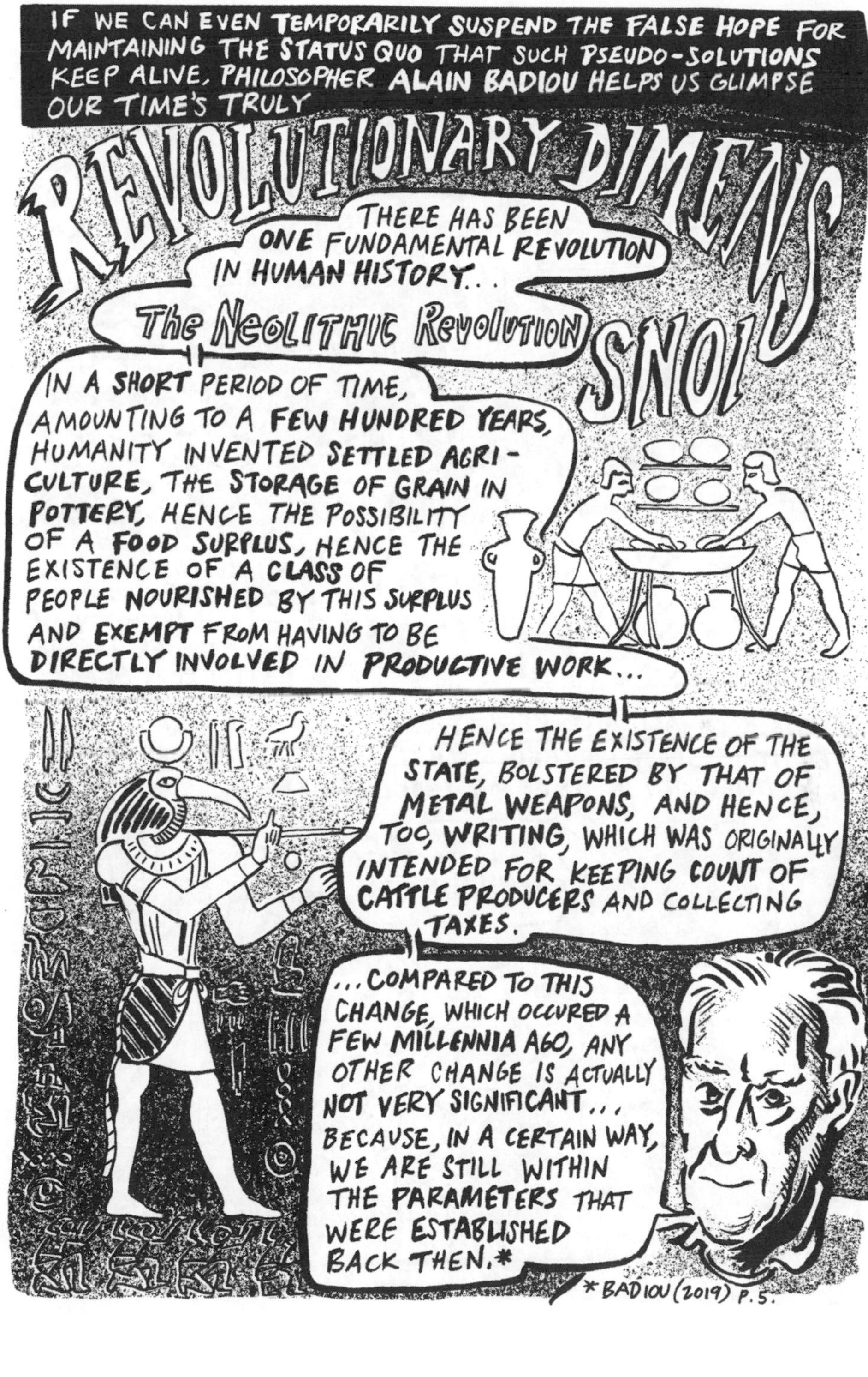

IF WE CAN EVEN TEMPORARILY SUSPEND THE FALSE HOPE FOR MAINTAINING THE STATUS QUO THAT SUCH PSEUDO-SOLUTIONS KEEP ALIVE, PHILOSOPHER ALAIN BADIOU HELPS US GLIMPSE OUR TIME'S TRULY
REVOLUTIONARY DIMENSIONS
THERE HAS BEEN ONE FUNDAMENTAL REVOLUTION IN HUMAN HISTORY...
The Neolithic Revolution
IN A SHORT PERIOD OF TIME, AMOUNTING TO A FEW HUNDRED YEARS, HUMANITY INVENTED SETTLED AGRICULTURE, THE STORAGE OF GRAIN IN POTTERY, HENCE THE POSSIBILITY OF A FOOD SURPLUS, HENCE THE EXISTENCE OF A CLASS OF PEOPLE NOURISHED BY THIS SURPLUS AND EXEMPT FROM HAVING TO BE DIRECTLY INVOLVED IN PRODUCTIVE WORK...
HENCE THE EXISTENCE OF THE STATE, BOLSTERED BY THAT OF METAL WEAPONS, AND HENCE, TOO, WRITING, WHICH WAS ORIGINALLY INTENDED FOR KEEPING COUNT OF CATTLE PRODUCERS AND COLLECTING TAXES.
...COMPARED TO THIS CHANGE, WHICH OCCURED A FEW MILLENNIA AGO, ANY OTHER CHANGE IS ACTUALLY NOT VERY SIGNIFICANT... BECAUSE, IN A CERTAIN WAY, WE ARE STILL WITHIN THE PARAMETERS THAT WERE ESTABLISHED BACK THEN.*
*BADIOU (2019) P. 5.

DESPITE THE INCREASES IN SURPLUSES AND TECHNOLOGIES BROUGHT ABOUT BY THE NEOLITHIC REVOLUTION, BADIOU'S POINT IS THAT DIVISIONS, INEQUITY AND CONFLICTS HAVE, IF ANYTHING, WORSENED.* BUT THIS VERY AWARENESS POINTS TO A FURTHER SOCIAL DEVELOPMENT THAT CAME ALONG WITH THE OTHERS...

* BADIOU (2019) Pg.11.

WHY DON'T YOU TRY THE OTHER FRUIT FIRST?

RACES — NATION STATES — CLASS DIVISIONS — ARMIES — WEAPONS AND MORE WEAPONS

POPULAR CULTURE

ALIENATED LABOUR

REVOLUTION

IDLE RULING CLASSES

THERE GOES MY DOCILE LABOUR FORCE.

SSSURPLUS

WHILE THE BIBLICAL EDEN STORY PRESENTS ITSELF AS THE EVENT THAT CAUSES HUMANS' FALL FROM GRACE,

PERHAPS IT ACTUALLY REGISTERS A MOMENT WHEN A NEOLITHIC STATE OF BEING THAT SUBJECTS HAD ALREADY BEEN DWELLING IN BECAME INTOLERABLE.

IN OTHER WORDS, PERHAPS IT REGISTERS THE TRAUMATIC EFFECTS OF A MOMENT OF CRITIQUE WHEN A HIGHER IDEAL INTERRUPTED THE DOMINANT NEOLITHIC CULTURAL FORMATION, PASSING JUDGMENT UPON IT FOR FALLING SHORT OF FULL HUMAN POTENTIAL.

YOU WILL TOIL IN DUST AND EVEN THE MIGHTY SURPLUS ENERGIES OF FOSSIL FUELS WILL NOT DELIVER YOU FROM STRIFE.

ANIMAL BLISS

HISTORY

IF SO, IT SEEMS AS THOUGH THE BIBLICAL RECORDING OF THIS MYTH ATTEMPTS TO RECLAIM ITS SUBVERSIVE CONTENT FOR A PRIESTLY DISCOURSE AFFIRMING HIERARCHIES VIA GUILT.

THOUGH FIRMLY **MATERIALIST**, **BADIOU'S** VISION IS IN KEEPING WITH THE **GENEAOLOGIES** OF **NEOLITHIC CRITIQUE** FOR WHICH THE **HEBREW BIBLE** PROVIDES ONE OF THE **EARLIEST** AND MOST **ENDURING ARCHIVES.**

YOUR LORD GOD IS NOT PARTIAL AND TAKES NO BRIBE. HE EXECUTES JUSTICE FOR THE ORPHAN AND THE WIDOW, AND LOVES THE STRANGERS, PROVIDING THEM FOOD AND CLOTHS.

DEUTERONOMY 10:18

HEBREW SCRIPTURE ADAPTED THE **NEOLITHIC** LANGUAGE OF **MIGHT, KIN** AND **KINGSHIP** TO **EXPRESS** AN **ALTERNATIVE** SET OF VALUES THAT **CHALLENGED** THE DOMINANT **CODES** OF **SOVEREIGNTY** AND **ETHNIC BELONGING.**

THOUGH THIS VISION REMAINS IN **UNEASY TENSION** WITH SOME OF THE INSTITUTIONS THAT ENSURED ITS **TRANSMISSION** AND **SURVIVAL** (A TENSION AND HISTORY PARTLY **RECORDED** IN THE SCRIPTURES THEMSELVES), IT **REMAINS** ONE OF THE FOUNDING EXPRESSIONS OF A **NEW** HISTORICAL **SENSIBILITY** AND **DIALECTIC** THAT IS STILL IN THE **PROCESS** OF BEING **WORKED** OUT. THE GUIDING **VISION** OF THIS ONGOING **STRUGGLE** EXCEEDS THE ORBIT OF **NEOLITHIC CULTURE.**

THEN, AS NOW, THE FIGURE OF **GENEROSITY EXTENDED** TO THE **HOMELESS REFUGEE** REMAINS THE **DEFINITIVE CHALLENGE** AND **TEST** BY WHICH WE **SUCCEED** OR **FAIL** TO LIVE UP TO THIS **ETHICAL VISION.**

IT IS ESTIMATED THAT BY **2050, CLIMATE CHANGE** WILL HAVE CAUSED THE **DISPLACEMENT** OF UPWARDS OF **200 MILLION PEOPLE.** *

IF THE **NEOLITHIC FIXTURES** OF STATES, **RACIAL** CONFLICT AND **CLASS ADVANTAGES** ARE UNABLE TO **ADDRESS** THIS CRISIS, AND INSTEAD SEEM BENT ON **RETRENCHING** THE VERY **WORST TENDENCIES** OF THE PAST **TEN THOUSAND YEARS,** PERHAPS WE ARE RUNNING UP AGAINST THE HISTORICAL **LIMITS** OF THE **NEOLITHIC ITSELF.**

*BROWN (2008).

HEBREW SCRIPTURE IS BY NO MEANS THE ONLY SOURCE OF OLD IDEAS THAT CHALLENGE NEOLITHIC LOGICS, AND WE SHOULD BE WARY OF TENDENCIES TOWARDS ESSENTIALIZING VISIONS OF HETEROGENEOUS INFLUENCES. FOR INSTANCE, INDIGENOUS PEOPLES OF NORTH AMERICA, WHOSE CULTURAL LEGACIES ON THE CONTINENT PREDATE NEOLITHIC DEVELOPMENTS BY MILLENNIA,* SHOWED GREAT GENEROSITY TO STRANGERS IN THEIR MIDST.

INDIGENOUS PEOPLES SHARED FOOD, MEDICINE AND TECHNOLOGIES FOR SURVIVAL WITH SETTLERS. THEY SHARED AND TRADED LAND, RESOURCES, CULTURE AND, AS DAVID GRAEBER ARGUES, LIKELY INFLUENCED THE PRACTICAL WORKING OF EARLY AMERICAN DEMOCRACY.**

* THE MOST CURRENT EVIDENCE PLACES THIS AT THE END OF THE LAST ICE AGE, 14,000 YEARS AGO. THE INDIGENOUS PHRASE, "FROM TIME IMMEMORIAL" IS JUST AS ACCURATE. SEE: KATZ (2017).

** SEE: GRAEBER (2007).

THE RESPONSE OF EUROPEAN SETTLERS TO THIS GENEROSITY IS WELL KNOWN: BROKEN PROMISES AND TREATIES, VIOLENCE AND GENOCIDE, ENACTED UNDER THE BANNER "CIVILIZATION." THE EXTENT TO WHICH CONTEMPORARY SETTLER CULTURE CYNICALLY ACCEPTS THESE TRAGEDIES AND AGGRESSIONS IS A MEASURE OF THE DEGREE TO WHICH WE HAVE LOST SIGHT OF THE ONLY IDEAL THAT CAN GIVE THE TERM "CIVILIZATION" MEANING.

BADIOU DESCRIBES THIS **IDEAL** AS **HUMAN UNITY** OR THE RECOGNITION OF OURSELVES AS PART OF A **UNIFIED SPECIES**. THIS IS INDEED AKIN TO WHAT **MARX DESCRIBED AS SPECIES BEING.** * IT IS ALSO A FORM OF AWARENESS THAT **CLIMATE CHANGE AND SPECIES EXTINCTION** FORCE US TO CONFRONT...

...IF WE SURVEY HUMAN **HISTORY** FROM ABOVE WITH THE IDEA THAT HUMANITY SHOULD AND **COULD** PRODUCE A **SOCIAL ORGANIZATION** WORTHY OF ITS BASIC **UNITY**, THAT IS, PRODUCE A CONSCIOUS **AFFIRMATION** OF ITSELF AS A **UNIFIED SPECIES**, THEN THE TOTAL **FAILURE** OF THAT ENDEAVOR WOULD **REDUCE** HUMANITY TO BEING JUST ONE **ANIMAL FIGURE** AMONGST OTHERS, TO BEING AN ANIMAL FIGURE THAT IS STILL **DOMINATED** BY THE **STRUGGLE FOR SURVIVAL, COMPETITION** AMONG INDIVIDUALS, AND THE **TRIUMPH** OF THE **FITTEST.**

PERHAPS THE PAST **TEN THOUSAND YEARS** HAVE MERELY BEEN A **LONG, PAINFUL** PROCESS OF WAKING UP TO HUMANITY'S **POTENTIAL** AND PLACE IN THE **UNIVERSE**...

...A PROCESS **ACCELERATED** BY **FOSSIL FUELS**, THE CUMULATIVE EFFECTS OF WHICH HAVE MADE IT **URGENTLY** NECESSARY THAT WE THINK **BEYOND THE LIMITS** OF OUR CURRENT SOCIAL FORMS.

WE ARE HERE

... THERE CLEARLY NEEDS TO BE, THERE WILL **HAVE** TO BE, IN THE CURRENT CENTURIES AND ON A SCALE THAT WE CAN'T **COMPREHEND**, A **SECOND REVOLUTION** AFTER THE **NEOLITHIC** REVOLUTION. A REVOLUTION THAT, BY ITS SHEER **MAGNITUDE**, WOULD BE ON PAR WITH THE NEOLITHIC REVOLUTION BUT THAT WOULD **RESTORE** HUMANITY'S **FUNDAMENTAL UNITY** IN THE PROPER ORDER OF THE IMMANENT **ORGANIZATION** OF SOCIETY. **

* SEE CHAPTER 5.   ** BADIOU (2019) Pg. 10.

BADIOU'S READ ON THE TRANSFORMATIVE POTENTIAL OF OUR TIMES HELPS US SEE HOW STOPGAP MEASURES, SUCH AS SWAPPING GAS VEHICLES FOR ELECTRIC ONES, OR "MAKING POLLUTERS PAY" WITH CARBON TRADING, FALL SHORT: THEY ALLOW US TO BELIEVE THAT CLIMATE CHANGE IS JUST ANOTHER TECHNICAL PROBLEM THAT ENGINEERS AND ECONOMISTS CAN FIX FOR US, WHILE KEEPING SOCIAL RELATIONS BASED ON THE PRIVATE APPROPRIATION OF SOCIAL SURPLUSES INTACT.

SUCH MAGICAL THINKING MERELY DISPLACES THE CORE PROBLEM. FOR INSTANCE, INCREASED DEMAND FOR LITHIUM, A KEY ELEMENT IN BATTERIES, IS POISED TO WREAK HAVOC ON THE ENVIRONMENT AND ECONOMY OF COUNTRIES LIKE CHILE AND PORTUGAL CREATING WHAT SOME HAVE CALLED THE "WHITE OIL" CURSE*

*O. BALCH, "THE CURSE OF WHITE OIL: THE ELECTRIC CAR'S DIRTY SECRET," THEGUARDIAN.COM DEC 8, 2020)

THE LARGER QUESTION WE SHOULD ASK IS: EVEN IF WE COULD NAVIGATE A GLOBAL ENERGY TRANSITION WHILE KEEPING CURRENT CULTURES AND SOCIAL RELATIONS INTACT,

WHY WOULD WE WANT TO???

GLOBALIZED PETROCULTURE, WITH ITS COMPULSION TO CONSTANT EXPANSION, ITS MASSIVELY UNEVEN DISTRIBUTIONS OF WEALTH, ITS CARPETS OF ASPHALT BOUNDED BY DYING OCEANS AND ITS BAN AGAINST RELATING TO EACH OTHER AS ANYTHING OTHER THAN COMPETING INDIVIDUALS IS NOT A RATIONAL ORDER, ONE BEFITTING CREATURES WITH SELF-AWARENESS, EMPATHY AND COMPASSION FOR ONE ANOTHER.

IT'S JUST SO DAMN BEAUTIFUL!

THIS BRINGS US TO WHAT IS PERHAPS THE **HEART** OF THE PROBLEM OF OUR **ATTACHMENT** TO **PETROCULTURE**. IF WE ARE SUPPOSEDLY RATIONAL ACTORS PURSUING OUR INDIVIDUAL SELF-INTEREST, AS MUCH CONTEMPORARY ECONOMIC THEORY HOLDS, WHY DO WE INDULGE IN SUCH SELF-AND WORLD-DESTROYING BEHAVIOUR?

IT JUST **FEELS RIGHT**.

FOLLOWING THE WORK OF SABINA SPIELREIN, SIGMUND FREUD THEORIZED A "DEATH DRIVE" THAT LEADS HUMANS TO PURSUE **REPETITIVE, PAINFUL** AND **DESTRUCTIVE BEHAVIOURS**, IN **EXCESS** OF THE INTERESTS OF SELF-PRESERVATION (WHICH HE CALLED "EROS," THE LIFE DRIVES.)

THOUGH FREUD REVISITS AND REFINES THE IDEA FROM 1920 TO THE END OF HIS CAREER, HE NEVER SATISFACTORILY EXPLAINS DESTRUCTIVE COMPULSIONS TO REPEAT. INSTEAD, HE SETTLES ON A **DUALISTIC** MODEL OF LIFE ENERGIES WHERE "EROS" AND "THANATOS" (DEATH DRIVE) CONTEND WITH EACH OTHER.

LIFE SIMPLY INCLINES TOWARDS DEATH, AND EVERY DEATH IS INTERNALLY MOTIVATED BY THE ORGANISM, EVEN THAT OF MY BELOVED SOPHIE.

CIVILIZATION MUST CONSTANTLY STIFLE THE DEATH DRIVE AND THAT IS WHY INDIVIDUALS CAN NEVER BE FULLY HAPPY. BUT WE CAN SMOKE.

WHAT IN HIS **EARLIER WORKS** SEEMS TO BE A WAY OF GRAPPLING WITH **GRIEF** OVER THE DEATH, BY SPANISH FLU, OF HIS **FAVOURITE DAUGHTER** BECOMES, IN HIS **LATE WORK**, A PHILOSOPHICAL VISION OF "CIVILIZATION AND ITS DISCONTENTS."

PHILOSOPHER SLAVOJ ŽIŽEK FOLLOWS LACAN TO OFFER A MORE NUANCED AND USEFUL UNDERSTANDING OF THE DEATH DRIVE, ONE THAT CHALLENGES FREUD'S OWN INITIAL IDEAS ABOUT IT:

"... WE SHOULD NOT CONFUSE THE DEATH DRIVE WITH THE SO-CALLED 'NIRVANA-PRINCIPLE,' THE THRUST TOWARDS DESTRUCTION OR SELF-OBLITERATION: THE FREUDIAN DEATH DRIVE ... IS, ON THE CONTRARY, THE VERY OPPOSITE OF DYING - A NAME FOR THE 'UNDEAD' ETERNAL LIFE ITSELF, FOR THE HORRIBLE FATE OF BEING CAUGHT IN THE ENDLESS REPETATIVE CYCLE OF WANDERING AROUND IN GUILT AND PAIN."*

SUCH WANDERING IS ILLUSTRATED BY TRAVIS BICKLE (ROBERT DENIRO) IN TAXI DRIVER (1976), WHO, DISTURBED BY THE DEPRAVITY AND VIOLENCE HE WITNESSES IN THE STREETS OF NEW YORK, BEGINS TO WRESTLE WITH VIOLENT, VIGILANTE FANTASIES.

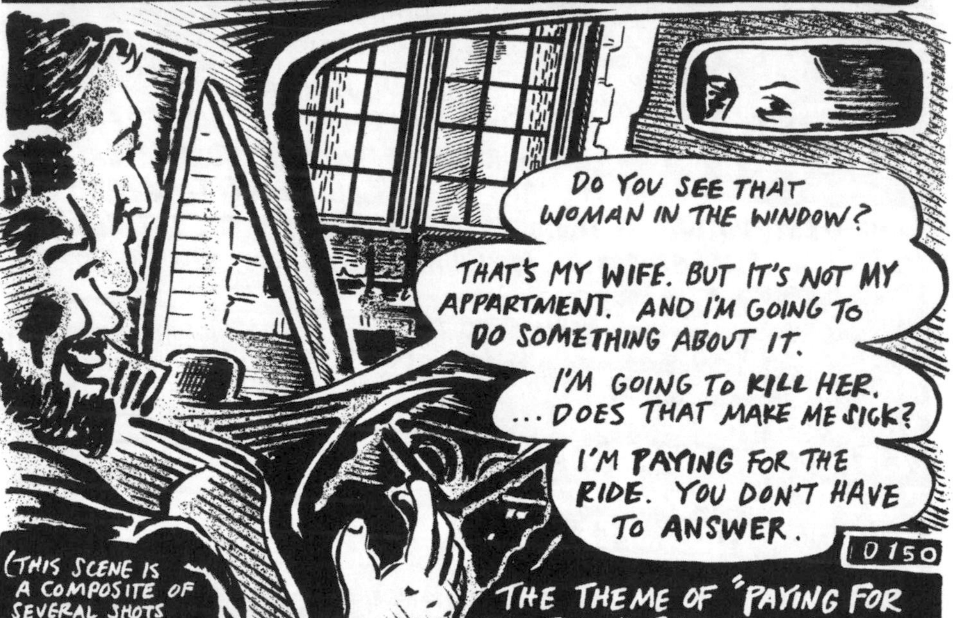
DO YOU SEE THAT WOMAN IN THE WINDOW?
THAT'S MY WIFE. BUT IT'S NOT MY APPARTMENT. AND I'M GOING TO DO SOMETHING ABOUT IT.
I'M GOING TO KILL HER. ... DOES THAT MAKE ME SICK?
I'M PAYING FOR THE RIDE. YOU DON'T HAVE TO ANSWER.
0150

(THIS SCENE IS A COMPOSITE OF SEVERAL SHOTS AND MOMENTS IN THE FILM.)

THE THEME OF "PAYING FOR THE RIDE" RETURNS AT THE END OF THE FILM, DRAWING ATTENTION TO THE SURPLUS ENJOYMENT OF WHICH BICKLE'S TAXI IS THE VEHICLE; BEYOND THE TRANSPORTATION SERVICE IT PROVIDES, THE TAXI'S CIRCULATION OF THE STREETS OFFERS VOYEURISTIC PLEASURES CHARGED WITH SICKENING, TRANSGRESSIVE ENERGY.

* ZIZEK (2009), Pg 62.

FROM INSIDE HIS TAXI, BICKLE WATCHES THE ROILING STREET LIFE OF NEW YORK, BUT HIS REAR-VIEW MIRROR ALLOWS US TO REFLECT UPON BICKLE'S GAZE ITSELF AS BEING A DETERMINATIVE PART OF WHAT HE VIEWS.

AS A VIETNAM VETERAN SUFFERING FROM ACUTE INSOMNIA TRYING TO REINTEGRATE INTO AMERICAN SOCIETY, BICKLE VIGOROUSLY IDENTIFIES WITH HIS ROLE AS A NIGHT CABBIE; ATTEMPTING TO TURN HIS AFFLICTION INTO EXCESSIVE INDUSTRY, BILKLE CANNOT ESCAPE THE SENSE OF ALIENATION THAT DOGS HIM

BICKLE FANTASIZES ABOUT CLEANING UP THE "FILTH AND SCUM" OF THE STREETS, BUT HE SIMULTANEOUSLY FEELS EXCLUDED FROM THE SOCIAL LIFE HE SEES AROUND HIM. A CLASS-BASED STIGMA THUS HAUNTS HIS GAZE, WHICH HE TRIES TO REMEDY WITH WORK.

BICKLE IS IMPRESSED BY CHARLES PALANTINE (LEONARD HARRIS), A PRESIDENTIAL CANDIDATE WHOSE POPULIST SLOGAN, "WE ARE THE PEOPLE," MOBILIZES THE PROMISE OF A UNIFIED POPULACE, BUT WHOSE ASIDES BETRAY THE PERSISTENT EXISTENCE OF CLASS DISTANCES.

BICKLE ADMITS TO BEING IGNORANT ABOUT POLITICAL ISSUES, BUT WHEN PALANTINE PRESSES, HE DOES HAVE ONE GRIPE...

THIS CITY IS LIKE AN OPEN SEWER; IT'S FULL OF FILTH AND SCUM...WHOEVER BECOMES PRESIDENT SHOULD JUST REALLY CLEAN IT UP... YOU SHOULD JUST FLUSH IT RIGHT DOWN THE FUCKING TOILET!

THE SENSE OF DIGNITY AND CONNECTION BICKLE SEEKS BY DRIVING CAB IS UNDERMINED BY THE TRAUMA OF SOCIAL DISTANCE ITSELF, AND HE TRIES TO COMPENSATE FOR HIS LOWLY AND LONELY STATUS BY ASSUMING A CRITICAL DISTANCE FROM THE ENVIRONMENT OF WHICH HE IS A PART... A MINIMUM DISTANCE WHICH THE TAXI ITSELF PROVIDES.

THE PARADOX OF THE FREUDIAN "DEATH DRIVE" IS THAT IT IS FREUD'S NAME FOR ITS VERY OPPOSITE, FOR THE WAY IMMORTALITY APPEARS WITHIN PSYCHOANALYSIS, FOR AN UNCANNY EXCESS OF LIFE, FOR AN "UNDEAD URGE" WHICH PERSISTS BEYOND THE (BIOLOGICAL) CYCLE OF LIFE AND DEATH, OF GENERATION AND CORRUPTION.*

FIZZZZ

A REPRESENTATION OF THIS IS PROVIDED BY THE MILKY, SIZZLING BROMIDE WATER INTO WHICH BICKLE PEERS. HIS NAUSEA ABOUT THE "EXCESS" OF THE STREETS (A PLACE-HOLDER FOR THE SURPLUS DENIED HIM DUE TO CLASS STATUS) BECOMES HIS ENJOYMENT ITSELF, BECOMES HIS DEATH DRIVE.

* ZIZEK (2009) PG. 62

THE ULTIMATE LESSON OF PSYCHOANALYSIS IS THAT HUMAN LIFE IS NEVER JUST "LIFE"; HUMANS ARE NOT SIMPLY ALIVE, THEY ARE POSSESSED BY THE STRANGE DRIVE TO ENJOY LIFE IN EXCESS, PASSIONATELY ATTACHED TO A SURPLUS WHICH STICKS OUT AND DERAILS THE ORDINARY RUN OF THINGS.*

THE PRODUCTION, MANAGEMENT AND DISTRIBUTION OF THIS SURPLUS IS A KEY POLITICAL ISSUE, AND TAXI DRIVER SHOWS US HOW THIS UNDEAD SURPLUS IS MANAGED FOR A WORKING MAN IN LATE 20TH-CENTURY AMERICAN PETROCULTURE: BY SUBSTITUTING DRIVE (THE PURSUIT/ENJOYMENT OF SURPLUS) FOR DESIRE. THE APOLITICAL AND UNDEREDUCATED BICKLE BECOMES FIXATED ON BETSY (CYBILL SHEPHERD), A VOLUNTEER FOR PALANTINE'S PRESIDENTIAL BID.

Sometime Sweet Susan

YOU'RE TAKING ME HERE?

I'VE SEEN LOTS OF COUPLES COMING HERE.

BETSY IS BOTH INTIMIDATED AND FASCINATED BY BICKLE, BUT WHEN ON THEIR SECOND DATE HE TAKES HER TO A PORN THEATRE, SHE IS REPULSED AND REJECTS HIM. THOUGH BICKLE'S MISSTEP APPEARS INNOCENT, IT HAS AN UNCANNY INTENTIONALITY THAT ALLOWS BETSY TO BECOME HIS "LOST OBJECT.".

A METONYMIC STAND-IN FOR THE VOID OF THE IMPOSSIBLE THING: IT IS IN DESIRE THAT THE ASPIRATION FOR FULLNESS IS TRANSFERRED TO PARTIAL OBJECTS.*

BETSY BECOMES THE SUBSTITUTE FOR THE POLITICAL COHESION PROMISED IN PALANTINE'S "WE" SLOGAN (THE IMPOSSIBLE/LOST UNITY), SPECIFICALLY...

YOU KNOW, YOU HAVE BEAUTIFUL EYES.

BUT IT IS ACTUALLY BETSY'S FASCINATION FOR BICKLE— THE IMAGE OF HIMSELF HE IMAGINES IN HER EYES— THAT BECOMES HIS PARTIAL OBJECT; A STAND IN FOR THE BLOCKED POLITICAL AVENUES FOR ADRESSING THE REDISTRIBUTION OF SURPLUSES & STATUS.

* ZIZEK (2019) Pg. 62.

199

MORE SPECIFICALLY, IT IS THE **FASCINATION** BICKLE BELIEVES HE SEES FOR HIMSELF IN BETSY'S EYES AS SUMMONED BY ACTS OF MASCULINE **BRAVADO** AND **AGGRESSION** THAT THE FILM REVEALS TO BE THE **FANTASY** MODULATING BETWEEN DRIVE AND DESIRE.

YOU PEOPLE ARE LIVING IN HELL, AND YOU'LL DIE IN HELL!

ALL OF BICKLE'S **ACTING OUT** IN THE FILM IS AN ATTEMPT TO **REGAIN HIS LOST OBJECT** — BETSY'S ADMIRING GAZE.

BUT THIS GAZE IS **ACTUALLY** THE SPOT FROM WHICH BICKLE IMAGINES **WATCHING HIMSELF** IN ORDER TO **ELEVATE HIS LOWLY STATUS.** THUS, BICKLE'S **REJECTION** BY BETSY, FAR FROM **CAUSING** THE SERIES OF **VIOLENT** ACTS THAT **FOLLOW,** IS WHAT HE **SECRETLY WANTED,** FOR IT ALLOWS HIM TO RE-STAGE THE **LOSS** HE HAS **ALREADY SUFFERED** AS A **DISENFRANCHISED** WORKER AND VETERAN, WHILE AVOIDING CONFRONTING THE **HUMILIATING CLASS VOID** AT THE **HEART** OF **AMERICAN LIFE** ITSELF.

HAVEN'T YOU EVER LOOKED AT YOUR OWN EYEBALLS IN THE MIRROR?

MASCULINE VIOLENCE CLOAKED IN THE FANTASY OF RESCUING WOMEN IS THE COMPENSATION TACITLY OFFERED BY SOCIAL NORMS IN EXCHANGE FOR BICKLE'S EXILE FROM ACTUAL POLITICAL LIFE. AS THE FANTASY SOLUTION TO A REAL PROBLEM OF SURPLUS DISTRIBUTION, IT IS **NOT MEANT TO SUCCEED.**

WHEN BICKLE **FAILS TO RESCUE"** BETSY, HE FIXATES UPON THE TWELVE – YEAR-OLD **RUNAWAY** AND SEX WORKER, IRIS (JODI FOSTER).

NAMED AFTER THE **APERTURE OF THE EYE ITSELF, IRIS** IS THE PART OF BICKLE'S FANTASY THAT **SEES THROUGH HIM** WITH HER OWN **TRAUMATIZED** AND **KNOWING GAZE.** FAR FROM A HELP-LESS DAMSEL IN NEED OF SAVING, **IRIS** PROVIDES HOPE THAT A **YOUNGER GENERATION** MIGHT FIND, EVENTUALLY, **ALTERNATIVES** TO THE **CYNICAL SOCIETY** IN WHICH THEY LIVE.

For all its gripping PATHOS, largely thanks to the acting of DeNiro, Foster and Harvey Keitel (who plays the sleazy pimp, Sport), the vigilante sequences of Taxi Driver's Third Act never escape the orbit of Bickle's violent, masculinist fantasy.

His attempt to assassinate Palantine is thwarted by the same desire for recognition that motivates it, supporting Zizek's claim that the death drive is not truly aimed at self-destruction.

You looking at me?

PROHIBIT

When Bickle finally succeeds to find an action to express his frustration it comes in the form of spectacular violence that succeeds in further traumatizing Iris under the pretext of saving her.

"We Are The People"

Furthermore, it is violence directed at an underclass— the pimp, Sport, and his operation — that serves to deflect attention from structural issues, such as the poverty and familial violence hinted at in Iris' background, in favour of an emergent, "tough on crime" discourse for which Bickle becomes a pseudo-revolutionary folk hero.

How much for the ride?

The fiction of solidarity and cohesion —Palantine's "We are the People" slogan — is produced by the redirection of Bickle's class-based frustration towards the violent suppression of the underclass. Paradoxically, it is Bickle's own contribution to the sleazy and seedy excesses of the same urban underbelly he despises that finally succeeds in making him respectable to the establishment. He also wins back the fascinated gaze of Betsy, who now becomes the safely inaccessible object validating his fantasy.

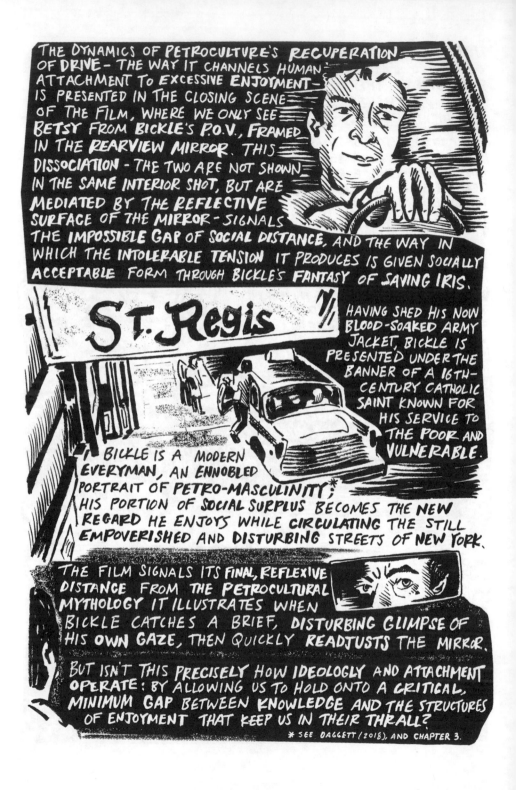

THE DYNAMICS OF PETROCULTURE'S RECUPERATION OF DRIVE - THE WAY IT CHANNELS HUMAN ATTACHMENT TO EXCESSIVE ENJOYMENT - IS PRESENTED IN THE CLOSING SCENE OF THE FILM, WHERE WE ONLY SEE BETSY FROM BICKLE'S P.O.V., FRAMED IN THE REARVIEW MIRROR. THIS DISSOCIATION - THE TWO ARE NOT SHOWN IN THE SAME INTERIOR SHOT, BUT ARE MEDIATED BY THE REFLECTIVE SURFACE OF THE MIRROR - SIGNALS THE IMPOSSIBLE GAP OF SOCIAL DISTANCE, AND THE WAY IN WHICH THE INTOLERABLE TENSION IT PRODUCES IS GIVEN SOCIALLY ACCEPTABLE FORM THROUGH BICKLE'S FANTASY OF SAVING IRIS.

St. Regis

HAVING SHED HIS NOW BLOOD-SOAKED ARMY JACKET, BICKLE IS PRESENTED UNDER THE BANNER OF A 16TH-CENTURY CATHOLIC SAINT KNOWN FOR HIS SERVICE TO THE POOR AND VULNERABLE.

BICKLE IS A MODERN EVERYMAN, AN ENNOBLED PORTRAIT OF PETRO-MASCULINITY; HIS PORTION OF SOCIAL SURPLUS BECOMES THE NEW REGARD HE ENJOYS WHILE CIRCULATING THE STILL EMPOVERISHED AND DISTURBING STREETS OF NEW YORK.

THE FILM SIGNALS ITS FINAL, REFLEXIVE DISTANCE FROM THE PETROCULTURAL MYTHOLOGY IT ILLUSTRATES WHEN BICKLE CATCHES A BRIEF, DISTURBING GLIMPSE OF HIS OWN GAZE, THEN QUICKLY READJUSTS THE MIRROR.

BUT ISN'T THIS PRECISELY HOW IDEOLOGLY AND ATTACHMENT OPERATE: BY ALLOWING US TO HOLD ONTO A CRITICAL, MINIMUM GAP BETWEEN KNOWLEDGE AND THE STRUCTURES OF ENJOYMENT THAT KEEP US IN THEIR THRALL?

* SEE DAGGETT (2018), AND CHAPTER 3.

THE LESSON TO DRAW FROM THIS IS NOT THAT EXCESS IS BAD; IT IS AN INESCAPABLE AND DETERMINATIVE COMPONENT OF HUMAN PSYCHOLOGY AND SOCIETIES.

THE PROBLEM IS WITH THE SPECIFIC WAYS IN WHICH PETROCULTURE COMPENSATES FOR THE PRIVATIZED APPROPRIATION OF SOCIAL SURPLUSES BY A SMALL MINORITY, BY DIVERTING CLASS-CONFLICT INTO ENJOYMENT-INFUSED PREJUDICES OF A RACIALIZED AND GENDERED NATURE THAT STRUCTURE SHARED SOCIAL SPACES.

DON'T BLACK LIVES MATTER

PETROCULTURE BEGUILES US THROUGH AN IMMENSE AND UNEVENLY DISTRIBUTED PRODUCTION OF WASTED SPACE, RESOURCES AND LIVES. THIS ANALYSIS COMPLICATES MALM'S DISTINCTION BETWEEN CONSUMPTION OF FOSSIL FUELS BASED ON UTILITY AND THAT WHICH GENERATES PROFITS*: THOUGH THE LATTER IS RESPONSIBLE FOR THE LION'S SHARE OF EMISSIONS, THE FORMER — FUEL BURNT FOR PERSONAL USE WITHOUT RECUPERATION OF PROFIT — IS RESPONSIBLE FOR OUR ATTACHMENT TO PETROCULTURE.

FURTHERMORE, IT IS PRECISELY ITS GRATUITOUS AND WASTEFUL NATURE, ITS EXCESSIVENESS, THAT CEMENTS THIS ATTACHMENT AS ONE OF THE FEW FORMS OF CARNIVALESQUE PLEASURE AFFORDED US IN REAL, "SHARED" SOCIAL SPACE, OUTSIDE OF VIRTUAL ENTERTAINMENTS AND COMMUNICATION.

* SEE, MALM (2016) Pg. 315 AND CHAPTER 2 OF THIS BOOK.

THIS REALM OF CONSUMPTION IS WHERE PETROCULTURE PLAYS A KEY ROLE IN CAPTURING THE CONSENT OF ORDINARY PEOPLE, AND TRYING TO CONVINCE US THAT IT IS HYPOCRITICAL AND EVEN NIHILISTIC TO IMAGING ALTERNATIVES TO THE PETROLEUM ECONOMY.

WAKING UP FROM THIS DREAM SET IN CONCRETE AND ASPHALT WILL REQUIRE PROVIDING ALTERNATIVES TO THE SPECIFIC KINDS OF EXCESS THAT PETROCULTURE HAS SO SUCCESSFULLY CAPTURED AND CONDITIONED,

THIS IS A STUMBLING BLOCK UPON WHICH MUCH CONTEMPORARY "GREEN" ACTIVISM FALTERS: IT TURNS PARTICIPATION IN THE SAME OLD PETROCULTURE (OR ONE'S ESCAPE FROM IT) INTO FURTHER SIGNIFIERS OF CLASS STATUS, ON ONE HAND, WHILE THREATENING TO EXACERBATE AUSTERITY AND DEPRIVATION ON THE OTHER.

ELECTRIC

COLLECT THEM ALL!

DISCOURSES OF CONSERVATION AND CONSTRAINT THAT REMAIN WITHIN AN EXPANSIVE, MARKET-ORIENTED FRAMEWORK ARE ALMOST GUARANTEED TO KINDLE AGGRESSIVE, SEEMINGLY IRRATIONAL RESISTANCE FROM PEOPLE WHOSE REMAINING SHARE OF LUXURY IS PROVIDED BY PETROCULTURAL HABITS AND INFRASTRUCTURE.

WE IMAGINE THAT THE END OF OIL SPELLS THE END OF OUR EASE AND PLEASURES...

WELCOME TO THE EDGE OF THE UNIVERSE NO SHOPPING CARTS BEYOND THIS POINT!

...WHEN PERHAPS WHAT WE NEED IS A NEW WAY OF UNDERSTANDING AND RELATING TO THE REALITIES OF ENERGY AND SURPLUS THEMSELVES.

THE FRENCH PHILOSOPHER **GEORGES BATAILLE'S** UNDERSTANDING OF ENERGY IS INDISPENSABLE FOR COMING TO TERMS WITH THE EXCESSIVE AND SEEMINGLY CONTRADICTORY DRIVES THAT CHARACTERIZE OUR CONTEMPORARY ATTACHMENT TO THE **PETROCULTURES** THAT ARE DESTROYING THE PLANET.

I WILL BEGIN WITH A BASIC FACT: THE LIVING ORGANISM, IN A SITUATION DETERMINED BY THE PLAY OF ENERGY ON THE SURFACE OF THE GLOBE, ORDINARILY RECEIVES MORE ENERGY THAN IS NECESSARY FOR MAINTAINING LIFE... *

WHAT BATAILLE CALLS THE "GENERAL ECONOMY" IS A UNIVERSAL NORM OF EXPENDITURE WITHOUT RECUPERATION: THE PURE, PLAYFUL SQUANDERING OF ENERGY, FOR WHICH THE SUN PROVIDES A MODEL: THIS IS THE ENERGIC REALITY IGNORED BY WHAT BATAILLE CALLS THE "RESTRICTED ECONOMY" OR THE MAJORITY OF MODERN ECONOMIC THEORIES BASED ON RATIONAL SELF-INTEREST.

... EXCESS ENERGY (WEALTH) CAN BE USED FOR THE GROWTH OF A SYSTEM (e.g., AN ORGANISM); IF THE SYSTEM CAN NO LONGER GROW, OR IF THE EXCESS CANNOT BE COMPLETELY ABSORBED IN ITS GROWTH, IT MUST NECESSARILY BE LOST WITHOUT PROFIT; IT MUST BE SPENT WILLINGLY OR NOT, GLORIOUSLY OR CATASTROPHICALLY. *

THIS ENERGY/WEALTH THAT CANNOT BE ABSORBED IN GROWTH BATAILLE CALLS **The ACCURSED SHARE**

THE MANNER IN WHICH THIS SHARE IS DISSIPATED SHAPES THE PARTICULAR CHARACTER OF PEOPLE AND CULTURES...

* BATAILLE (1998) Pg. 21.

...AS WELL AS THEIR MOST DESTRUCTIVE TENDENCIES...

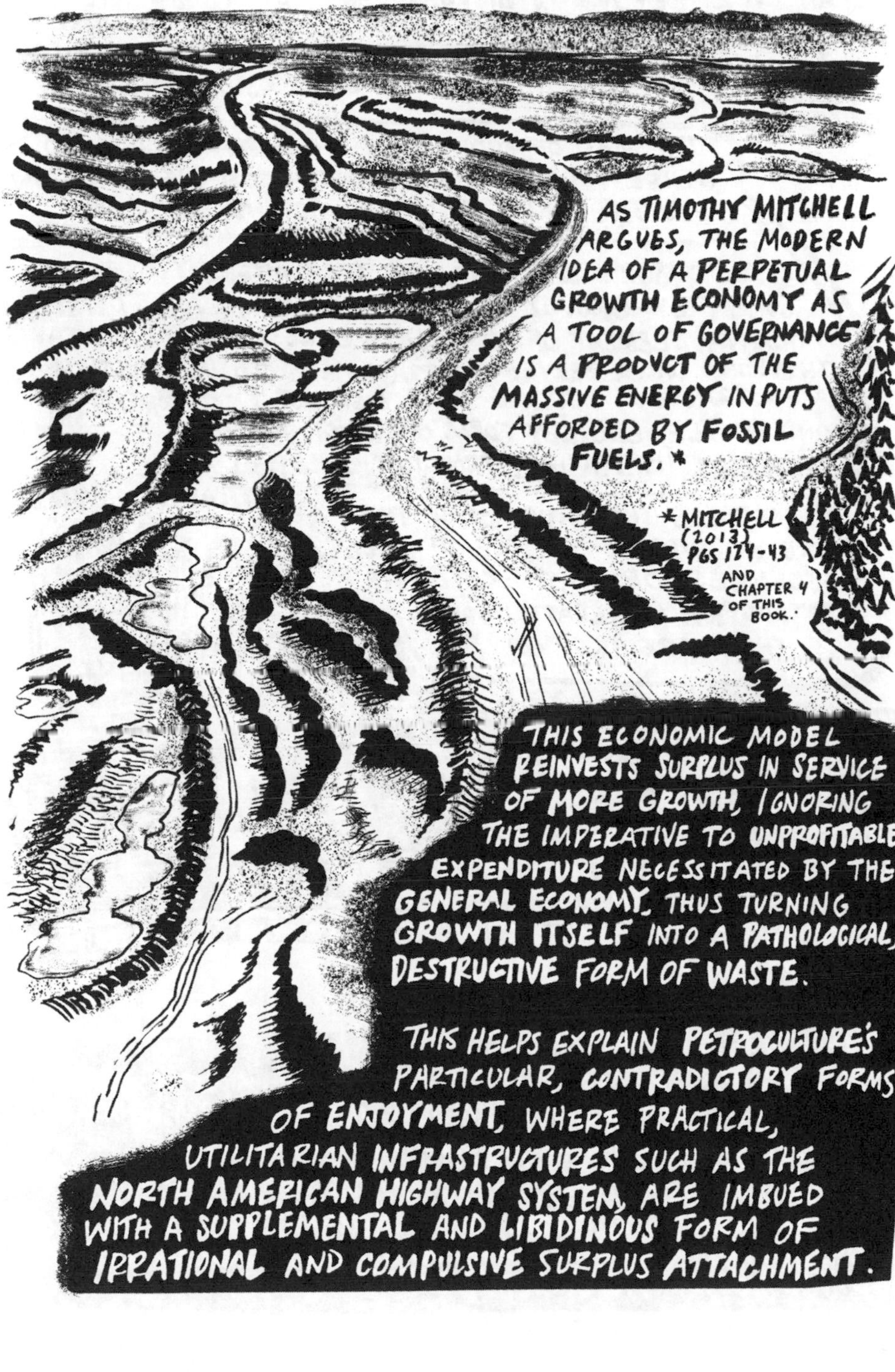

THE GLOBAL PRODUCTION OF SURPLUS WEALTH IS GREATER THAN EVER BEFORE IN HISTORY, AND YET THESE SPOILS HAVE NOT PROVIDED GREATER SECURITY OR SOCIAL MOBILITY IN EVEN THE MOST AFFLUENT NATIONS. FAITH IN THE "FREE MARKET" SUPPLIES NO OTHER SET OF GOALS ASIDE FROM BLIND GROWTH.

THE MAN OF INDUSTRIAL GROWTH - HAVING NO OTHER PURPOSE THAN GROWTH - ON THE CONTRARY IS THE EXPRESSION OF SOMNOLENCE. *

A SUPPOSEDLY RATIONAL SELF-INTEREST DEFINED SOLELY BY GROWTH IGNORES THE LARGER AND DETERMINATIVE ELEMENT OF PROFLIGATE EXCESS - WHICH THUS TAKES THE FORM OF A PERVERSE ATTACHMENT TO DESTRUCTION, A PROTRACTED, MASSIVE WAR AGAINST ENVIRONMENTS AND PEOPLE, ONE KEY FORM OF WHICH IS THE SEEMINGLY UTILITARIAN, PROSAIC CIRCULATION OF TRAFFIC.

RELIGION IS THE SATISFACTION THAT A SOCIETY GIVES TO THE USE OF EXCESS RESOURCES, OR RATHER TO THEIR DESTRUCTION (AT LEAST INSOFAR AS THEY ARE USEFUL). **

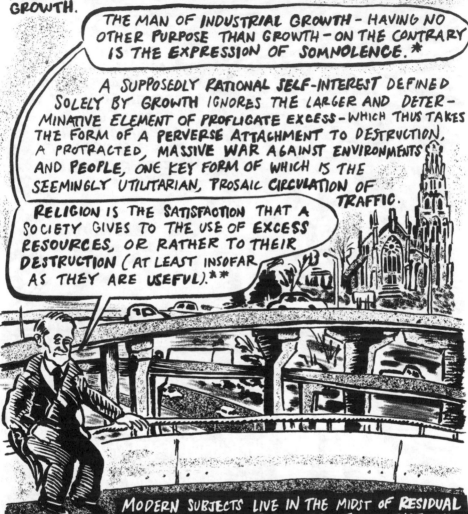

MODERN SUBJECTS LIVE IN THE MIDST OF RESIDUAL MONUMENTS TO OLDER CULTURAL FORMS THAT DID REALIZE, HOWEVER IMPERFECTLY, AN ORDER OF PURE EXPENDITURE AMIDST THEIR CONSCIOUSLY GUIDING PRINCIPLES.

OUR OWN DISAVOWAL OF THE GENERAL ECONOMY CREATES A LARGELY UNCONSCIOUS MODE OF CATASTROPHIC SURPLUS EXPENDITURE DISGUISED AS "PROGRESS." *BATAILLE (1991) Pg.137. ** Pg. 120.

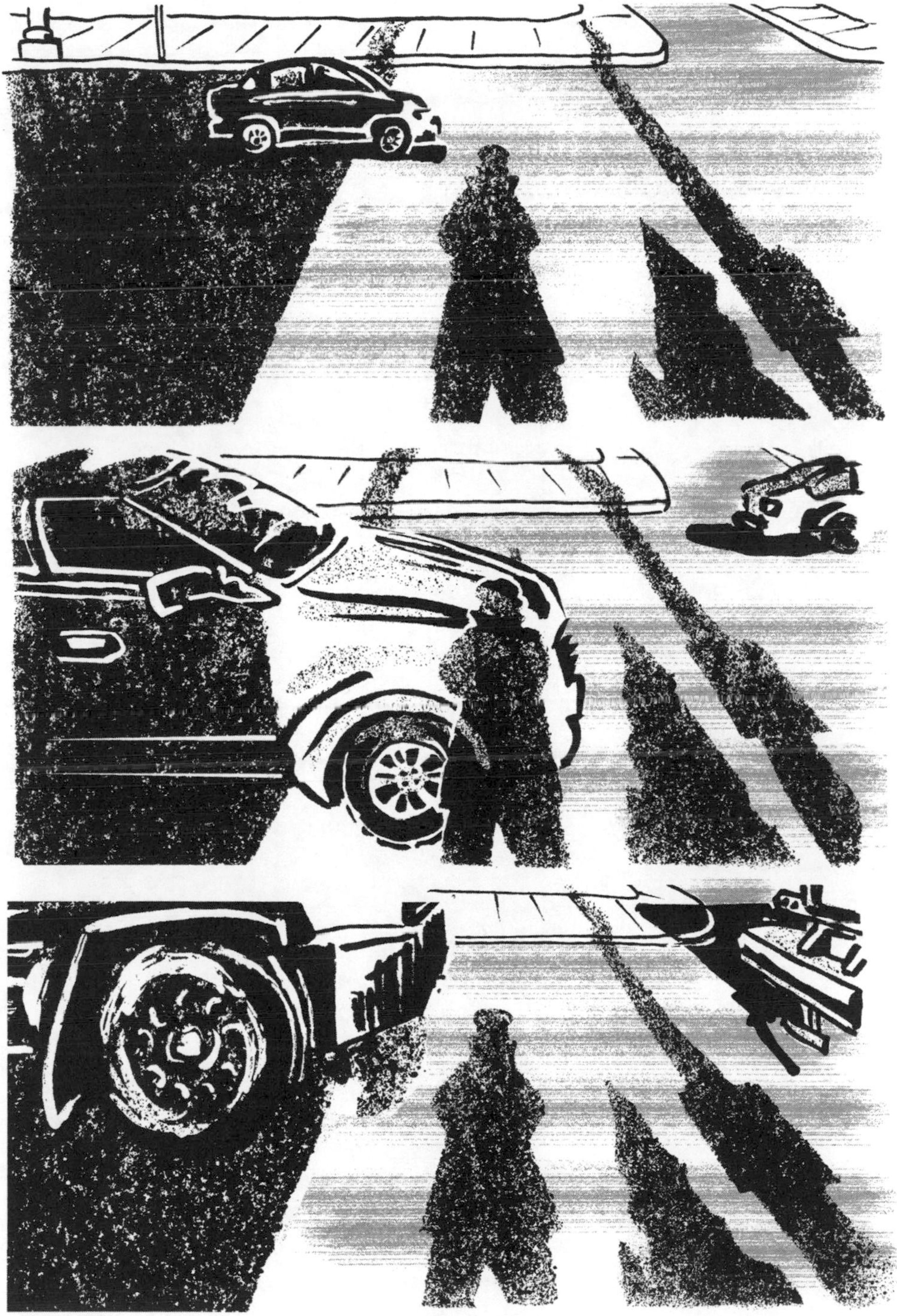

Chapter 8
The Beach

Chapter 8

"The Menace

AS ANDREW PENDAKIS POINTS OUT... WHENEVER CINEMA REQUIRES AN IMAGE OF "BEING ITSELF," AN IMAGE OF THINGS AS THEY ARE IN THE BROADEST POSSIBLE SENSE, IT USES A STANDARD TRICK...

... THE CAMERA IS SITUATED IN SUCH A WAY AS TO SIMPLY RECORD A FLOW OF TRAFFIC...

FORTINI'S
MARKET WITH HEART

DOLLAR ZONE | CATS! DOGS!

TIMMY'S

410

BEING & OIL

... AS IF BY MAGIC THE SIGHT OF CARS PASSING IN QUICK SUCCESSION GENERATES A THOUGHT OF EXISTENCE AS SUCH, CAPTURED IN ITS MOST RELAXED AND UNSELFCONSCIOUS STATE. *

TRAFFIC IS THE ONTOLOGICAL BASELINE OF MODERN CINEMA, ARGUES PENDAKIS. RATHER THAN CLOUDS OR RIVERS, WE RECOGNIZE STREAMS OF TRAFFIC AS REAL.

* PENDAKIS "BEING & OIL.." (2017) P. 377.

CONVERSLEY, MANY HORROR FILMS USE OVERHEAD PANS OF CARS NAVIGATING LONELY ROADS SURROUNDED BY TREES OR FIELDS TO GENERATE A VAGUE SENSE OF UNEASE AND DREAD...

PERHAPS THE OPENING SCENES OF FILMS LIKE STANLEY KUBRIC'S THE SHINING ARE EXPRESSING THE ISOLATING AFFECTIVE REALITY OF DRIVING WITH THESE TABLEAUS.

LEGIONS OF CAR COMMERCIALS DEPICT THE TROPE OF "VEHICLES IN NATURE" IN A DECIDEDLY MORE TRIUMPHALIST AND ROMANTIC REGISTER, BUT THE SAME SET OF BINARIES, NATURE AND CULTURE, REMAIN INTACT.

THE BITTER IRONY OF THESE COMMERCIALS IS THAT THEY MOBILIZE IMAGES OF A PRISTINE NATURE THAT DOESN'T EXIST IN SERVICE OF FURTHER DESTROYING THE ACTUALLY EXISTING WORLD.

OBSCURED BY THE DICHOTOMY BETWEEN A REALM OF "NATURAL FREEDOM" TO WHICH DRIVING SUPPOSEDLY PROVIDES ACCESS AND A SECOND, CONCRETE WILDERNESS FROM WHICH SO MANY CAR COMMERCIALS PROMISE PROTECTION, IS A THIRD OPTION...

AS A POETIC TERM FOR THAT WHICH PERSISTS, UNOWNED AND UNOWNABLE DESPITE THE PRIVATIZATION AND SUBSUMPTION OF OUR SHARED WORLD BY A VORACIOUS PETROCULTURE...

...LET'S BORROW A SLOGAN FROM THE REVOLUTIONARY ENERGIES OF MAY, 1968...

AND JUST CALL IT

THE BEACH

THAT LIMINAL SHIFTING SPACE BETWEEN LAND AND WATER, BEATEN BY WAVES AND WARMED BY SUNLIGHT...

PROVIDES A FITTING FIGURE FOR THE COMMON WORLD THAT CONTINUES TO SUSTAIN US DESPITE MODERNITY'S RELENTLESS DRIVE TO SUFFOCATE ITS EXISTENCE.

IT'S NOT AS THOUGH CONTEMPORARY BEACHES ARE PARTICULARLY SHARED SPACES — MANY ARE PRIVATIZED AND COMMODITIZED.

PRIVATE PROPERTY

BUT EVEN THE MOST COMMERCIALIZED AND SPOILED BEACHES CAN REMIND US OF RELATIONSHIPS, GENEALOGIES AND RHYTHMS THAT PETROCULTURE AND MODERN LIFE HAVE TEMPORARILY MUTED.

THE BEACH REMINDS US OF THE COMMON OCEANIC ORIGINS OF ALL LIFE...

JUST AS RISING WATER LEVELS REMIND US OF OUR SHARED(?) PRECARIOUS FUTURE.

AS THE POETS AND ACTIVISTS OF MAY 68 REMIND US, THE BEACH IS EVERYWHERE, LOCKED BENEATH THE PAVEMENT STONES WAITING TO BE RELEASED

ONE OF MY EARLIEST EXPERIENCES OF THE BEACH OCCURRED IN THE MID 1980S. STREET SKATING - SKATEBOARDING IN PUBLIC PLACES RATHER THAN PRIVATE SKATE PARKS - WAS JUST STARTING TO CATCH ON.

I PRACTICED ALL THE TIME AND WORE OUT A PAIR OF SHOES EVERY COUPLE OF WEEKS.

I HAD A SMALL GROUP OF SKATING FRIENDS. ONE AFTERNOON AS WE WERE SKATING DOWNTOWN, MORE AND MORE SKATERS STARTED JOINING US FROM SIDE STREETS AND ALLEYWAYS.

THERE WERE KIDS WE DIDN'T KNOW, FROM OTHER SCHOOLS, BUT WE SHARED A COMMON PASSION.

SOON WE WERE A MASS OF SKATERS TAKING OVER THE MAIN STREET, RUMMBLING ALONG ON OUR BOARDS, STOPPING TRAFFIC.

THE FUTURE OF PHONES

Mar SAM SAMI

RUMMMMM MBBB

THERE, IN DOWNTOWN BARRIE, ONTARIO, WE HAD FOUND THE BEACH.

SKATEBOARD WHEELS ARE MADE FROM POLYURETHANE, AN OIL-BASED SUBSTANCE.

WHEN THEY ROLL OVERTOP THE IRREGULARITIES OF STREETS THE SOUND IS AMPLIFIED AND BROADCAST BY THE WOODEN BODY OF THE SKATEBOARD DECK.

THE SOUND HAS ALWAYS REMINDED ME OF THE ROARING OF OCEAN WAVES.

RWWOAWRR

IN A WORLD THAT HAS BEEN MADE OVER IN THE IMAGE OF CARS AND PETROLEUM, STREET SKATING USES THE SAME TECHNOLOGIES AND INFRASTRUCTURES TO HELP THE STREETS REMEMBER THE BEACH

BENEATH THE IMPETUS TO MARKET A WHITE, MASCULINIST VERSION OF CALIFORNIAN SURFER REBELLION TO MIDDLE-CLASS SUBURBAN YOUTH, WHATEVER TRULY COUNTER-CULTURAL ELEMENTS SKATEBOARDING FOSTERS LAY IN THE *ALTERNATIVE RELATIONSHIPS* IT ALLOWS PEOPLE TO FORM WITH *EACH OTHER* AND THE *ENVIRONMENT.*

INFRASTRUCTURES DESIGNED TO PROMOTE FANTASTICAL AND INDIVIDUALIZED FREEDOM OF MOBILITY ARE *SUBVERTED* BY *SKATEBOARDERS* TO GENERATE A *HUMAN-POWERED,* AFFECTIVE *LIBERATION* AND SENSE OF *PLAY,* OFTEN COUPLED WITH AND *REINFORCED* BY THE *CAMARADERIE* OF *OTHER SKATERS.*

BUT THIS EXPERIENCE OF *THE BEACH* REMAINS TIED TO THE SAME INFRASTRUCTURES SKATING *MOMENTARILY* AND *FUGITIVELY* SUBVERTS.

THE QUESTION REMAINS: HOW MIGHT WE FIND A SIMILAR SENSE OF *ENJOYMENT* AND *LIBERATION* IN ASSOCIATION WITH *POST-OIL INFRASTRUCTURES?*

OR PERHAPS THIS IS THE **WRONG QUESTION** TO ASK.

WE CAN'T KNOW **AHEAD** OF TIME WHAT LIFE UNDER A **DIFFERENT ENERGY SYSTEM** WILL **LOOK** OR **FEEL** LIKE.

IT WILL SURELY BRING NEW **RELATIONSHIPS**, **OPPORTUNITIES** AND **STRUGGLES**. BUT IMAGINE, FOR INSTANCE, **WORK** THAT IS NOT **COERCED** AND **EXPLOITATIVE**. WHAT MIGHT THAT **FEEL** LIKE, AND WOULD WE EVEN **CALL** IT **WORK**?

HERE WE MIGHT RECALL THE JOKE: HOW MANY **SKATEBOARDERS** DOES IT TAKE TO CHANGE A LIGHTBULB?

JUST **ONE**, BUT YOU HAVE TO GIVE HIM **TWENTY** TRIES.

A SKATER'S COMPULSION TO REPEAT IS JUST AS MONOTONOUS AS THE MOST MUNDANE OF JOBS, BUT SKATEBOARDERS DO NOT OFTEN SEE IT AS "WORK."

BUILDING A SUSTAINABLE AND EQUITABLE FUTURE, ONE CAPABLE OF REPAIRING THE DAMAGE AND TRAUMA THAT LONG LEGACIES OF VIOLENCE, INJUSTICE AND NEGLECT HAVE PRODUCED, REQUIRES THE WORK OF MANY HANDS...

THE ENGRAINED HABITS AND VICES OF CENTURIES AND MILLENNIA WILL NOT CHANGE EASILY OR OVERNIGHT. THERE WILL YET BE MANY FAILURES AND SETBACKS...

...BUT, AS THE ZEN PROVERB SAYS,

FALL DOWN FIVE TIMES, GET UP SIX.

LIKE THE DOGGED ACTIVITY OF SKATEBOARDERS, THESE FAILURES CONTRIBUTE TO THE UNPREDICTABLE, WONDROUS MOMENT WHEN LONG EFFORTS COALESCE INTO A NEWLY INTERNALIZED ABILITY TO DO WHAT PREVIOUSLY SEEMED IMPOSSIBLE.

AND YET, NEITHER THE "MANY HANDS" RHETORIC WE MIGHT ASSOCIATE WITH INDUSTRIAL UNIONISM, NOR THE NEOLIBERAL, INDIVIDUALIZED MODES OF VIRTUOSITY AND SELF-FULFILLMENT THROUGH WORK (IN A SOCIETY STRIPPED OF THE PRO-TECTIONS AND SECURITIES HARD-WON BY THE FORMER) CAN ADEQUATELY CAPTURE THE STAKES AND POTENTIALS OF OUR CURRENT PREDICAMENT.

WHICH OF THE FOLLOWING BEST DESCRIBES YOU AS A PERSON? (CHECK ALL THAT APPLY.)

☐ SELF-STARTER
☐ EDUCATED
☐ EBUILLIENT
☐ PROBLEM SOLVER
☐ MOTIVATED
☐ WELL GROOMED
☐ RELIABLE
☐ WATER RESISTANT
☐ AGREEABLE
☐ PEPPY
☐ AGILE
☐ DETAIL ORIENTED
☐ ARTISTIC
☐ COURTEOUS
☐ RESILIENT

☐ TEAM PLAYER
☐ EAGER
☐ CONNECTED
☐ CAREFULL
☐ HIGHLY MOTIVATED
☐ STEADFAST
☐ SOLVENT
☐ SINGULAR
☐ MULTIFACETED
☐ INDEPENDENT
☐ PREPARED
☐ PERSISTENT
☐ PUNCTUAL
☐ UNASSUMING
☐ POSEABLE

☐ WILLING TO WORK WEEKENDS AND HOLIDAYS

THE NEW SUBJECTIVITIES THAT MIGHT EMERGE THROUGH STRUGGLES FOR POLITICAL AND SOCIAL TRANSFORMATION MUST BE COLLECTIVE ON A GLOBAL SCALE AT THE LEVEL OF SPECIES. THIS WILL REQUIRE RETHINKING CATEGORIES LIKE ETHNICITY, GENDER, CLASS AND CULTURE THEMSELVES.

AT THE SAME TIME, THESE STRUGGLES MUST BE LOCALLY NUANCED — A MODALITY THAT MARKET LOGICS CAN ONLY EVER RECOGNIZE AS FORMS OF VALUE TO BE EXTRACTED, COMMODITIZED AND ULTIMATELY DESTROYED. AS GREG BROWN SINGS...

CAN'T GO TO THE COUNTRY — THE COUNTRY ISN'T THERE. IT GOT CHOPPED UP AND MORTGAGED AND VANISHED INTO THIN AIR. IT'S A PAINT-BY-NUMBER AND IT COSTS A MILLION BUCKS DOWN AT THE PAWN...

...I WAS LOOKING FOR WHAT I LOVED WHATEVER IT WAS, IT'S GONE.

WITH HUMAN POTENTIALS BLOCKED BY AND UNREALIZABLE DUE TO PETROCULTURAL CONTRADICTIONS, THE FOUNDATIONAL POLITICAL ACTION CONSISTS OF LIBERATING THE SPACE, TIME AND RESOURCES NEEDED FOR SOMETHING TRULY NEW TO EMERGE.

SUPERMAN DON'T LIVE HERE ANYMORE

IN THIS PROJECT, THE VERY DE-RAILMENT OF OUR HOPES AND EXPECTATIONS MIGHT PROVIDE THE NECESSARY GAP, THE FAVOURABLE CONDITIONS, FOR SUBSTANTIAL CHANGE.

I TRIED TO ESCAPE PETROCULTURE BUT ALL I GOT WAS SOME AIR

OUR SUBJECTIVITIES ARE SPLIT BETWEEN IMPOSSIBLE INJUNCTIONS TO ADAPT TO A PATHOLOGICAL, ALIENATING PETROCULTURE AND WHATEVER TOEHOLDS OF RESISTANCE AND FREEDOM WE MANAGE TO UNCOMFORTABLY AND TEMPORARILY NAVIGATE.

BUT WHAT IF WE ALL JUST STOPPED?

GIVEN PETRO-MODERNITY'S REFINED TECHNIQUES FOR USURPING PAST, PRESENT AND FUTURE RESERVES OF TIME, SPACE AND ENERGY, ANY ALTERNATIVE FORMATIONS MUST BE GROUNDED IN THE THREE 'R's: REAPPROPRIATION, REDISTRIBUTION AND REFUSAL

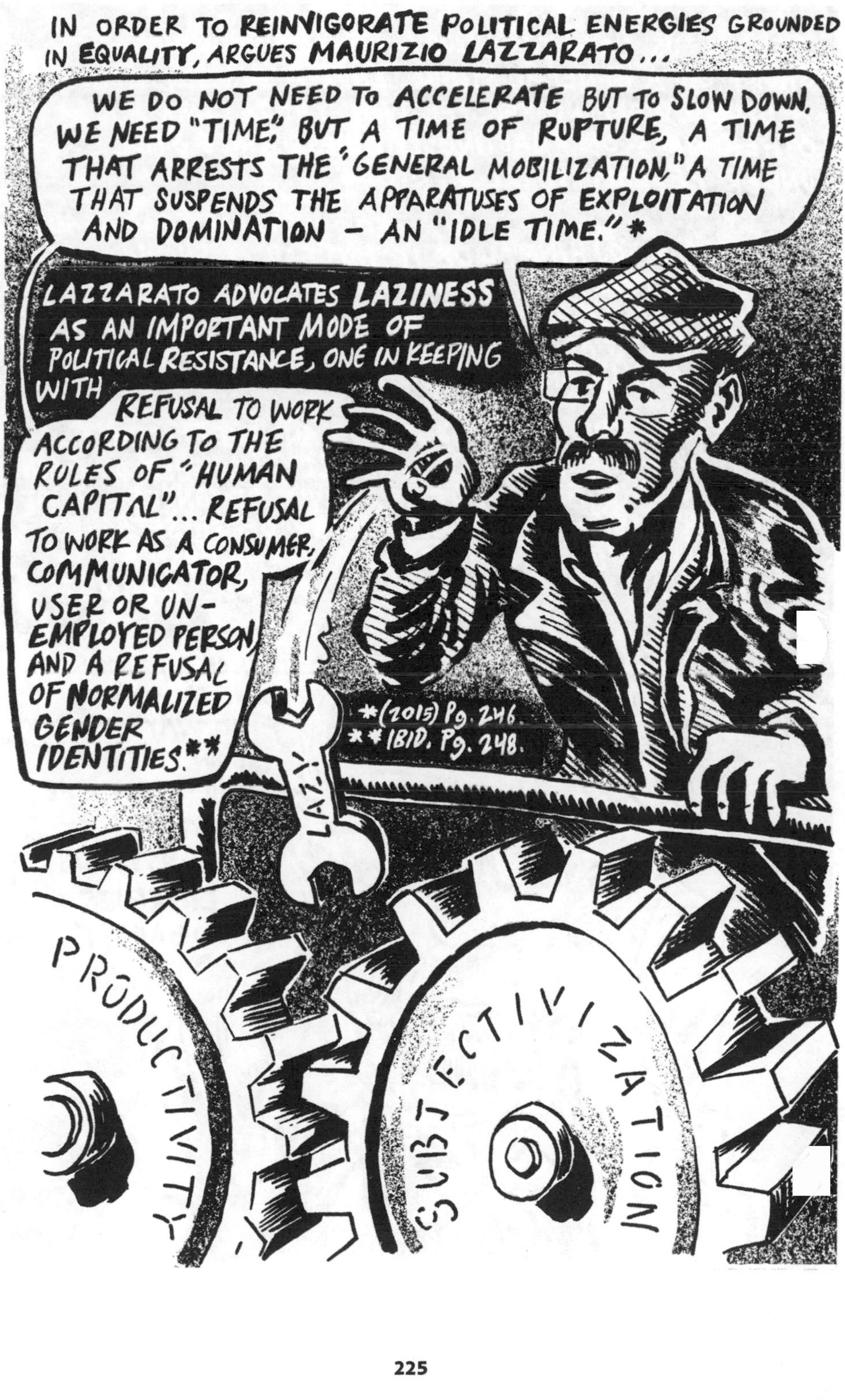

IN ORDER TO REINVIGORATE POLITICAL ENERGIES GROUNDED IN EQUALITY, ARGUES MAURIZIO LAZZARATO...
WE DO NOT NEED TO ACCELERATE BUT TO SLOW DOWN. WE NEED "TIME," BUT A TIME OF RUPTURE, A TIME THAT ARRESTS THE "GENERAL MOBILIZATION," A TIME THAT SUSPENDS THE APPARATUSES OF EXPLOITATION AND DOMINATION – AN "IDLE TIME."*
LAZZARATO ADVOCATES LAZINESS AS AN IMPORTANT MODE OF POLITICAL RESISTANCE, ONE IN KEEPING WITH
REFUSAL TO WORK ACCORDING TO THE RULES OF "HUMAN CAPITAL"... REFUSAL TO WORK AS A CONSUMER, COMMUNICATOR, USER OR UN-EMPLOYED PERSON, AND A REFUSAL OF NORMALIZED GENDER IDENTITIES.**
*(2015) Pg. 246.
**IBID. Pg. 248.
LAZY
PRODUCTIVITY
SUBJECTIVIZATION

FEW OF US HAVE THE LUXURY OF NOT WORKING. BUT SHORT OF A GENERAL STRIKE (NOT A BAD IDEA FROM A GLOBAL WARMING PERSPECTIVE) THERE REMAIN OTHER WAYS OF ENACTING LAZINESS WHILE STILL UNDER PETROCULTURAL REGIMES.

FOR INSTANCE, DEAR READER, SINCE YOU HAVE MADE IT THIS FAR, I SHOULD NOTE THAT THIS BOOK IS THE PRODUCT OF HUNDREDS OF HOURS OF EXCESSIVE LABOUR. COMICS ARE A TERRIBLY INEFFICIENT WAY TO EXPRESS IDEAS AND RESEARCH, FROM A TIME AND ENERGY PERSPECTIVE.

BUT IT IS THIS VERY EXCESSIVE AND INEFFICIENT MEDIUM — THE ARTISTRY CAREFULLY LAVISHED ON EACH IMAGE AS THE ARGUMENT IS SLOWLY ADVANCED — THAT CONSTITUTES THE UNIQUE CHARACTER OF THESE PAGES FULL OF BORROWED IDEAS AND THE DESIRE FOR CHANGE.

IN SHORT, IF YOU HAVE TO WORK, FIND WAYS TO SLOW IT DOWN AND DIRECT THE SYSTEM'S MONSTROUS ENERGIES AGAINST ITSELF.

JUST LIKE "OIL CONSUMPTION" IS OFTEN DEPLOYED AS A HOMOGENEOUS TERM, THEREBY COVERING OVER VARIOUS DIFFERENT RELATIONSHIPS TO ENERGY, SO TOO DOES THE IDEOLOGY OF "WORK" SPURIOUSLY EQUATE MANY DIFFERENT KINDS OF ACTIVITY...

THE SOLAR ADVANTAGE

FROM THE ENERGIES EXPENDED TO MAINTAIN CONTROL OVER WORKERS AND RESOURCES...

GASOLINE DREAMS

TO THE ENERGY EXPENDED IN SERVICE OF MERELY REPRODUCING ONE'S ABILITY TO SHOW UP AGAIN AT A JOB...

...TO THE ARTISTIC ACTIVITY OF WRESTLING WITH IDEAS, FORMS AND DEADLINES.

ALL OF THESE ACTIONS ARE DESCRIBED AS "WORK," BUT THEY ALL **FEEL** DIFFERENT BECAUSE OF THE DIFFERENT POWER RELATIONSHIPS THAT STRUCTURE AND INFORM THEM.

I'VE BEEN SITTING HERE FOR OVER TWO YEARS, MAKING THIS BOOK. IT'S MOST SURELY **WORK**, BUT IT'S ALSO **SOMETHING MORE**: A **PRAYER**, A **HOPE**, A **MEDITATION** AND A **SCREAM** TOWARDS THE **TRAFFIC** THAT DAILY PASSES OUTSIDE MY WINDOW...

WAKE UP!

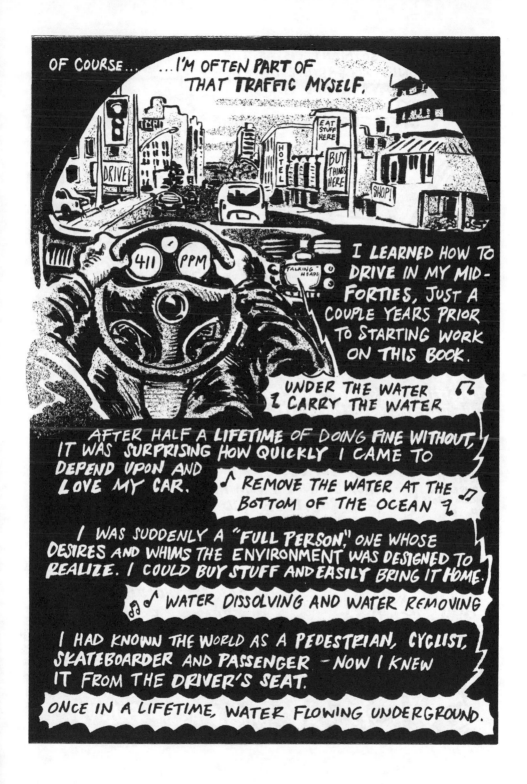

OF COURSE... ...I'M OFTEN **PART OF** THAT **TRAFFIC MYSELF**.

EAT STUFF HERE

HOTEL

BUY THINGS HERE

SHOP!

DRIVE

411 PPM

TALKING HEADS

I LEARNED HOW TO DRIVE IN MY MID-FORTIES, JUST A COUPLE YEARS PRIOR TO STARTING WORK ON THIS BOOK.

UNDER THE WATER
I CARRY THE WATER

AFTER HALF A **LIFETIME** OF DOING **FINE WITHOUT**, IT WAS **SURPRISING** HOW QUICKLY I CAME TO DEPEND UPON AND LOVE MY CAR.

REMOVE THE WATER AT THE BOTTOM OF THE OCEAN

I WAS SUDDENLY A "**FULL PERSON**," ONE WHOSE DESIRES AND WHIMS THE ENVIRONMENT WAS DESIGNED TO REALIZE. I COULD BUY STUFF AND EASILY BRING IT HOME.

WATER DISSOLVING AND WATER REMOVING

I HAD KNOWN THE WORLD AS A **PEDESTRIAN, CYCLIST, SKATEBOARDER** AND **PASSENGER** – NOW I KNEW IT FROM THE **DRIVER'S SEAT**.

ONCE IN A LIFETIME, WATER FLOWING UNDERGROUND.

THERE ARE SO MANY VISTAS THAT ARE ONLY ACCESSIBLE FROM HIGHWAYS WHERE THE SKYLINE AND SENSE OF OPEN SPACE ARE SUBLIME.

THE WINDSHIELD BECAME MY SCREEN, TRANSFORMING THE WORLD INTO A VAST MOTION PICTURE.*

* SEE: ROSS (1995) Pgs. 22-54. FOR THE ORIGINS OF THIS PARALLEL.

AND EVEN WHEN THE CAR FAILS TO DELIVER ON WHAT KRISTIN ROSS IDENTIFIES AS THE "AMERICAN MYTH OF SPEED AND FREEDOM,"** DUE TO EVER MORE CONGESTED STREETS AND CITIES, IT PROMISES

** ROSS Pg. 46.

*** THIS QUOTE IS CONDENSED FROM, ROSS Pg. 55.

... COMPESATORY MYTHS OF THE CAR AS A PROTECTED INTERIOR SPACE, QUASI-DOMESTIC (BUT ALSO ANTI-DOMESTIC), A HOME AWAY FROM HOME, A PLACE FOR SOLITUDE AND INTIMACY. ***

PERHAPS THE FINAL MUTATION IN CAR MYTHOLOGY WILL BE THE SPACE OF QUIET SOLITUDE AND CINEMATIC PERSPECTIVE IT OFFERS FOR WATCHING THE WORLD AS IT BURNS..

WHICH RETURNS US TO THE START OF THIS BOOK, WHERE EVAN MAURO AND I WERE DRIVING THROUGH THE SMOKE-FILLED STREETS OF VANCOUVER.

...THE HIGHWAY IS YOUR GIRLFRIEND AS YOU GO BY QUICK, SUBURBAN TREES, SUBURBAN SPEED...

ALONGSIDE CHECKING OUT NEW HIGHWAY INFRASTRUCTURE, WE WERE ON A TOUR OF HISTORIC VANCOUVER SKATEBOARD PARKS...

GONNA DRIVE TO THE STOP 'N SHOP WITH THE RADIO ON AT NIGHT...

ONE OF WHICH IS A SKATER-BUILT SPACE IN AN ABANDONED TRANSIT TUNNEL. LEESIDE PARK IS NAMED AFTER LEE MATASI, A SKATER AND ARTIST WHO HELPED DISCOVER AND TRANSFORM THE SPACE, BEFORE HE WAS TRAGICALLY MURDERED IN 2005.*

THE SPACE REMINDS ME OF DELEUZE'S FIGURES OF THE MOLE AND SERPENT.**

TRYING TO HOLD HOLD OUT FOR NOW... WITH THE ICE CAPS MELTING DOWN...

THE FLOWING, UNEVEN CONTOURS OF LEESIDE, ADORNED WITH GRAFFITI, CAPTURES BOTH THE MOLE'S UNDERGROUND ACTIVITIES AND THE FLUID MOVEMENTS OF THE SERPENT.

...WITH THAT TRANSISTOR SOUND OF AND MY CHEVROLET TERRA PLANE GOING ROUND, ROUND, ROUND...

* ROBINSON (2011).
** (1992) AND CHAPTER 2 OF THIS BOOK.

231

PERHAPS SUBCULTURAL SPACES LIKE THIS ARE WHAT HAPPENS WHEN THE SUBVERSIVE ENERGIES OF THE MOLE ARE SWALLOWED BY THE FLUID CONTROL STRUCTURES OF THE SERPENT...

EACH IS TRANSFORMED TO SOME EXENT BY THE OTHER, BUT THE RESULT IS ALTERIOR SPACES OF FASCINATION AND BEAUTY THAT DON'T DIRECTLY THREATEN THE STATUS QUO,...

AND MIGHT EVEN REINFORCE DOMINANT VALUES UNDER THE GUISE OF REBELLION,

PERHAPS A SIMILAR FATE WILL BEFALL THE TRANSFORM- ATIVE POTENTIAL OF THE SHIFT AWAY FROM OIL: THE OPPORTUNITY TO BUILD A MORE EQUITABLE, LESS DESTRUCTIVE AND EXPLOITATIVE WORLD WILL BE CO-OPTED BY THE SAME EXTRACTIVE AND VIOLENT TENDENCIES THAT CHARACTERIZE PETRO-CULTURE.

AS IMRE SZEMAN POINTS OUT, SOLAR IDEOLOGIES
HINGE UPON TWO KEY PROMISES:
ENERGY WITHOUT FUEL (I.E., WITHOUT
BURNING MATTER IN SOME FORM),
AND INFINTE ENERGY; BUT THIS IS
REALLY JUST THE PROMISE OF BUSINESS-AS-
USUAL: IN THE WEST, UNDER PETROCULTURE,
"WE HAVE ALWAYS USED ENERGY AS
ENERGY AND NOT FUEL; AND WE HAVE ALSO
TREATED ENERGY AS IF IT WERE
INFINITE." *

WITHOUT CRITICAL
AND POLITICAL INTERVENTIONS,
THE SHIFT TO RENEWABLES
PROMISES TO FURTHER
PETROCULTURAL LOGICS OF
EXTRACTION, VIOLENCE,
ENCLOSURE OF THE
COMMONS AND UNEVEN
DEVELOPMENT.

* SZEMAN
(2020) Pg. 9.

** AFTER OIL
(2019) Pg. 2.

"APPROACHING
SOLAR IN
THIS WAY, AS
AN ENERGY
SOURCE
IMMEDIATELY
AVAILABLE,
INFINITE IN SUPPLY
AND NEGLIGIBLE
IN COSTS IS TO
SETTLE UPON THE
SUN AS THE LAST
FRONTIER OF AN EXTRACTIVE
ENTERPRISE WHOSE NAMES HAVE BEEN
SLAVERY, COLONIALISM, INDUSTRIAL
CAPITALISM, AND IMPERIALISM." **

233

AND YET, **SUNLIGHT** IN ITS NON-FOSSILIZED FORM COULD BE OUR **GREATEST ALLY** IN REVERSING THE EFFECTS OF GLOBAL WARMING, BUT SUN AND WIND CANNOT BE **COMMODITIZED** AND TRANSPORTED WITH THE SAME SCALE, EASE AND **MASSIVE** RETURNS ON INVESTMENT THAT FOSSIL FUELS PROVIDE. AS **ANDREAS MALM** OBSERVES, THE SUN'S ENERGY IS A **FREE GIFT** OF NATURE...

THE ONLY THING THAT HAS EXCHANGE VALUE IS THE TECHNOLOGY FOR CAPTURING, CONVERTING AND STORING THE ENERGY OF THE FUEL, AND LIKE ALL TECHNOLOGIES, IT IS SUBJECT TO ECONOMIES OF SCALE: MASS PRODUCTION SLASHES THE COSTS OF PANELS AND TURBINES.*

FOSSIL CAPITAL

THE **HIGH INITIAL INVESTMENTS** REQUIRED BY **RENEWABLES** ARE NOT APPEALING TO PRIVATE INVESTORS WHO CAN MAKE MUCH GREATER **PROFITS** FROM THE EXISTING PETROL ECONOMY.

CAPITAL DID NOT ENGAGE IN THE **TRANSITION** AS MANY HAD EXPECTED IT WOULD, LARGELY BECAUSE THE ENERGY FROM THE [SOLAR AND WIND] **FLOW** LOST SO MUCH OF ITS EXCHANGE-VALUE AT THE VERY SAME TIME THAT ITS SOCIAL USE-VALUE — SLOWING DOWN CLIMATE CHANGE — ROSE TOWARDS PRICELESS HEIGHTS**

*MALM, 2016, PG. 369 ; **IBID. PG. 371.

234

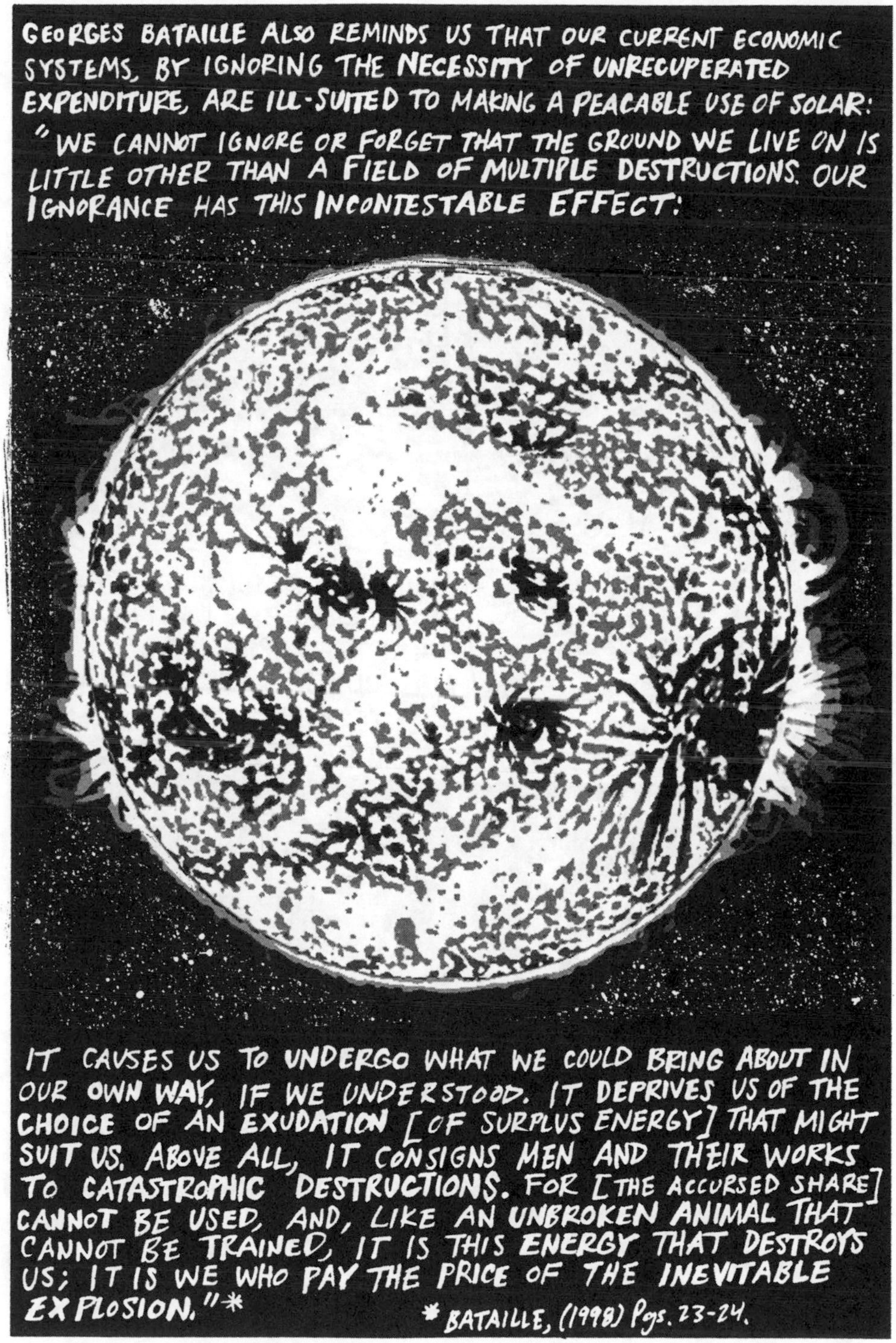
GEORGES BATAILLE ALSO REMINDS US THAT OUR CURRENT ECONOMIC SYSTEMS, BY IGNORING THE NECESSITY OF UNRECUPERATED EXPENDITURE, ARE ILL-SUITED TO MAKING A PEACABLE USE OF SOLAR:
"WE CANNOT IGNORE OR FORGET THAT THE GROUND WE LIVE ON IS LITTLE OTHER THAN A FIELD OF MULTIPLE DESTRUCTIONS. OUR IGNORANCE HAS THIS INCONTESTABLE EFFECT:
IT CAUSES US TO UNDERGO WHAT WE COULD BRING ABOUT IN OUR OWN WAY, IF WE UNDERSTOOD. IT DEPRIVES US OF THE CHOICE OF AN EXUDATION [OF SURPLUS ENERGY] THAT MIGHT SUIT US. ABOVE ALL, IT CONSIGNS MEN AND THEIR WORKS TO CATASTROPHIC DESTRUCTIONS. FOR [THE ACCURSED SHARE] CANNOT BE USED, AND, LIKE AN UNBROKEN ANIMAL THAT CANNOT BE TRAINED, IT IS THIS ENERGY THAT DESTROYS US; IT IS WE WHO PAY THE PRICE OF THE INEVITABLE EXPLOSION."*
* BATAILLE, (1998) Pgs. 23-24.

SOLAR ENEREY IS LIKELY TO BECOME A KEY SITE OF STRUGGLE, THE OUTCOMES OF WHICH WILL DEFINE **POLITICAL**, ECONOMIC AND CULTURAL FORMS IN RELATION TO OTHER RENEWABLE ENERGY SOURCES.

WILL THE RESULTS OF THESE STRUGGLES BE " CONTINUOUS WITH THE CAPITALIST, MASCULINIST, RACIST, COLONIALIST, AND IMPERIALIST EXTRACTIVE ENTERPRISES THAT DEFINED THE FOSSIL-FUEL ERA ECONOMY."? *

THIS IS ONE POSSIBLE FUTURE DESCRIBED BY THE TERM

SOLARITY

HOWEVER, WITH ITS SONIC ECHOES OF "SOLIDARITY," THE TERM ALSO DESCRIBES A HOPE FOR, AND COMMITTMENT TO, MATERIALIZING "DIFFERENT WAYS OF BEING IN RELATION TO ONE ANOTHER AND THE PLURALITY OF NON-HUMAN OTHERS WITH WHOM OUR FATES ARE ENTANGLED."*

* AFTER OIL, "SOLARITY..." (2019) Pg.3.

IN THE HIERARCHICAL, INIQUITOUS SOCIETIES THAT HAVE CHARACTERIZED THE PAST TEN THOUSAND YEARS, EXCESS ENERGY HAS OFTEN TAKEN FORMS OF MONUMENTAL GRANDEUR, RITUALIZED INDULGENCE AND WAR — PRACTICES IMBUED WITH MESMERIZING SURPLUS ENJOYMENT.

THE PETROCULTURES OF THE PAST LONG CENTURY HELPED REPLACE THE OLD, CELESTIAL GODS TO WHOM EXCESS WAS CONSIGNED WITH A NEW, SECULAR RELIGION OF SEEMINGLY MAGICAL, AIMLESS MOBILITY AND CONSUMPTION.

THESE INDIVIDUALISTIC FORMS OF RITUAL EXCESS CONSTITUTE A MASSIVE, PROTRACTED WAR AGAINST THE PLANET AND ITS INHABITANTS. DISGUISING THIS WAR AS "PROGRESS" HAS BEEN ONE OF PETROCULTURE'S CHIEF ACHIEVEMENTS.

THIS RUSE HAS OBSCURED THE WORKINGS OF THE GENERAL ECONOMY IN FAVOUR OF A FANTASY OF CONSTANT GROWTH. THE COST OF OUR COLLECTIVE IGNORANCE ABOUT NECESSARY, UNRECUPERATED EXPENDITURE IS A RAPID, DAILY NARROWING OF FUTURE PROSPECTS FOR LIFE.

WHAT IF THE NEXT TEN THOUSAND YEARS WERE CHARACTERIZED, NOT BY PAYING TRIBUTE TO IMAGINARY BEINGS, OR THE SUBJUGATION OF TIME, SPACE AND LIFE ITSELF, BUT TO SQUANDERING OUR COLLECTIVE SURPLUSES BY BEING GENEROUS AND KIND TO ONE ANOTHER AND THE PLANET?

FACED WITH AN UNCERTAIN AND PRECARIOUS FUTURE, OUR FALTERING PETROCULTURES ARE ABLE TO DO LITTLE MORE THAN CYCLE THROUGH THE HOPES, DREAMS AND NIGHTMARES OF THE PAST.

THE TRUE ADVENTURES LIE AHEAD.

ALL THE APOCALYPSES MULTIPLYING ON OUR SCREENS AND IN OUR IMAGINATIONS ARE DISGUISES FOR THINGS THAT HAVE ALREADY HAPPENED TO US.

WHAT YET REMAINS IS THE ADVENTURE OF LEARNING HOW TO LIVE HUMANELY AND WELL ON THIS RARE AND PRECIOUS GLOBE.

AFTERWORD

Especially arresting among the many memorable images that pulse throughout *Gasoline Dreams: Waking Up from Petroculture*, Simon Orpana's mesmerizing handbook on our fossil-fueled emergency, is the tableau with which the introduction concludes. Here Orpana punctuates the crucial insight motivating his project—that urgent changes required to limit global warming to manageable levels are not simply technological or even political but also, and everywhere, cultural—with a brilliant riff on an art-historical classic: call it *Laocoön at the Gas Bar*. In this update of ancient myth, the serpents sent to punish the Trojan priest for warning his fellow citizens about the dangers posed by the enormous wooden horse left as a seeming gift at the gates of Troy have become serpentine fuel pumps, their deadly poison now the combustible petroleum energy that today makes everything go. *Laocoön at the Gas Bar* is a casual masterpiece, a tragedy-as-farce double take that, in limning fossil fuel as our era's Trojan Horse, underscores the grim punchline of petromodernity: careful what you wish for.

This image, like so many others in the pages of *Gasoline Dreams*, delivers the kind of condensed, defamiliarizing shock that, for Walter Benjamin, constitutes *dialectics at a standstill*: a mode of showing and seeing "wherein what has been comes together in a flash with the now to form a constellation."* This

---

* Walter Benjamin, "Convolute N: On the Theory of Knowledge, Theory of Progress," N2a,3, *The Arcades Project*, trans. Howard Eiland and Kevin McLaughlin (Cambridge, Mass.: Harvard University Press, 1999), 462

aesthetic strategy will signal Orpana's abiding concern with the key place of perceptual habits amidst the array of cultural challenges posed by petroculture. Sometimes, these habits get formed by dynamics of visibility and invisibility: the refinery infrastructure that blights the edge of an urban landscape; the drill-rig way offshore that barely registers on the horizon; the derailment spill or pipeline protest that, for a time, rivets attention on-screen; or the futures trading that turns the prospect of oil-to-come into so many abstruse figures. At other moments and in other ways, these habits have instead to do with the seen and the unseen—with blindnesses both known and unknowing. Here we might think instead of all those givens, nondescript, unremarkable, all-too easy to overlook, that texture the petrocultural everyday: drive to work; cloud computing; vacation plans; pet chew toy. This sort of perspective on the seen and unseen in fossil-fueled life invites an understanding of energy as not just brute input but also social and cultural relation: a matter of values, habits, practices, affects, and beliefs that, at first glance, might seem completely unrelated to questions of energy. In today's world—albeit in powerfully dissymmetrical ways—we are all creatures of oil. The challenge, when confronting this circumstance, is not just what but also *how* to see. The telling power in *Gasoline Dreams* has everything to do with its capacity to embrace that challenge: to proffer a visceral, unnerving, and vital idiom for rendering and so reckoning the contemporary petrocultural condition.

Transition in Energy, Culture and Society (TECS), the multiyear collaborative research endeavor at the University of Alberta to which Orpana has contributed so immensely and within which he began the project that has become *Gasoline Dreams*, implicitly turns on an unstated precept: *see differently*. Following the lead set by the Petrocultures Research Group (PCRG) and After Oil (AO), TECS frames the petrocultural problem less as one of content—of absent or insufficient knowledge—and more as one of form—of mode and method. Contemporary publics have access to a surfeit of information about energy use as it bears on climate crisis . . . and yet nothing seems to change. The bid of TECS (as of PCRG and AO) involves a shift in the content of the form: that qualitative approaches from the arts and humanities might bite in ways and to ends that quantitative data, to date, seems unable to do. Whether this bid can succeed will remain, for now, an open question—but Orpana's wonderful project epitomizes its ambition and great promise.

One of the many current preoccupations of the TECS crew involves energy impasse, whereby despite overwhelming scientific consensus about the environmental consequences of oil societies, petroculture persists and—with every new ring road, pipeline, fracking rig, and plastic plant—redoubles. Energy impasse evokes blockage: those malign politicians and obtuse municipal governments and outdated building codes that, while impeding energy transition in the here and now, represent mere obstacles for contemporary societies to overcome. More consequentially and troublingly, though, energy impasse entails *stuckness*: the perpetuation of sameness in which any bypass of blockage will not solve, and might in fact compound, the conditions of impasse. Whereas blockage means impediment, stuckness equals mire. *Laocoön at the Gas Bar* encapsulates the mire—and thus makes vivid the superlative challenges posed by the stuckness of energy impasse today.

Yet if *Laocoön at the Gas Bar* provides our entry, by way of such stuckness, into the petrocultural dilemmas depicted so vividly in *Gasoline Dreams*, it nevertheless does not foreclose all hope of change. Quite the opposite: Orpana's riveting account of petroculture manages to seed, by way of its imaginative aesthetic, an abundance of possibilities athwart and beyond our fossil-fueled present. At stake, as on offer, is one means by which we might reconceive and so recalibrate the future.

Mark Simpson
English and Film Studies
University of Alberta

ACKNOWLEDGMENTS

If this book provides useful perspectives on the cultures, challenges, and possibilities of our times, it does so perched on the shoulders of a multitude of scholars, researchers, writers, activists, and artists who are doing ground-breaking work on the cultural, political, and social dimensions of energy. Some of these visionaries appear in this book, and many more do not. I am deeply grateful to all who are working to help us face the single greatest challenge our species has known, and to courageously meet it as an opportunity to fashion a better world.

This book began during a two-year Fellowship with Transitions in Energy, Culture and Society, part of the Future Energy Systems research initiative at the University of Alberta, where the Department of English and Film Studies graciously supported the work. Very special thanks go to Imre Szeman (now at the University of Waterloo) for encouragement, input, and insight. This book would not have come about, nor taken the form that it did, without your tireless help, intelligence, and enthusiasm. I am also deeply grateful for Mark Simpson's patient guidance, support, insights, and friendship. Thank you to administrators Dianne Johnson and Annett Gaudig-Rueger and to Cecily Devereux, Chair of English and Film Studies at U of A, for supporting this project while I toiled in my studio, several provinces away. Special thanks go to FES Research Associate Jordan Kinder for his assistance during this project and for his ongoing friendship and inspiration.

The community of people working on petrocultures is diverse and expansive. I can only apologize, in advance, to the many whom I do not specifically name here. Heartfelt thanks go to Graeme Macdonald and the other gracious hosts of the Petrocultures 2018 conference, "Transitions," at the University of Glasgow, Scotland, and to the many presenters there whose ideas helped inspire and shape this book. Special thanks to Eva-Lynn Jagoe and Lisa Moore for including me in the panel "Creative Writing in the Age of Derangement," and to Brent Ryan Bellamy, Ian Clarke, Bob Johnson, Tom Laughlin, Tanja Riekkinen, and Sheena Wilson for their kindness, collegiality, and friendship. To the many other friends and colleagues I met in Scotland: thank you.

I am grateful to Darin Barney of McGill University and to the staff at the Canadian Centre for Architecture in Montreal for hosting *After Oil School 2* in May of 2019. Special thanks go to the hosts of the Imagining Indigenous Solarities workshop, Maize Longboat (Kanien'kehá:ka) and Waylon Wilson (Tuscarora Nation), and to participants Emilee Gilpin, Derek Gladwin, Jordan Kinder, Melina Laboucan-Massimo, Liz Miller, Shirley Roburn, Kyle P. Whyte, and Darin Barney; the work we did and the conversations we had during those two days have greatly shaped this book.

These pages could not have been made without a safe, warm place in which to work. I would like to acknowledge that my studio sits on the traditional territories of the Erie, Neutral, Huron-Wendat, Haudenosaunee, and Mississaugas. The land is covered with the Dish with One Spoon Wampum Belt Covenant, which recognizes the Great Lakes as an important resource that must be cared for in a spirit of sharing, cooperation, and humility. As a member of a settler nation, I am grieved by how our actions repeatedly fail to respect the treaties and agreements by which Indigenous people welcomed Europeans to their lands. So many times, the petitions of Indigenous leaders to meet and talk, in a spirit of equality, about land and recognition disputes have been met with brutal governmental and legal force rather than the conversations and conciliation these complex histories call for. I hope that this book can contribute, in some small way, to building better relationships and futures.

Special thanks go to Cymene Howe and Dominic Boyer of Rice University, whose Cultures of Energy podcast provided the soundtrack to countless hours of drawing and introduced me to many of the thinkers and ideas featured in these pages. Your voices and those of your guests greatly heartened me in this work.

Warm thanks go to the members of the Spare Time Reading Group in Hamilton, Ontario, for friendship and support, and for indulging my petrocultural reading requests: Calla Churchward, Rufus Hickok, Jennifer Hambleton, Carolyn Veldstra, Tina Wilson, and many others. We are grateful to the Workers Arts and Heritage Centre for hosting our meetings. Thanks, as well, to CUPE 3906 for their solidarity and support; keep fighting the good fight!

I am so very grateful for the ongoing friendship and inspiration of colleagues at McMaster University: Christina Baade, Sarah Brophy, Daniel Coleman, Amber Dean, Grace Kehler, Rick Monture, Chris Myhr, Susie O'Brien, Liss Platt, Peter Walmsley, Lorraine York, Eugenia Zuroski, and many others are the caretakers of a wonderful and supportive community. The untimely passing of Joe Adamson and Don Goellnicht has left a keen absence in our hearts. Special thanks go to Mary O'Connor, my Ph.D. supervisor, whose encouragement and guidance deeply inform the combination of art, scholarship, and theory that has made this book possible.

Thank you to Joe Ollmann and Alana Traficante for including pages from this book in the groundbreaking exhibit *This Is Serious: Canadian Indie Comics* at the Art Gallery of Hamilton in 2019. I am also grateful for the friendship of artists Dave Collier, Matt McInnes, Sylvia Nickerson, and poet Darrell Epp: your unique perspectives and talents continue to amaze and inspire. Thank you to the skateboarders of Beasley Park in Hamilton and particularly Grant Coates, Andrea Varvara Biggs, Peter "Popeye" Hanson, Landon Haggerty, and Derek "Oldschool" Lapierre. More thrashing and less driving make the world a better place!

I am grateful, as well, for friend and colleague Evan Mauro, who bought a new skateboard when I forgot my own, and whose tour of historic Vancouver skateboard parks helped get this book off the ground. Thank you to Genevieve Verité for encouragement and driving photographs of road trips, and to Maryna Bunda for gifting me the best pencil sharpener available on the Internet.

To my neighbors in Hamilton, Cynthia Belaskie Dan Horner, Jake and Heidi Veri, Peter Karuna, thank you; I feel lucky to live in the midst of such a wonderful and inspiring group of people. Thank you, as well, to former neighbors Luseadra McKerracher, Bjarke Skaerlund Risager, Niki K. Boyd, and Paul Huebener: we miss you in the hood. Thank you to Laura Wiebe and Adam Wills for donating their old Wacom tablet and pen when I had lost my own.

And no acknowledgment of Hamilton influences would be complete without warmly recognizing the wonderful members of the Brightside Neighbourhood Project, who have shown me that memory and relationships are stronger than the destruction wrought by cities and industry.

I would like to acknowledge that this book was written during a period in which I began to actively treat psychological depression that has shaped my life since adolescence. The financial security offered by the FES Fellowship and the opportunity to pursue a meaningful project greatly enabled this healing journey. I have been helped in this ongoing work by precious friends such as Emory and Natalie Baird, Zak Baird, Nancy Bouchier, Emily Hill, Rebecca Godderis, Rob Kristofferson, and Irene Loughlin. My parents, Valerie and Bob Orpana, and my sister Heather Orpana have likewise been constant sources of love and support. Love and thanks to you all.

Thank you to Shelley Streeby and Daniel Worden for offering astute insight and encouragement on earlier drafts of this book. Thanks, as well, to Kate Cunningham for encouragement on a draft of this book. At Fordham University Press, I am extremely grateful to Richard Morrison for believing in this work and seeing it through to publication. Thank you to Eric Newman for further editorial help and to Mark Lerner for his gifts and expertise at book design.

Finally, heartfelt thanks to my partner and companion, Amy Gullage. Your love, kindness, intelligence, humor, and wisdom are a constant source of strength, growth, and amazement. Thank you for talking me through the Friday blues.

NOTES

Wherever possible, I have attempted to provide credits and context for the reference photos used in making many of the drawings in this book. My apologies to any photographers or artists whom I did not credit.

Dedication page. This image is based on a photo by Imre Szeman from a reception for the first After Oil School in August 2015.

Page 4. Scattered throughout this book are references to the parts per million (ppm) measurement of atmospheric carbon dioxide. On May 9, 2013, atmospheric CO_2 surpassed 400 ppm for the first time since we began keeping records. On completing this book, in 2021, atmospheric CO_2 had reached 417 ppm. Numbers within this range, hidden throughout the book, serve as a kind of CO_2 time stamp, registering the ppm measurement for the day when the page was created.

Page 13. This image of an oil refinery was adapted from a photo of Total's oil refinery in Antwerp, Belgium, by Jonathan Raa (Zuma Press).

Page 38. (Top) Image adapted from the film *Star Wars: Episode VII—The Force Awakens*, directed by J. J. Abrams, 2015. (Bottom) Image adapted from the Netflix series *Sex Education*, created by Laurie Nunn (2019).

Page 39. (Bottom) Image of zombies adapted from the film *Dawn of the Dead*, directed by George A. Romero (1978).

Page 40. (Top) Image adapted from the film *Night of the Living Dead*, directed by George A. Romero (1968). (Bottom) Image adapted from *The Walking Dead* television series by Frank Darabont and Angela Kang (2010).

Page 41. Image of spaceship on this page adapted from *The Empire Strikes Back*, directed by Irvin Kershner (1980).

Page 42. The image of Amitav Ghosh is adapted from a photo by Ivo van der Bent.

Page 51. This image is adapted from a cover illustration by Frank Ingoglia, *Motor* magazine (June 1952).

Page 52. (Middle) Image adapted from a photo of a woman walking across oil pipelines in Okrika, Nigeria, by Ed Kashi. Wurthmann (2006) points out how "in Nigeria, which has reaped an estimated US$600 billion in oil revenue since 1960, 70 percent of the people live on less than a dollar a day" (6).

Page 53. (Top) Image adapted from a 1908 photo of child coal miners in Gary, West Virginia, USA.

Page 56. The assembly of valves, casting spools, and fittings used to regulate the flow of pipes in fracking is called a "Christmas tree."

Page 59. (Bottom). Image adapted from an illustration of "scavengers and piercers at work" that appeared in Edward Baines's book *The History of Cotton Manufacture* (1835).

Page 60. (Top) Image adapted from a photograph of Victorian London (Welgos/Getty Images).

Page 61. (Top) Image adapted from a c. 1902 lithograph, "La sortie de l'opéra en l'an 2000." (Bottom) Image adapted from a c. 1843 wood engraving by G. Stiff from G. W. M. Reynolds's book *The Mysteries of London* (Project Gutenberg).

Page 65. (Bottom) Imaged based on the television series *The X-Files*, which ran from 1993 to 2008.

Page 71. The image on this page is adapted from an undated ad for the Assam Oil Company ("It's a BIG job") from the BP Archive at the University of Warwick, England (ARC134875). The term "big Other" is borrowed from the psychoanalytic ideas of Jacques Lacan (1901–81) for whom the term described the radical alterity of the symbolic order (such as law and language) insofar as it interpellates each individual subject.

Page 75. (Bottom) The dinosaurs here were modeled after a 1931 ad for Sinclair Motor Oil ("Mellowed A Hundred Million Years") from the BP Archive at the University of Warwick, England (ARC203163).

Page 79. While the dictionary definition of "jouissance" is "physical or intellectual pleasure, delight, or ecstasy," Lacan's use of the term as, roughly, "extreme enjoyment" emphasizes destructive, excessive, repetitive, and unpleasant elements. For a more detailed explanation of the term, see https://nosubject.com/Jouissance.

Page 80. Althusser influentially described ideology as "the imaginary relationship of individuals to their real conditions of existence" (109).

Page 84. The lyrics on this page are from the song "Jocko Homo," by Devo (1978). For more on the idea of "energy slaves," or thinking about energy consumption in terms of the equivalent number of human "slaves" that fossil fuels put at our disposal, see Nikiforuk (2012).

Page 88. (Bottom) Image inspired by the music video for the song "In Cars," by Gary Numan (1979).

Page 90. (Top) The composition of this image was inspired by an illustration by Jasiyot Singh Hans accompanying a story by Erik Oritz, "Inside 100 Million Police Traffic Stops: New Evidence of Racial Bias," *NBC News* (March 13, 2019).

Page 93. (Bottom) Image adapted from a Jan. 1909 photo of "Doffer Boys" in Macon, Georgia, USA, by Lewis W. Hine (Getty Images). For more on Illich's work on energy and how it can provide a starting point for creating an energy commons, see Szeman, "Energy Commons" (2019).

Page 96. This image was adapted from a poster for the film *Planes, Trains and Automobiles*, directed by John Hughes (1987).

Page 104. For more information on the history of Claiborne Ave., see Reckdahl (2018) and Kaplan-Levenson (2016). The images on this page were based on contemporary and historical photos from a news article and documentary by Charisse Gibson, "Tremé: How 'Urban Renewal' destroyed the cultural heart of New Orleans" (2019).

Page 114. The image at the bottom of this page is adapted from the cover of the comic book *Fantastic Four* 1, no. 271, written and drawn by John Byrne (1984). This comic features a monster called the Gormuu who grows larger (but not heavier) the more energy it consumes.

Page 117. The idea of a "quilting point" is adapted from Jacques Lacan, whose phrase "*point de caption*" (literally: "upholstery button") describes the key discursive points at which the fluid relationships between language and the world are held in place. I use the term to indicate the additional possibility of a point of intersection for diverse modes of activism, at those spots where petroculture has fixed key shared elements of culture temporarily in place.

Page 120. (Top) Image adapted by a Feb. 19, 2019, photo of the United We Roll convoy in Ottawa by Andrew Meade in the National Observer.

Page 122. (Top) Image adapted from a photo of a National Citizens Alliance Public Rally in downtown Edmonton, by Larry Wong (Postmedia Network).

Page 123. (Bottom) Image adapted from a photo of a Yellow Vest protest in Paris on Dec. 1, 2018 (Getty Images).

Page 124. The zombie image was adopted from the film *Return of the Living Dead*, directed by Dan O'Bannon, 1985.

Page 126. *Terra Nullius* (from Latin meaning "nobody's land") was a principle used in international law to justify claims that a territory may be claimed by a state's occupation of it.

Page 127. The image on this page is inspired by elements of a painting by the American artist William Henry Powell, "Discovery of the Mississippi by De Soto" (1853), which hangs in the United States Capitol rotunda. My use of satire and anachronism to challenge the colonial and racist elements of historical paintings is inspired by the work of Kent Monkman.

Page 130. (Bottom) Image adapted from a photo by the Unist'ot'en Camp accompanying a story by Elizabeth McSheffrey, "What You Need to Know about the Unist'ot'en-Pipeline Standoff," *Vancouver Observer* (Aug. 31, 2015).

Page 131. Image adapted from a photo from the Unist'ot'en webpage "No Pipelines," https://unistoten.camp/no-pipelines/.

Page 133. (Top) Image adapted from a photo from the Unist'ot'en webpage: https://unistoten.camp/.

Page 134. (Top) Image adapted from an uncredited photo accompanying a news story by Jesse Winter, Perrin Gruaer, and Alex McKeen, "What You Haven't Heard from Inside the Battle of the Gidimt'en Checkpoint," *Toronto Star* (Jan. 12, 2019). (Bottom) Image adapted from an uncredited photo accompanying a news story by Perrin Grauer and Jesse Winter, "RCMP Force a Retreat at Wet'suwet'en Barricade," *Toronto Star* (Jan. 7, 2019).

Page 137. (Top) Image adapted from a photo of the North Dakota pipeline protests by Indian Country Today Media Network. (Bottom) Image adapted from a photo of a North Dakota pipeline protests by Tom Stromme (Associated Press).

Page 139. The image of the oil gusher was adapted from a 1930 photo of the "Wild Mary" well in Oklahoma City, Oklahoma, from the Metropolitan Library System.

Page 143. The image of the two men fighting is adapted from the painting "Fight with Cudgels," by Franciso Goya (1820–23) in the Museo del Prado, Madrid.

Page 144. (Bottom) Image adapted from Pablo Picasso's 1937 painting "Guernica" in the Museo Reina Sofia, Madrid.

Page 156. Thanks to Shawn and Sheri Selway for gifting me the souvenir jar of oil from Oil Springs, Ontario, on which the drawing at the top of this page is based.

Page 159. Image adapted from the painting "The Double Secret," by Rene Magritte (1927).

Page 181. The monster on this page was inspired and adapted from the film *Monsters*, directed by Gareth Edwards (2010).

Page 191. (Bottom) Image adapted from a 2019 photo by UN Women/Allison Joyce of families being relocated due to flooding and landslides in a refugee camp in Bangladesh. While Brown's 2008 figure of two hundred million climate refugees by 2050 is often cited, more recent estimates predict as many as one billion people displaced by climate change by this date (see Institute for Economics and Peace 2020).

Page 192. (Top) Image adapted from a 1777 cartouche by William Faden (Library and Archives Canada). (Bottom) Image adapted from a Feb. 1940 photo of a classroom at Cross Lake Indian Residential School in Manitoba, Canada (Library and Archives Canada).

Page 194. (Top) Image adapted from a photo by Iván Alvarado of brine pools and processing areas of the Rockwood lithium plant on the Atacama salt flat, Chile (Reuters).

Page 195. Freud first advances the theory of the death drive in 1920, in *Beyond the Pleasure Principle* (Freud 1989).

Page 201. (Top) We might wonder why, if Bickle's true aim was to assassinate Palantine, he makes such a spectacle of himself at the rally with his appearance and behavior. (Bottom) Betsy's actual quote from the end of the film, "How much was it?," has been slightly adjusted here for clarity. Her words recall those, earlier in the film, of the passenger who planned to kill his wife, a character played by the director himself, Martin Scorsese. Both quotes point to the "cost" of Bickle's surplus enjoyment, which goes over and above the mere price of the cab ride. In the age of global climate change, the costs of our attachment to fossil fuels go well beyond the price of gasoline, cars, and roads.

Page 207. Image adapted from a photo of the Alberta oilsands by Louis Bockner (Sierra Club BC).

Page 215. Another more generally used term for this idea would be "the commons," for which there exists an extensive scholarly and activist literature. Just for starters, see Federici (2012), Harvey (2011), Hardt and Negri (2009), Klein (2001), Linebaugh (2014), and the essays collected in the *Minnesota Review* 2019, no. 93 (Nov. 2019).

Pages 219–20. The skateboarder image on these pages was adapted from a 1988 photo by Grant Brittain of the legendary street skating pioneer Natas Kaupas. The photo was originally published in *Transworld* magazine. Copies of a similar, alternative photo can be purchased from the website https://jgrantbrittainphotos.com/products/natas-kaupas-fire-hydrant-alternate-angle-18x24-photo.

Page 223. The lyrics quoted here are from the song "Whatever It Was," by Greg Brown (1997).

Page 224. The image on this page was adapted from a 1991 photograph of skateboarder Mike Youssefpour by Mark Waters.

Page 229. The lyrics quoted here are from the song "Once in a Lifetime," by Talking Heads (1980).

Page 231. The lyrics quoted here are from the songs "Roadrunner" by the Modern Lovers (1972) and "Gamma Ray" by Beck (2008).

Page 236. For more resources on the idea of solarity, see the essays collected in *South Atlantic Quarterly* 120, no. 1 (January 2021).

BIBLIOGRAPHY

Abrams, J. J., dir. 2015. *Star Wars: Episode VII—The Force Awakens*. Burbank, Calif.: Lucasfilm.

After Oil. 2019. "Solarity: Energy and Society after Oil." *afteroil.ca*. http://afteroil.ca/ solarity-energy-and-society-after-oil/.

Althusser, Louis. 2001. *Lenin and Philosophy and Other Essays*. Translated by Ben Brewster. New York: Monthly Review Press.

Amnesty International. 2016. *Out of Sight, Out of Mind: Gender, Indigenous Rights, and Energy Development in Northeast British Columbia, Canada*. London. https://www .amnesty.ca/sites/amnesty/files/, Out of Sight Out of Mind EN FINAL web.pdf.

Badiou, Alain. 2019. *I Know There Are So Many of You*. Translated by Susan Spitzer. Medford MA: Polity Press.

Balch, Oliver. 2020. "The Curse of 'White Oil': Electric Vehicles' Dirty Secret." *Guardian*. Dec. 8. https://www.theguardian.com/news/2020/dec/08/ the-curse-of-white-oil-electric-vehicles-dirty-secret-lithium.

Bataille, Georges. 1991. *The Accursed Share: An Essay on the General Economy*. Vol. 1. New York: Zone.

Beck, "Gamma Ray." 2008. Track 2 on *Modern Guilt*. DGC, compact disk.

Berlant, Lauren. 2011. *Cruel Optimism*. Durham, N.C.: Duke University Press.

Boyer, Dominic. 2011. "Energopolitics and the Anthropology of Energy." *Anthropology News* (May): 5, 7.

Boyer, Dominic, and Cymene Howe. 2019. "166—Kyle Powys Whyte." *Cultures of Energy*. February 28. Podcast, 1:05. http://culturesofenergy.com/ 166-kyle-powys-whyte/.

Brown, Greg. 1997. "Whatever It Was." Track 1 on *Slant Six Mind*. Red House Records, compact disk.

Brown, Oli. 2008. *Migration and Climate Change*. Geneva: International Organization for Migration.

Byrne, John. 1984. *Fantastic Four*. Vol. 1, no. 271. New York: Marvel Comics Group.

Canadian Petroleum Hall of Fame. 2019. "James Miller Williams." http://www .canadianpetroleumhalloffame.ca/james-williams.htmlb.

Cariou, Warren. 2017. "Aboriginal." In *Fuelling Culture: 101 Words for Energy and Environment*, edited by Imre Szeman, Jennifer Wenzel and Patricia Yaeger, 17–20. New York: Fordham University Press.

Chakrabarty, Dipesh. 2009. "The Climate of History: Four Theses." *Critical Inquiry* 35, no. 2 (Winter): 197–222. https://doi.org/10.1086/596640.

Chrisafis, Angelique. 2018. "Who Are the Gilets Jaunes and What Do They Want?" *Guardian*, Dec. 16. https://www.theguardian.com/world/2018/dec/03/ who-are-the-gilets-jaunes-and-what-do-they-want.

Connerton, Paul. 1989. *How Societies Remember*. Cambridge: Cambridge University Press.

Cooper, Melinda. 2010. "Turbulent Worlds: Financial Markets and Environmental Crisis." *Theory, Culture & Society* 27, no. 2–3: 167–90.

"Country Overshoot Days 2019." 2019. *overshootday.org* (May). https://www .overshootday.org/content/uploads/2019/05/2019_Country_Overshoot_Days-1000 .jpg.

Cox, Alex, dir . 1984. *Repo Man*. Edge City.

Crutzen, Paul J., and Eugene F. Stoermer. 2000. "The 'Anthropocene.'" *Global Change Newsletter*, no. 41 (May): 17–18. http://www.igbp.net/ download/18.316f18321323470177580001401/1376383088452/NL41.pdf.

Daggett, Cara. 2018. "Petro-Masculinity: Fossil Fuels and Authoritarian Desire." *Millennium: Journal of International Studies* 47, no. 1: 25–44. https://doi.org/10.1177/0305829818775817.

Darabont, Frank and Angela Kang, creators. 2010. *The Walking Dead*. New York: American Movie Classics (AMC).

Davies, Kert. 2016. "Top Ten Documents Every Reporter Covering ExxonMobil Should Know." *climateinvestigations.org* (May 23). https://climateinvestigations.org/ top-ten-documents-every-reporter-covering-exxon-should-know/.

Deleuze, Gilles. 1992. "Postscript on the Societies of Control." *October* 59 (Winter): 3–7. https://www.jstor.org/stable/778828.

Delgamuukw v. British Columbia. 1997. 23799, 3 SCR 1010 (SCC 1997).

Democracy Now! 2018. "Trump Won in 2016 Thanks to Voter Suppression Says Carol Anerson, Author of 'One Person, No Vote'." *democracynow.org*. Oct. 16. https://www.democracynow.org/2018/10/16/trump_won_in_16_thanks_to.

Devo. "Jocko Homo." 1978. Track 6 on *Q: Are Not Men? A: We Are Devo!* Warner Bros. Vinyl LP.

Descartes, René. 1901. *Descartes: The Method, Meditations, and Philosophy*. Translated by John Vetch. London: Universal Classics Library.

Duffer, Matt, and Ross Duffer, creators. 2018. *Stranger Things*. Season 1. 21 Laps Entertainment. https://www.netflix.com/ca/title/80057281.

Edwards, Gareth, dir . 2010. *Monsters*. London: Protagonist Pictures.

Environmental Defence Canada. 2019. "The Biggest Barrier to Climate Action in Canada: The Oil and Gas Lobby." *environmentaldefence.ca*. October. https://environmentaldefence.ca/report/oil_barrier_climate_action_canada/.

Favreau, Jon, creator. 2019. *The Mandalorian*. Fairview Entertainment.

Federici, Sylvia. 2012. "Feminism and the Politics of the Commons." In *The Wealth of the Commons: A World Beyond Market & State*, edited by David Bollier and Silke Helfrich. Commons Strategy Group,

Fisker, Jacob Lund. 2005. "The Laws of Energy." In *The Final Energy Crisis*, edited by Andrew McKillop and Sheila Newman, 74–86. Ann Arbor, Mich.: Pluto.

Fleming, Victor, dir . 1939. *The Wizard of Oz*. Beverly Hills, Calif.: Metro-Goldwyn-Mayer.

Fordnation. 2019. "United We Roll! Stop the Carbon Tax and Let's Get Those Pipelines Built!" *facebook.com*. Feb. 15. YouTube video, Accessed Jan 18, 2021. https://www.facebook.com/watch/?v=812800695725173.

Freud, Sigmund. 1961. *Civilization and Its Discontents*. Translated by James Strachey. New York: W. W. Norton.

———. 1989. *Beyond the Pleasure Principle*. Translated by Gregory Zilboorg. New York: Norton.

———. 1995. *The Interpretation of Dreams*. Translated by A. A. Brill. New York: Quality Paperback Book Club.

Ghosh, Amitav. 2016. *The Great Derangement: Climate Change and the Unthinkable*. Chicago: University of Chicago Press.

Gibson, Charisse. 2019. "Tremé: How 'Urban Renewal' Destroyed the Heart of New Orleans." *wwltv.com*. Nov. 26. https://www.wwltv.com/article/news/local/orleans/trem-how-the-i-10-destroyed-a-thriving-black-neighborhood/289-a73ddc1e-dff1-468a-97e0-00392898a658.

Gibson, G., K. Yung, L. Chisholm, and H. Quinn, with Lake Babine Nation and Nak'azdli Whut'en. 2017. *Indigenous Communities and Industrial Camps: Promoting Healthy Communities in Settings of Industrial Change*. Victoria, B.C.: Firelight Group. https://firelight.ca/wp-content/uploads/2016/03/Firelight-work-camps-Feb-8-2017_FINAL.pdf.

Graeber, David. 2007. *Possibilities: Essays on Hierarchy, Rebellion and Desire*. United Kingdom: AK.

Guzikowski, Aaron. 2020. *Raised by Wolves*. Film Afrika Worldwide.

Hardt, Michael, and Antonio Negri. 2009. *Commonwealth*. Cambridge, Mass.: Belknap Press of Harvard University Press.

Harvey, David. 2011. "The Future of the Commons." *Radical History Review* 2011, no. 109 (Winter): 101–7.

Honor the Earth. "Sexual Violence in Extraction Zones." 2021. *honorearth.org*. Accessed Jan. 20, 2021. http://www.honorearth.org/ sexual_violence_in_extraction_zones_past.

Hopper, Dennis, dir . 1969. *Easy Rider*. Pando Company.

Howe, Cymene. 2014. "Anthropocenic Ecoauthority: The Winds of Oaxaca." *Anthropological Quarterly* 87, no. 2 (Spring): 381–404.

Hughes, John, dir . 1987. *Planes, Trains & Automobiles*. Los Angeles: Paramount Pictures.

Huson, Freda. "Background of the Campaign." 2017. *unistoten.camp*. Uist'ot'en Camp. https://unistoten.camp/no-pipelines/background-of-the-campaign/.

Illich, Ivan. 1974. *Energy and Equity*. New York: Harper & Row.

Institute for Economics & Peace. 2020. *Ecological Threat Register 2020: Understanding Ecological Threats, Resilience and Peace*. Sydney: IEP. https://www.visionofhumanity. org/wp-content/uploads/2020/10/ETR_2020_web-1.pdf.

Intergovernmental Panel on Climate Change. "Global Warming of 1.5° C." 2018. https://www.ipcc.ch/sr15/.

Jameson, Fredric. 1994. *The Seeds of Time*. New York: Columbia University Press.

Kaplan-Levenson, Laine. "<HS>'The Monster': Claiborne Avenue Before and After the Interstate." wwno.org. May 5, 2016. https:// www.wwno.org/podcast/tripod-new-orleans-at-300/2016-05-05/ the-monster-claiborne-avenue-before-and-after-the-interstate.

Katz, Brigit. "Found: One of the Oldest North American Settlements." 2017. *Smithsonian*, April 5. https://www.smithsonianmag.com/smart-news/ one-oldest-north-american-settlements-found-180962750/.

Kershner, Irvin, dir . 1980. *The Empire Strikes Back*. Burbank, Calif.: Lucasfilm.

Klein, Naomi. 2013. "Dancing the World into Being: A Conversation with Idle No More's Leanne Simpson." *Yes*, March 6. https://www.yesmagazine.org/social-justice/2013/03/06/ dancing-the-world-into-being-a-conversation-with-idle-no-more-leanne-simpson/.

Klein, Naomi. 2001. "Reclaiming the Commons." *New Left Review* 9 (May/June): 81–89.

Kolb, Carolyn. 2013. *New Orleans Memories: One Writer's City*. Oxford: University of Mississippi Press.

Kransinski, John, dir . 2018. *A Quiet Place*. Los Angeles: Paramount Pictures.

Kubrick, Stanley, dir . 1980. *The Shining*. Warner Bros.

Lacan, Jacques. 2007. *The Seminar of Jacques Lacan*. Book XVII: *The Other Side of Psychoanalysis*. Translated by Russell Grigg. New York: W. W. Norton.

Latour, Bruno. 2018a. *Down to Earth: Politics in the New Climatic Regime*. Translated by Cathy Porter. Cambridge: Polity Press.

———. 2018b. "On a Possible Triangulation of Some Present Political Positions." *Critical Inquiry* 44, no. 2 (Winter): 1–14.

Lazzarato, Maurizio. 2015. *Governing by Debt*. Translated by Joshua David Jordan. South Pasadena, Calif.: Semiotext(e).

Linebaugh, Peter. 2014. *Stop, Thief! The Commons, Enclosures, and Resistance*. San Francisco: PM.

Lucas, George, dir . 1977. *Star Wars*. Lucasfilm.

Macdonald, Graeme. 2016. "Improbability Drives: The Energy of SF." *Strange Horizons*. Feb. 15. http://strangehorizons.com/non-fiction/articles/improbability-drives-the-energy-of-sf/.

Malm, Andreas. 2016. *Fossil Capital: The Rise of Steam Power and the Roots of Global Warming*. New York: Verso.

Marx, Karl. 1978. "Economic and Philosophic Manuscripts of 1844." In *The Marx-Engels Reader*, 2nd ed., edited by Robert C. Tucker, 66–125. New York: W. W. Norton.

———. 2008. *The 18th Brumaire of Louis Bonaparte*. New York: International.

Marx, Karl, and Friedrich Engels. 1978. "Manifesto of the Communist Party." In *The Marx-Engels Reader*, 2nd ed., edited by Robert C. Tucker, 469–500. New York: W. W. Norton.

Milmam, Oliver. 2020. "How SUVs Conquered the World—at the Expense of Its Climate." *Guardian*, Sept. 1. https://www.theguardian.com/us-news/2020/sep/01/suv-conquered-america-climate-change-emissions.

Mitchell, Timothy. 2013. *Carbon Democracy: Political Power in the Age of Oil*. New York: Verso.

McKibben, Bill. "How Extreme Weather Is Shrinking the Planet." 2018. *New Yorker*, Nov. 16. https://www.newyorker.com/magazine/2018/11/26/how-extreme-weather-is-shrinking-the-planet.

Modern Lovers. 1972. "Roadrunner." Track 1 on *The Modern Lovers*. Beserkly, vinyl LP.

Moore, Jason W. 2016. "Name the System! Anthropocenes & the Capitalocene Alternative." *Jason W. Moore* (blog), Oct. 9. https://jasonwmoore.wordpress.com/2016/10/09/name-the-system-anthropocenes-the-capitalocene-alternative/.

Morton, Timothy. 2017. "Ecology." In *Fuelling Culture: 101 Words for Energy and Environment*, edited by Imre Szeman, Jennifer Wenzel, and Patricia Yaeger, 117–19. New York: Fordham University Press.

NASA. 2021a. "Facts." *Global Climate Change: Vital Signs of the Planet*. nasa.gov. Accessed Jan. 5. https://climate.nasa.gov/vital-signs/global-temperature/.

———. 2021b. "2020 Tied for Warmest Year on Record, NASA Analysis Shows." *nasa.gov.* Jan. 14. https://www.nasa.gov/press-release/2020-tied-for-warmest-year-on-record-nasa-analysis-shows.

National Asphalt Pavement Association. 2011. "Fast Facts." *asphaltpavement.org.* Feb. 14. https://www.asphaltpavement.org/uploads/documents/GovAffairs/NAPA%20Fast%20Facts%2011-02-14%20Final.pdf.

Nikiforuk, Andrew. 2012. *The Energy of Slaves: Oil and the New Servitude.* Vancouver: Greystone,.

Nixon, Rob. 2011. *Slow Violence and the Environmentalism of the Poor.* Cambridge, Mass.: Harvard University Press.

Nunn, Laurie, creator. 2019. *Sex Education.* Episode eleven. https://www.netflix.com/ca/title/80197526.

O'Bannon, Dan, dir . 1985. *Return of the Living Dead.* Cinema <APOS>84.

O'Brien, Susie. 2016. "We Thought the World was Makeable: Scenario Planning and Postcolonial Fiction." *Globalizations* 13, no. 3: 329–44.

Petrocultures Research Group. 2016. *After Oil.* Edmonton: Petrocultures. http://afteroil.ca/resources-2/after-oil-book/.

Pendakis, Andrew. 2017. "Being and Oil: Or, How to Run a Pipeline through Heidegger." In *Petrocultures: Oil, Politics, Culture,* edited by Sheena Wilson, Adam Carlson and Imre Szeman, 377–88. Montreal, QC: McGill-Queens University Press.

Raney, Tracey, and Mackenzie Gregory. 2019. "Women Climate Leaders Face 'Green Race' Attacks." *Tyee,* Sept. 16. https://thetyee.ca/Analysis/2019/09/16/Green-Rage-Against-Women/.

Reckdahl, Katy. 2018. "A Divided Neighborhood Comes Together under an Elevated Expressway." *nextcity.org.* Aug. 20. https://nextcity.org/features/view/a-divided-neighborhood-comes-together-under-an-elevated-expressway.

Refn, Nicolas Winding, dir . 2011. *Drive.* Los Angeles: FilmDistrict.

RiseCanada. 2019. "Faith Goldy Unleashed at United We Roll." *bitchute.com.* Feb. 19. https://www.bitchute.com/video/z6LEMGkeP_U/.

Robinson, Matthew. 2011. "Leeside Skate Park, Lee's Domain." *Tyee,* Sept. 28. https://thetyee.ca/News/2011/09/28/Leeside-Skate-Park/.

Romero, George A., dir . 1968. *Night of the Living Dead.* Pittsburgh: Image Ten.

———. 1978. *Dawn of the Dead.* Laurel Group.

Ross, Kristin. 1995. *Fast Cars, Clean Bodies: Decolonization and the Reordering of French Culture.* Cambridge, Mass.: MIT Press.

Salminen, Antti, and Tere Vadén. 2015. *Energy and Experience: An Essay in Nafthology.* Chicago: M-C-M1. http://www.mcmprime.com/files/Energy-and-Experience.pdf.

Scheer, Andrew. 2019. "Canadian Energy Workers Deserve a Government That Supports Their Energy Industry." *facebook.com.* Feb. 19. https://fb.watch/35q9DcfWYs/.

Schopenhauer, Arthur. 1958. *The World as Will and Idea*. Vol. 2. Translated by E. F. J. Payne. New York: Dover.

Schroeder, Robert. 2019. "Trump Climate Advisor Compared 'Demonization' of Carbon Dioxide to Jews' Treatment under Hitler." May 28. https://www.marketwatch.com/story/trump-climate-advisor-compared-demonization-of-carbon-dioxide-to-jews-treatment-under-hitler-2019-05-28.

Scorsese, Martin, dir . 1976. *Taxi Driver*. Culver City, Calif.: Columbia Pictures.

Serres, Michel. 1990. *The Natural Contract*. Translated by Elizabeth MacArthur and William Paulson. Ann Arbor: University of Michigan Press.

Shell International. 2008. *Shell Global Scenarios to 2050*.

Simpson, Mark. 2017. "Lubricity: Smooth Oil's Political Frictions." In *Petrocultures: Oil, Politics, Culture*, edited by Sheena Wilson, Adam Carlson, and Imre Szeman, 287–318. Montreal QC: McGill-Queens University Press.

Smith, Adam. 2007. *Wealth of Nations*. Edited by Charles J. Bullock. New York: Cosimo Classics.

Smith, Charlie. 2015. "Video: RCMP Blocked from Entering Unist'ot'en Camp." Georgia *Straight*. July 19. https://www.straight.com/blogra/492176/video-rcmp-blocked-entering-unistoten-camp.

Steffen, Will et al. 2018. "Trajectories of the Earth System in the Anthropocene." *Proceedings of the National Academy of Sciences of the United States of America* 115, no. 33: 8252–59. https://doi.org/10.1073/pnas.1810141115.

Straus, Mark. 2014. "Climate-Denying Physicist Compares Carbon Dioxide to Jews." *gizmodo.com*. Oct. 18. https://io9.gizmodo.com/climate-change-denying-physicist-compares-carbon-dioxid-1607297863.

Sunderland, Mitchell. 2017. "People Think Women Are Worse Drivers Than Men—Statistics Say Otherwise." *Vice*, Jan. 13. https://www.vice.com/en/article/qvdpgv/people-think-women-are-worse-drivers-than-menstatistics-say-otherwise.

Szeman, Imre. 2014. "Conclusion: On Energopolitics." *Anthropological Quarterly* 87, no. 2 (March): 453–64.

——. 2019a. "Energy Commons." *Minnesota Review*, 93 (November): 94–101.

——. 2019b. *On Petrocultures: Globalization, Culture and Energy*. Morgantown: West Virginia University Press.

——. 2020. "On Solar Futures." *Tilting* (2), no.7 (May): 9.

Szeman, Imre, and Jeff Diamanti. 2017. "Beyond Petroculture: Strategies for a Left Energy Transition." *Canadian Dimension*, Feb. 17. https://canadiandimension.com/articles/view/beyond-petroculture-strategies-for-a-left-energy-transition.

Talking Heads. 1980. "Once in a Lifetime." Track 4 on *Remain in Light*. Sire Records, vinyl LP.

Thompson, Clive. 2016. "No Parking Here." *Mother Jones*, January/February. https://www.motherjones.com/environment/2016/01/future-parking-self-driving-cars/.

"Unist'ot'en and the Limits of Reconciliation in Canada." 2019. *The Conversation*, Jan. 20, 2019. https://theconversation.com/unistoten-and-the-limits-of-reconciliation-in-canada-109704.

Van Sant, Gus, dir. 2012. *Promised Land*. Universal City, Calif.: Focus Features.

Virilio, Paul. 2016. *Speed and Politics*. Translated by Mark Polizzotti. Cambridge, Mass.: MIT Press.

Wack, Pierre. 1985. "Scenarios: Uncharted Waters Ahead." *Harvard Business Review*. September. https://hbr.org/1985/09/scenarios-uncharted-waters-ahead.

Watts, Jonathan. 2018. "We Have 12 Years to Limit Climate Change Catastrophe, Warns UN." *Guardian*, Oct. 8. https://www.theguardian.com/environment/2018/oct/08/global-warming-must-not-exceed-15c-warns-landmark-un-report.

Watts, Vanessa. 2013. "Indigenous Place-Thought & Agency amongst Humans and Non-Humans (First Woman and Sky Woman Go on a European World Tour!)." *Decolonization: Indigeneity, Education & Society* 2, no. 1: 20–34.

Whyte, Kyle P. 2018. "Indigenous Science (Fiction) for the Anthropocene: Ancestral Dystopias and Fantasies of Climate Change Crisis." *Environment and Planning E: Nature and Space* 1, nos. 1–2: 224–42. https://doi.org/10.1177/2514848618777621.

World Meteorological Organization. 2018. *WMO Statement on the State of the Global Climate in 2017*. Geneva: World Meteorological Association.

Worrall, Eric. 2019. "Claim: Criticism of Climate Messiah Greta Thunberg Is Toxic Masculinity." *wattsupwiththat.com*, September 13. https://wattsupwiththat.com/2019/09/13/claim-criticism-of-climate-messiah-greta-thunberg-is-toxic-masculinity/.

Wurthmann, Geerd. 2006. "Ways of Using the African Oil Boom for Sustainable Development." Economic Research Working Paper no 84. African Development Bank.

Yeager, Patricia. 2011. "Editor's Column: Literature in the Ages of Wood, Tallow, Coal, Whale Oil, Gasoline, Atomic Power, and Other Energy Sources." *PMLA* 126, no. 2 (March): 305–10. https://www.jstor.org/stable/41414106.

Zalik, Anna. 2010. "Oil 'Futures': Shell's Scenarios and the Social Constitution of the Global Oil Market." *Geoforum* 41, no. 4: 553–64. https://doi.org/10.1016/j.geoforum.2009.11.008.

Žižek, Slavoj. 2009. *The Parallax View*. Cambridge Mass.: MIT Press.

Simon Orpana is an artist and educator. His work explores the political and historical dimensions of popular culture, and his writing has appeared in such collections as *Zombie Theory: A Reader* and *Skateboarding: Subcultures, Sites and Shifts*. He is also the co-author of *Showdown! Making Modern Unions*, a graphic history of labor organizing.

Imre Szeman is University Research Chair of Environmental Communication and Professor of Communication Arts at the University of Waterloo.